Webster's New World™ Dictionary

of **Acronyms** and **Abbreviations**

Auriel Douglas

Michael Strumpf

Webster's New World
New York

WEBSTER'S NEW WORLD

Simon & Schuster, Inc.
Gulf + Western Building
One Gulf + Western Plaza
New York, NY 10023

DISTRIBUTED BY PRENTICE HALL TRADE

Manufactured in the United States of America

   2 3 4 5 6 7 8 9 10

Library of Congress Cataloging-in-Publication Data

```
Webster's new world dictionary of
  acronyms and abbreviations /
(editors) Auriel Douglas,
  Michael Strumpf.
      p.    cm.
ISBN 0-13-947136-7.
1. Abbreviations, English--Dictionaries.
2. Acronyms--Dictionaries.
I. Douglas, Auriel.  II. Strumpf, Michael.
PE1693.W44  1989
423'.1--dc20                        89-8943
                                        CIP
```

CONTENTS

Introduction   vi

Dictionary of Acronyms and
Abbreviations   1

Common Words/Acronyms and
Abbreviations   209

Introduction

The number of abbreviations and acronyms used in English continues to grow, with new ones being added almost daily from the media, the sciences, government, and many other sources. *Webster's New World Dictionary of Acronyms and Abbreviations* is designed to supply readers with an up-to-date, easily used key to these shortened word forms. In this book, the term *abbreviation* means the shortened form of a word or phrase, e. g., *Mr.* for *Mister*, *St.* for *Saint*, *Song of Sol.* for *Song of Solomon* (Bible). *Acronyms* are words formed from the initial letter or letters of successive parts of a term. They derive from speech and should not contain or be followed by periods. Some are made up of all capital letters; others are all lowercase. Acronyms include names of organizations like NATO or OCAS, and technical terms like COBOL or LORAN. Some acronyms have joined the language as common words: *laser, radar, scuba, sonar.*

There is a tendency, in ordinary use, toward the elimination of periods in abbreviations, especially in units of measure such as *mph, lb,* or *hr.* In this book, style has been primarily chosen to conform to usage in *Words into Type*, Third Edition (Prentice Hall, Englewood Cliffs, New Jersey, 1974), a standard reference. In the following dictionary sections, the acronyms and abbreviations have been taken principally from the database used in compiling *Webster's New World Dictionary*, Third College Edition (Simon & Schuster, New York, New York 1988). Other terms have been selected from the United States Government Style Manual (US Government Printing Office).

The dictionary is divided into two sections. The first lists acronyms and abbreviations in alphabetical order, each followed by its definition. Since the same combinations of letters are frequently used for different terms, you will often find several definitions under one listing. The second section reverses the procedure. It lists common terms in alphabetical order, followed by their abbreviations or acronyms; these too will often present more than one variation.

The Editors

Key to Abbreviated Identifying Terms

astron	astronomy
cartog	cartography
chem	chemistry
CIA	Central Intelligence Agency
dipl	diplomacy
DOP	Department of Defense

elec	electronics
eng	engineering
FBI	Federal Bureau of Investigation
fin	finance
GB	Great Britain
hort	horticulture
ins	insurance
knit	knitting
lang	language
math	mathematics
med	medicine
met	meteorology
mil	military
mus	music
NASA	National Aeronautics and Space Administration
NATO	North Atlantic Treaty Organization
numis	numismatics
photo	photography
phys	physics
psych	psychology
typo	typography
UN	United Nations
UNESCO	United Nations Educational, Scientific, and Cultural Organization
USAF	United States Air Force
USDA	United States Department of Agriculture
USN	United States Navy

Dictionary of Acronyms and Abbreviations

–A–

a about; absolute; academy; ace; acid; acre; acting (rank); active; actual; address; adjective; adjutant; admiral; afternoon; age; air; alcohol; amateur; annual (hort); anode (elec); anonymous; answer; anterior; area

a. before [L *ante*]; in the year [L *anno*]

A adult; America; American; ampere; angstrom; atomic weight; August; Australia

AA Alcoholics Anonymous; anti-aircraft; author's alterations

A.A. Associate in Arts

AAA Agricultural Adjustment Administra-tion; Amateur Athletic/American Automobile Association; antiaircraft artillery

AAAL American Academy of Arts and Letters

A.A.A.S. Associate in Arts and Science

AAB Aircraft Accident Board; Army Air Base; Army Artillery Board

aaby as amended by

AAC Amateur Athletic Club; Army Air Corps; automatic amplitude control

AAF Army Air Force; Auxiliary Air Force

AAM air-to-air missile

aar against all risks; aircraft accident record/report; average annual rainfall

AARP American Association of Retired Persons

A.A.S. Associate in Applied Science

AASC Allied Air Support Command

AASF Advanced Air Striking Force

AAU Amateur Athletic Union

AAUW American Association of University Women

ab about

AB able-bodied seamen; advisory board; air board; Alberta

A.B. Bachelor of Arts

ABA American Bankers/Bar/Basketball/Booksellers Association

abbr abbreviated; abbreviation

abbrev abbreviated; abbreviation

ABC American Bowling Congress; American Broadcasting Company

abd abdicate; average body dose (radiation)

ABD all but dissertation

ab init. from the beginning [L *ab initio*]

abl ablative

ABM antiballistic missile

A-bomb atomic bomb

abr abridge; abridgement

abs absence; absent; absolute; absorbent; abstract

ABS American Bible Society

absol absolute

abs. re. the defendant being absent [L *absente reo*]

abstr abstract

abt about

ABT American Ballet Theatre

abv above

ac acre; activity; alternating current

a/c account; account current

Ac actinium (chem)

AC Air Corps; alternating current; Athletic Club; author's correction

A.C. before Christ [L *ante Christum*]; before meals (med) [L *ante cibum*]

A/C account; aircraft; aircraftman; air-conditioning

A & C addenda and corrigenda

ACBWS automatic chemical biological warning system

acc acceleration; accent; acceptance; accompanied; according; account; accusative

ACC administrative co-ordination committee; Agricultural Credit Corporation

accel accelerando (mus)

accom accommodation

accomp accompanied; accompaniment

accred accredited

acct account; accountant

acctd accented

accum accumulate

accus accusative

ACDA Arms Control and Disarmament Agency

ack ack anti-aircraft

ackgt acknowledgement

ACLU American Civil Liberties Union

acn all concerned notified

ACORN Association of Community Organizations for Reform Now

ACP American College of Physicians

acpt acceptance

acq acquire; acquittal

ACR advanced capabilities radar

acron acronym

ACRR American Council on Race Relations

ACS American Cancer Society; American Chemical Society; American College of Surgeons

act. acting; active; activities; actuary

ACT Advisory Council on Technology; American College Test/Testing

A.C.T. Australian Capital Territory

ACTH adrenocorticotropic hormone (antirheumatic drug)

Acts Acts of the Apostles (Bible)

acv actual cash value; air cushion vehicle

acy average crop yield

ad adapter; advantage; average deviation

AD accidental damage; active duty; administrative department; air defense; armament depot; autograph document; average deviation

A.D. in the year of our Lord [L *anno Domini*];

right ear [L *auric dexter*]

ADA acetone-dicarboxylic acid; Air Defense Agency; American Dental Association; Americans for Democratic Action; Atomic Development Authority

ADB accidental death benefit

ADC aide-de-camp; Aid to Dependent Children; Air Defense Command; automatic digital calculator

add. to be added, additional; address

ADD attention deficit disorder

addit additional

addl additional

ad effect. until effective (med) [L *ad effectum*]

ad inf. to infinity [L *ad infinitum*]

ad init. at the beginning [L *ad initium*]

ad int. in the meantime [L *ad interim*]

ADIZ air defense identification zone

adj adjective; adjacent;
adjourned; adjustment

Adj adjutant

Adj Gen adjutant gen-
eral

adl activities of daily
living

ad lib. at pleasure [L *ad
libitum*]

ad loc. at the place [L *ad
locum*]

adm admission; admit-
ted; average daily
membership

Adm admiral

admin administration;
administrator

ADP adenosine diphos-
phate; advanced/auto-
mated data processing

ad s. at the suit of [L *ad
sectam*]

ads. autograph docu-
ment signed

adv advance; adverb; advertisement; advice;
advise; advisory; advo-
cate

Adv Advent; advocate

ad val. according to
value [L *ad valorem*]

adv pmt advance pay-
ment

ADW air defense warn-
ing

AE adult education; aeronautical engineer/
engineering; age
exemption; army edu-
cation; atomic energy

AEA Actors' Equity Association; air efficiency
award; American Eco-
nomic Association;
Atomic Energy Author-
ity

AEC Atomic Energy
Commission

AECB Atomic Energy
Control Board

AEF American Expedi-
tionary Forces

aeq. equal; equals [L *aequales*]

Aer. E. Aeronautical Engineer

aero aeronautic; aeronautical

aet. of, or at, the age of [L *aetatis*]

AF audiofrequency

AFB Air Force Base

afc automatic frequency control

AFCE automatic flight control equipment

AFDC aid to families with dependent children

aff affairs; affectionate; affiliate; affirmative

afft affidavit

Afg Afghanistan

AFHC Air Force Headquarters Command

AFHQ Allied Force Headquarters

AFI American Film Institute

A1c airman, first class

AFL-CIO American Federation of Labor and Congress of Industrial Organizations

AFM American Federation of Musicians

Afr Africa; African

Afrik Afrikaans

aft. after; afternoon

AFTRA American Federation of Radio and Television Artists

Ag agent; agreement; agriculture; silver (chem) [L *argentum*]

AG *Aktiengesellschaft* [Ger]; attorney general

AGA Amateur Gymnastics Association; American Genetic Association

AGCA automatic ground-controlled approach

agcl automatic ground-controlled landing

agcy agency

agd axial gear differential; agreed

agg aggregate

AGI adjusted gross income

agit. ante su. shake before taking (med) [L *agita ante sumendum*]

agit-prop agitation and propaganda

agnos agnostic

agt agent; agreement

agw actual gross weight

Ah ampere-hour

A.H. in the Hebrew year; in the year of the Hegira

AHA American Heart Association

ahd ahead

AHS American Humane Society

a.i. in the meantime [L *ad interim*]

AI admiralty instruction; air interception; Amnesty International; army intelligence; artificial insemination

A & I Agricultural and Industrial

AIA American Institute of Architects

AIB American Institute of Banking

AICBM anti-intercontinental ballistic missile

AID Agency for International Development

AIDS Acquired Immune Deficiency Syndrome

AILAS automatic instrument landing approach system

AIME American Institute of Mining Engineers

AIW Atlantic-Intercoastal Waterway

AK Alaska

aka also known as

AKC American Kennel Club

Akr Akron

Al aluminium (chem)

AL Alabama; American League

Ala Alabama

ALA American Library Association

Alb Albania

alch alchemy

Alg algebra; Algeria; Algiers

ALGU Association of Land Grant Colleges and Universities

align. alignment

alk alkaline

alph alphabetical

ALR American Law Reports

als autograph letter signed

alt alteration; alternate; alternator; altimeter; altitude

alt. dieb. every other day (med) [L *alternis diebus*]

alt. noc. every other night (med) [L *alternis noctibus*]

ALU arithmetic logic unit

a.m. before noon [L *ante meridiem*]

Am americium (chem)

A/m ampere per meter

AM air marshal; air ministry; amplitude modulation; army manual

A.M. Hail Mary [L *Ave Maria*]; in the year of the world [L *anno mundi*]; Master of Arts

ama against medical advice

AMA American Management Association; American Medical Association

Amal amalgamated

Amb Ambassador; ambulance

AME African Methodist Episcopal

amend. amendment

Amer America; American

AmerInd American Indian

Amer Samoa American Samoa

Amer Std American Standard

Amex American Stock Exchange

Am.Inst.E.E. American Institute of Electrical Engineers

AMP advanced management program

AMPAS Academy of Motion Picture Arts and Sciences

amph amphibian; amphibious

Am.Soc.C.E. American Society of Civil Engineers

Am.Soc.M.E. American Society of Mechanical Engineers

amt amount

Amtrak National Railroad Passenger Corporation

amu atomic mass unit

AMVETS American Veterans of World War II, Korea, and Vietnam

an. above named

ANA American Nurses Association

anal analogy; analyse; analysis

anat anatomy; anatomical

ANC African National Congress

And. Andorra

ANF anti-nuclear factor; Atlantic Nuclear Force

ang angle; angular

Ang Angola

Angl Anglican

ann. in the year [L *anno*]; years [L *anni*]

anniv anniversary

annot annotate

annul. annulment

Annunc Annunciation

anon. anonymous

ANPA American Newspaper Publishers' Association

ANRC American National Red Cross

ans answer; autograph note signed

ant. antenna; antiquarian; antique; antiquity; antonym

Ant. Antarctica

ANTA American National Theatre and Academy

anthol anthology

anthrop anthropological; anthropology

antilog antilogarithm (math)

ANZAC Australian and New Zealand Army Corps

a/o (on) account of

AOL absent over leave

AOA Administration on Aging

ap about proof; advanced placement; apothecary; apparent; author's proof

Ap apostle; April

AP additional premium; Associated Press

A/P authority to pay/ purchase

APA American Pharmaceutical/Psychological/ Psychiatric Association

A-part alpha particle

APB all-points bulletin (law enforcement)

APC armored personnel carrier; aspirin, phenacetin, caffeine; automatic phase control

APD antisocial personality disorder

APHA American Public Health Association

API American Petroleum Institute

APL a programming language

apmi area precipitation measurement indicator

APO African People's Organization; Army post office

Apoc apocrypha; apocryphal

apos apostrophe

app apparatus; apparent; appeal; appended; appendix; applied; appoint; apprentice; approval; approximate

App Div Appellate Division

appl appeal; appellant; applicable; applied

appos appositive

appr apprentice

approx approximately

appt appoint; appointment

Apr April

APR annual percentage rate; annual progress report

Apt apartment

aq aqueous

a/r all risks

Ar argon (chem)

AR Arkansas

A/R account receivable

Aramco Arabian-American Oil Co

arb arbiter; arbitrary; arbitration

Arc Arctic

ARC AIDS-related complex, American Red Cross

arch. archaic; archery; archipelago; architect; architecture

Arch. archbishop; archdeacon; archduke

Arg Argentina

arith arithmetic

Ariz Arizona

Ark Arkansas

ARM adjustable rate mortgage

ARP air raid precautions

arr arrangement; arranger; arrivals; arrive

ARS Agricultural Research Service

art. article

Art.D. Doctor of Arts

As altostratus; arsenic (chem)

AS Anglo-Saxon

ASA American Standards Association

ASAP as soon as possible

ASCAP American Society of Composers, Authors and Publishers

ASCE American Society of Civil Engineers

ASCEA American Society of Civil Engineers and Architects

ASCII American Standard Code for Information Interchange

asdr airport surface-detection radar

asi air speed indicator

asl above sea level

ASL American Sign Language

ASM acting sergeant-major; air-to-surface missile

ASME American Society of Mechanical Engineers

ASN Army service number

ASPCA American Society for the Prevention of Cruelty to Animals

ASR airport surveillance radar; air-sea rescue

ass. assembly; association; assurance

Assn association

Assoc association; associate

ASSR Autonomous Soviet Socialist Republic

Asst assistant

AST Atlantic standard time

astrol astrology

astron astronomy

asyl asylum

at atmosphere (technical); atomic

At ampere-turn; astatine (chem)

AT Atlantic time

atc automatic temperature control

ATCO air traffic control officer

ATD actual time of departure

Atl Atlantic

atm atmosphere

ATM automated teller machine

at. no. atomic number

att attached

AT&T American Telephone and Telegraph

at. wt atomic weight

atty attorney

au astronomical units

Au angstrom unit; gold (chem) [L *aurum*]

Aug August

Aus Austria

AUS Army of the United States

Aust Australia

auth authentic; author; authority; authorize

av asset value

Av Avenue; average

AV Authorized Version (Bible)

A/V audiovisual

avdp avoirdupois

Ave Avenue

avg average

AWACS airborne warning and control system

awl absent with leave

awol absent without official leave

Az azimuth; azure

AZ Arizona

–B–

b bacillus; baryon scale; basso; bay; born; brother; brotherhood

B bachelor; bar; baron; Baume; bel; Bible; bin; bishop; boron (chem); brightness

b/a backache; boric acid; budget authorization

Ba barium (chem)

B.A.A. Bachelor of Applied Arts; Bachelor of Arts and Architecture

bac bacilli; bacillus; bacteria; bacterial antigen complex; bacteriology; blood-alcohol concentration

BACA Business and Consumer Affairs

bach bachelor

B.A.Chem. Bachelor of Arts in Chemistry

bact bacteria; bacteriology

BADAS Binary Automatic Data Annotation System

badc binary asymmetric dependent channel

B.Admin. Bachelor of Administration

B.A.E. Bachelor of Architectural Engineering; Bachelor of Arts in Education

B.A.Econ. Bachelor of Arts in Economics

B.A.Ed. Bachelor of Arts in Education

B.Ae.E. Bachelor of Aeronautical Engineering

ba & f budget, accounting, and finance

B.Ag.E. Bachelor of Agricultural Engineering

B.Ag.Eco. Bachelor of Agricultural Economics

B.Agr. Bachelor of Agriculture

B.Ag.Sc. Bachelor of Agricultural Science

Ba I Bahama Islands

B.A.J. Bachelor of Arts in Journalism

bal balance; balcony

BAL Basic Assembly Language; blood alcohol level

B.A.L.S. Bachelor of Arts in Library Science

B.A.Mus. Bachelor of Arts in Music

BANKPAC Bankers Political Action Committee

B.A.Nurs. Bachelor of Arts in Nursing

B.App.Arts Bachelor of Applied Arts

B.App.Sci. Bachelor of Applied Science

Bapt Baptist

bar. barometer; barometric; barrel

Bar. barrister; Baruch (Bible/Apocrypha)

BAR base address register (computer); Browning automatic rifle

Barb. Barbados

B.Arch. Bachelor of Architecture

Bart baronet

BART Bay Area Rapid Transit (San Francisco subway system)

B.A.S. Bachelor of Agricultural Science; Bachelor of Applied Science

B.A.Sc. Bachelor of Agricultural Science; Bachelor of Applied Science

BASIC Beginners' All-Purpose Symbolic Instruction Code (computer lang)

B.A.S.S. Bachelor of Arts in Social Science

bat. battalion; battle

b-a test blood-alcohol test

BATF Bureau of Alcohol, Tobacco, and Firearms

BATO balloon assisted take-off

bau basic assembly unit

bb ball bearing; bearer bonds; beer barrel; below bridges; books

b&b bed and board/breakfast

b to b back to back

BB bail bond; bank book; basketball; battleship; bill book; blue book; B'nai B'rith

B.B.A. Bachelor of Business Administration

bbb bed, breakfast and bath

BBB Better Business Bureau

BBC British Broadcasting Corporation

bbl barrel

bbq barbecue

bbt basal body temperature

BC British Columbia

B.C. before Christ

bcd binary-coded data

BCDIC Binary-Coded Decimal Interchange Code

B.C.E. Bachelor of Civil Engineering; before the common era

B.Ch. Bachelor of Surgery

B.Ch.E. Bachelor of Chemical Engineering

B.C.L. Bachelor of Civil Law

B.Comm. Bachelor of Commerce

B.C.S. Bachelor of Commercial Science

BCSE Board of Civil Service Examiners

BCU big close-up

bd board; bold; bond; bound; broad

b.d. twice a day (med) [L *bis die*]

b/d bank draft; barrels per day; bill discounted; brought down

b & d bondage and discipline

B.D. Bachelor of Divinity

bd ft board foot

BDS bomb disposal squad

B.D.Sc. Bachelor of Dental Science

b & e breaking and entering

Be Baume scale (chem); beryllium (chem)

B of E Board of Education

B.Ed. Bachelor of Education

B.E.E. Bachelor of Electrical Engineering

bef before

BEF British Expeditionary Forces

beg. beginning

bel below

Bel Belgium

B.E.M. Bachelor of Engineering of Mines; British Empire Medal

BENELUX Belgian-Netherlands-Luxembourg Committee

B.Eng. Bachelor of Engineering

B.Eng.Sci. Bachelor of Engineering Science

B.Eng.Tech. Bachelor of Engineering Technology

BEOG Basic Educational Opportunity Grant

B.E.P. Bachelor of Engineering Physics

BE & P Bureau of Engraving and Printing

beq bequeath

B.E.S. Bachelor of Engineering Science

bet. between

bev beverage

bf boldface; brief

B.F.A. Bachelor of Fine Arts

Bfo Buffalo

bft bio-feedback training

bg background; bag

Bg Bengal; Bengalese; Bengali

BG brigadier general

B.Gen.Ed. Bachelor of General Education

B-girl bar girl

Bgk Bangkok

bgl below ground level

bgm background music

BGN Board on Geographic Names

B/H bill of health

B of H Board of Health

bha basic helix angle

B.H.Adm. Bachelor of Hospital Administration

BHC benzene hexachloride

bhd beachhead; bulkhead

B.Hort. Bachelor of Horticulture

B.Hort.Sci. Bachelor of Horticultural Science

bhp brake horsepower

BHQ brigade headquarters

bhr basal heart rate

BHT butylated hydroxytoluene

B.Hyg. Bachelor of Hygiene

Bi bismuth (chem)

BI background information

BIA Bureau of Indian Affairs

Bib Bible; Biblical

bibl bibliographer; bibliographical; bibliography

bibliog bibliographer; bibliographical; bibliography

bicarb bicarbonate of soda

b.i.d. two times a day (med) [L *bis in die*]

B.I.E. Bachelor of Industrial Engineering

big. bigamist; bigamy

bil bilateral; billion

b-i-l brother-in-law

bilat bilateral

bim beginning of information marker

bi-m bi-monthly

bin binary (math)

bind. binding

biochem biochemical; biochemistry

biodeg biodegradable; biodegrade

biog biographer; biographical; biography

biol biological; biologist; biology

biomed biomedical; biomedicine

bionics biology + electronics

biophys biophysical; biophysics

BiP *Books in Print*

bis best in show

BIS Bank for International Settlements

BIT binary digit (computer)

bitum bituminous

biu basic income unit

biv bivouac

bi-w bi-weekly

B.J. Bachelor of Journalism

B.Jur. & Soc.Sc. Bachelor of Juridical and Social Science

bk bank; below the knee

Bk berkelium (chem)

bkbndg bookbinding

bkcy bankruptcy

bkd backward

bkfst breakfast

bkg banking; booking; bookkeeping

bkgd background

Bklyn Brooklyn

bkn broken

bkrpt bankrupt

bl baseline; blood loss; blue

BL baseline; black letter; building line

B.L. Bachelor of Law

B/L bill of lading

bld   bold; boldface

bldg   building

B.Lib.Sci.   Bachelor of Library Science

B.Lit(t).   Bachelor of Letters; Bachelor of Literature

blk   black; block

BLM   Bureau of Land Management

blr   breech-loading rifle

BLS   Bureau of Labor Statistics

blt   built

BLT   bacon, lettuce and tomato

Blvd   Boulevard

bm   board measure

BM   basal metabolism; bench mark; bowel movement

B.M.   Bachelor of Music; British Museum

BMD   ballistic missile defense; births, marriage and deaths

bme   biomedical engineering

B.M.E.   Bachelor of Mechanical Engineering; Bachelor of Mining Engineering

B.Med.   Bachelor of Medicine

bmi   ballistic missile interceptor

BMI   Broadcast Music Incorporated

BMOC   Big Man on Campus

BMR   basal metabolic rate

BMT   Brooklyn and Manhattan Transit (NYC Subway)

B.M.T.   Bachelor of Medical Technology

B.M.V.   Blessed Mary the Virgin

BMWS   ballistic missile weapon system

bn   beacon; been; born

Bn   battalion

BN   binary number

B.N.   Bachelor of Nursing

B of N   Bureau of Narcotics

Bngl. Bangladesh

B.N.Sc. Bachelor of Nursing Science

bo body odor; blackout; box office

b/o back order

BOB best of breed

Bol Bolivia

B.Opt. Bachelor of Optometry

bor borough

bot botanical; botanist; botany; bottle; bottom

Bots Botswana

BOV best of variety

bp birthplace; boiling point

b/p baking powder; bills payable

b of p balance of payments

Bp bishop

BP beautiful people; below proof; blood pressure; blueprint; bonus point British Petroleum

B.P. Bachelor of Pharmacy; Bachelor of Philosophy; before the present

bpb bank post bills

B.P.E. Bachelor of Physical Education

B.Ph. Bachelor of Philosophy

B.Pharm. Bachelor of Pharmacy

B.Phil. Bachelor of Philosophy

B.Phys.Thy. Bachelor of Physical Therapy

bpi bits per inch (computer)

bpl birthplace

b pt boiling point

BPOE Benevolent & Protective Order of Elks

bps bytes per second

bpu base production unit

BPW Board of Public Works

br bearing; bombardier; brief; brig; brigade; brother; brown; bugler

Br bromine (chem)

BR bank rate; bedroom; bill of rights; book of reference; British Railways

B/R bills receivable

Braz Brazil

brf brief

brg bearing; bridge

Brig brigadier

Brig Gen brigadier-general

Brit Britain; British

brkwtr breakwater

brm barometer

brn brown

Bro brother

brok broker; brokerage

brom bromide

Bros brothers

Brun Brunei

BRV ballistic reentry vehicle

bs back stage; bags; balance sheet; bales; bill of sale

B.S. Bachelor of Science; Bachelor of Surgery (GB)

B/S balance sheet; bill of sale

BSA Boy Scouts of America

B.S.A. Bachelor of Agricultural Science

bsc basic

B.Sc. Bachelor of Science

B.Sc.Acc. Bachelor of Science in Accounting

B.Sc.App. Bachelor of Applied Science

B.Sc.Dent. Bachelor of Science in Dentistry

B.S.Ch. Bachelor of Science in Chemistry

B.Sci. Bachelor of Science

bscn bit scan (computer)

B.S.Ed. Bachelor of Science in Education

bsh bushel

BSI British Standards Institute

B.S.Med. Bachelor of Science in Medicine

B.S.Met. Bachelor of Science in Metallurgy

bsmt basement

B.S.N. Bachelor of Science in Nursing

B.S.P.H. Bachelor of Science in Public Health

bt beat; bent; boat; bought

Bt baronet

BT basic training; bedtime; brain tumor

B of T balance of trade

bta better than average

btf balance to follow

b/tf balance transferred

B.Th. Bachelor of Theology

btl bottle

btn baton; battalion; button

btp body temperature and pressure

bts back to school

Btu British thermal unit

btwn between

bu base unit; bureau; bushel

Bul Bulgaria

bull. bulletin

BUN blood, urine, nitrogen

bur bureau; buried

Burm Burma; Burmese

burg burgess; burgomaster

burs bursar

bus. business

bus. mgr business manager

BV book value

BVI British Virgin Islands

B.V.M. Bachelor of Veterinary Medicine

B.V.Sc. Bachelor of Veterinary Science

Bvt brevet

B/W black and white

bwd backward

BWI British West Indies

bx box

BX base exchange

byo bring your own

Byz Byzantine

Bz benzoyl (chem)

–C–

c candle (phys); capacity; carat; cathode; centi- (math); century; city; cloudy; conductor; constant; consul; continental; contralto; copy; cubic; currency; cycle (radio); velocity of light

c. approximately [L *circa*]; with [L *cum*]

C calorie; capacitance (elec); carbon (chem); Catholic; Celsius; Centigrade; chancellor; Christ; Christian; circuit; circumference; clockwise; cocaine; Congress; coulomb

ca. cases (legal); circa

Ca calcium (chem); California; Canada

CA California; cancer; cardiac arrest; Central America; chartered accountant; court of appeal

C/A capital/credit/current account

CAB Citizens Advice Bureau; Civil Aeronautics Board

CACD computer-aided circuit design

CACM Central American Common Market

CAD computer-assisted design

caic computer-assisted indexing and classification

cal calendar; caliber; calorie

Cal California

calc calculate; calculator; calculus

Calif California

Cam Cameroon

Camb Cambodia

can. canal; cancel; cannon; canon; canto (mus)

Can Canada; Canadian;

CAN customs assigned numbers

canc cancellation; cancelled

cand candidate

Cand.jur. doctor of law [L *Candidatus juris*]

cap. capacity; capital; capital letter; capitalize; foolscap

CAP Civil Air Patrol

caps. capital letters; capsule

capt caption

Capt captain

car. carat; cargo

CAR Central African Republic; Civil Air Regulations; cloudtop altitude radiometer

carb carbon; carbonate

CARE Cooperative for American Remittances to Everywhere, Inc

CARICOM Caribbean Community

CARIFTA Caribbean Free Trade Area

cas castle; casual; casualty

cat. catalogue; catamaran; cataplasma (med); catapult; catechism; caterpillar tractor; cattle

CAT Civil Air Transport; compressed air tunnel; computer aided typesetting; computer of average transients

cath cathedral; cathode; Catholic

CAT-scan computerized axial tomography

CATV community access/antenna television

Cau Caucasian

cav cavalier; cavalry; caveat; cavity

c.a.v. the court desires to consider (legal) [L *curia advisare vult*]

Cb columbium (chem)

CB cash book; circuit breaker; citizens' band (radio); compass bearing; continuous breakdown

CBAT College Board Admission Test

cbc combined blood count

cbd cash before delivery

CBE Commander of Order of British Empire

CBF cerebral blood flow

cbi complete background investigation

CBI Central Bureau of Identification; China, Burma, India; computer based information; cumulative book index

CBIS computer-based information system

cb/l commercial bill of lading

CBS Columbia Broadcasting System

CBT Chicago Board of Trade

CBW chemical and biological warfare

cc carbon copy; cash credit; change course; cubic centimeter

Cc. chapter [L *capita*]

CC compass course; control computer; county clerk

C of C chamber of commerce; coefficient of correlation

CCA Circuit Court of Appeals

ccc command control console; computer-command control

CCC Civilian Conservation Corps; Commodity Credit Corporation

CC & C Command Control and Communications (USAF)

CCF chronic heart failure

C Cls Court of Claims

CCP Chinese Communist Party

CCPA Court of Customs and Patents Appeals

CCR Commission on Civil Rights

CCTV closed circuit television

CCU coronary care unit

ccw counter clockwise

cd candela; carried down; cash discount; cum dividend (fin); certificate of deposit

c & d collection and delivery

Cd cadmium (chem)

CD certificate of deposit; compact disc

C/D customs declaration

CDAS Civil Defense Ambulance Service

CDC Center for Disease Control

cd/in² candela per square inch

c div cum dividend (fin)

cd/m² candela per square meter

Cdr commander

CD-ROM compact disc read only memory

cdt cadet; commandant

Ce cerium (chem)

C.E. Chemical/Civil Engineer; common era

CEA Council of Economic Advisors

CEF Canadian Expeditionary Forces

Cel Celsius

cen central

Cen Afr Rep Central African Republic

cent. centigrade; central; centrifugal; century

Cento Central Treaty Organization

CEO chief executive officer

CEP circular error probability (computer)

cert certificate; certified

cesr conduction electron spin resonance

CET computerized emission tomogram

CETA Comprehensive Employment and Training Act

CETI communication with extraterrestrial intelligence

cf carried forward; center fielder; center forward; coast and freight; communication factor; cubic feet

cf. compare, or see [L *confer*]

c/f carried forward (accounting)

Cf californium (chem)

CFA Chartered Financial Analyst; College Football Association

cfh cubic feet per hour

cfm confirm; confirmation; cubic feet per minute

CFR Code of Federal Regulations

c ft cubic feet

CFTC Commodity Futures Trading Commission

cg centigram

CG coast guard; combat group; consul general

CGA certified general accountant

CGC coast guard cutter

cgi corrugated galvanized iron

CGI computer generated imagery

cgt capital gains tax

ch candle hour; central heating; chapter

c-h candela-hour

Ch chairman; chancellor; check; chief; church

CH center halfback; central heating; clearing house; custom house

char. character; characteristic; charity; charter

Ch.B. Bachelor of Chemistry

CHD coronary heart disease

Ch.D. Doctor of Chemistry

chem chemical; chemist; chemistry

Chem.E. Chemical Engineer

chemo chemotherapy

ch fwd charges forward

chg charge

Chi Chicago

Chin. China

Ch.M. Master of Surgery

Chmn chairman

ch ppd charges prepaid

chr Chrome

c hr candle hour

chron chronicle; chronology; chronometry

1 Chron 1 Chronicles (Bible)

2 Chron 2 Chronicles (Bible)

Chtr charter

CHU centigrade heat unit

c & i cost and insurance

Ci curie

CI Channel Island; chief inspector; counter intelligence

CIA Central Intelligence Agency; Culinary Institute of America

CIC Commander-in-Chief; Command Information Center; Counter Intelligence Corps

CICU cardiology intensive care unit

cif cost, insurance and freight

cif&c cost, insurance, freight and commission

C-in-C commander-in-chief

CIM computer input microfilm; computer integrated manufacturing

CIO Congress of Industrial Organization

CIP cataloging in publication

circ circle; circuit; circular; circulation; circumference; circus

circum circumference

CIS cataloging in source

cit citadel; citation; cited; citizen; citrate

CIT California/Carnegie Institute of Technology

civ civil; civilian; civilization

CJ Chief Justice

C.J. body of law [L *corpus juris*]

ck cask; check; cook

c/l cash letter

cL centiliter

Cl chlorine (chem)

CLC Cost of Living Council

CLEP College Level Examination Program

clin clinic; clinical

clr clear; color; cooler

cm centimeter

c/m cycles per minute

cm² square centimeter

cm³ cubic centimeter

Cm curium (chem)

CM circular measure; countermark; court martial

C.M. Master in Surgery

CMA cash management account; consolidated metropolitan statistical area

Cmdre commodore

cmil circular mil

cmpd compound; compounded

cm p s centimeters per second

CMR common mode rejection

CNO Chief of Naval Operations

CNS central nervous system

CNSG consolidated nuclear steam generator

co company; county

c/o carried over; cash order; change over; in care of

Co cobalt (chem); company

CO Colorado; commanding officer; conscientious objector

C/O certificate of origin; chief officer; commanding officer; Commissioner's office; conscientious objector

c.o.b. close of business

COBOL Common Business Oriented Language (computer lang)

COC Chamber of Commerce; combat operations center

cod. codicil; codification

c.o.d. cash/collect on delivery

COE Corps of Engineers

c.o.h. cash on hand

col collect; collection; college; colon; colony; column

Col Colombia; colonel; Colossians (Bible)

COLA cost-of-living adjustment

coll collect; colloquial

collab collaborate; collaborator

collect. collective; collectively

colloq colloquial; colloquialism

Colo Colorado

com comedy; commercial; committee; common; communication; community

comb. combination; combine; combustible

Comdr commander

COMECON Council for Mutual Economic Assistance (Soviet Union)

COMEX New York Commodity Exchange

Comintern Communist International

comm command; commentary; commerce; commission; commissioner; common; communication

comp companion; company; compare; compensation; compilation; complete; composition; compound; comprehensive

compar comparative

Comsat communication satellite

con concentration; concerning; conclusion; con-man; connection; consolidate; continued

con. against [L *contra*]

Con Congo

CONAD Continental Air Defense Command

concr concrete

cond condense; condition; conditional; conduct; conductivity; conductor

conf. compare [L *confer*]

cong congregation; congress

conj conjugation; conjunction

conn connected

Conn Connecticut

conq conquer; conqueror

Conrail Consolidated Rail Corporation

cons consecrate; consecutive; consequence; conservation; consignment; consolidated; consonant; construction; consult

Cons conservative; consul

consgt consignment

consid consideration

const constant; constituency; constitution; construction

constr construct; construction; construe

cont containing; contents; continent; continue; continuing; continuum; contract; contraction; control; controller

contd contained; continued

contemp contemporary

contr contract; contraction; contrary; control

cont. rem. let the medicine be continued (med) [L *continuantur remedia*]

CONUS Continental United States

conv convenient; convent; convention; conventional; conversation; converter; convertible; convocation

co-op cooperative

copr copyright

cor corner; cornet; coroner; corpus; correct; correlative; correspondent; corrupt

1 Cor 1 Corinthians (Bible)

2 Cor 2 Corinthians (Bible)

CORE Congress of Racial Equality

coroll corollary

corp corporal; corporation

corr correct; correlative; correspondence; correspondent

correl correlative

corresp corresponding

Cor Sec corresponding secretary

cos cosine

c.o.s. cash on shipment

cot cotangent

cp candlepower; center of pressure; chemically pure; constant pressure

cP centipoise

C.p. with the solo part (mus) [It *colla parte*]

CP cerebral palsy; civil power; civil procedure; command post; common pleas; common prayer; Communist Party; constant pressure

CPA certified public accountant; critical path analysis (computer)

CPB Corporation for Public Broadcasting

CPC city planning commission

cpi characters per inch

CPI Consumer Price Index

Cpl corporal

CP/M Control Program/Microcomputers

cpn coupon

CPR cardiopulmonary resuscitation

cps characters per second (computer)

CPS certified professional secretary

CPSC Consumer Product Safety Commission

CPSU Communist Party of the Soviet Union

cpt captain

CPU central processing unit

cr credit; creditor; creek; crown; cruise

Cr chromium (chem)

CR Costa Rica

crim criminal; criminologist

crit criterion; critic; critical; critically; criticism

Cr P criminal procedure

CRT cathode-ray tube

cs caesarean section

Cs cesium (chem)

csc cosecant

cSt centistokes

CST central standard time

ct carat; caught; cent; certificate; circuit

Ct court

CT central time; computerized tomograph; Connecticut

ctn carton

Ctr contribution; contributor

cu cubic

Cu copper (chem)

cu ft cubic foot

cu in cubic inch

cul culinary

CVA cerebrovascular accident

C&W country and western (mus)

CWO chief warrant officer

cwt hundredweight

Cy cyanide

cyber cybernetics

cyl cylinder; cylindrical

Cyp Cyprus

CZ Canal Zone

Czech Czechoslovakia

–D–

d day; daughter; dead; deceased; defeated; degree; delete; delivery; density; depart; depth; deuteron; dexter; diameter; died; dime; disease; distance; divorced; dollar; dose; duration

D December; Democrat; Democratic; destroyer; deuterium (chem); doctor; dowager

da deka (prefix, 10)

DA delayed action; Department of the Army; deposit account; digital-to-analog; district attorney

DAC digital-to-analog converter

dad dispense as directed

D.Adm. Doctor of Administration

D.Ae. Doctor of Aeronautics

DAE Dictionary of American English

dag dekagram

D.Ag. Doctor of Agriculture

Dah Dahomey

daL dekaliter

dam dekameter

dam² square dekameter

dam³ cubic dekameter

Dan Daniel (Bible); Danish

D.App.Sci. Doctor of Applied Science

DAPS Direct-Access Programming System

DAR Daughters of the American Revolution

DARE Dictionary of American Regional English

dat dative; datum

DAT Dental Aptitude Test; digital audio tape

datacom data communications

datacor data correction

datanet data network

datap data transmission and processing

dau daughter

DAV Disabled American Veterans

dB decibel

DB database; delayed broadcast

D & B Dun and Bradstreet

dba doing business as

D.B.A. Doctor of Business Administration

D.Bi.Chem. Doctor of Biological Chemistry

D.Bi.Sc. Doctor of Biological Sciences

DBMS data base management system

dBu   decibel unit

dc   direct current

d/c   double-column (bookkeeping)

DC   District of Columbia

D&C   dilatation and curettage (surgical procedure)

D.C.E.   Doctor of Civil Engineering

dcl   decaliter; declaration; decline

D.C.L.   Doctor of Civil Law

D.Com.   Doctor of Commerce

D.Com.L.   Doctor of Commercial Law

D.C.P.   Diploma in Clinical Pathology

DCPA   Defense Civil Preparedness Agency

D.C.S.   Doctor of Commercial Sciences

dd   dated; dedicated; delivered; drilled

DD   day's date; delayed delivery; dishonorable discharge; due date

D.D.   Doctor of Divinity

D and D   drunk and disorderly

DDC   Dewey Decimal Classification

ddi   digital data indicator; document disposal indicator

DDI   Deputy Director, Intelligence (CIA)

ddl   digital data link

DDL   data definition language

ddp   digital data processor

DDP   Data Distribution Point (NATO); distributed data processing

D.D.S.   Doctor of Dental Science/Surgery

D.D.Sc.   Doctor of Dental Science

DDT   dichlorodiphenyltrichloroethane (pesticide)

d/e   date of establishment

DE   Delaware

D.E.   Doctor of Engineering

D of E Department of Energy

DEA Drug Enforcement Administration

deb debenture; debit; debut; debutante

dec decade; deceased; decimal; declaration; declension; decompose decorative; decrease

Dec deceased; December

D.Ec. Doctor of Economics

decaf decaffeinated

decd deceased

decel deceleration

decid deciduous

decl declaration; declension

decn decontamination

decomp decomposition; decompression

D.Econ. Doctor of Economics

decr decrease

ded dedicated; dedication

D.Ed. Doctor of Education

def defendant; defense; deficit; definite; definition

def art. definite article

deg degree

del delegate; delegation; delete; delivery

Del Delaware

DEL delete character (data processing)

Deleg delegation

delib deliberate; deliberation

delin delineate; delineation

dely delivery

dem demand; democracy; democratic; demonstrate

Dem Democrat

demo demonstration

demon demonstrate; demonstrative

den denier; denotation; denouement; dental; dentist; dentistry

Den Denmark

D.Eng. Doctor of Engineering

denom denomination

dep depart; department; departure; dependant; dependency; dependent; deponent; depose; deposit; depositor; depot; deputy

depr depreciation

dept department; deponent; deputy

DER Department of Environmental Resources

deriv derivation; derivative; derive

derm dermatitis; dermatology

des desert; design; designate; designation; designer; desire; dessert

desc descend; descendant; descent; describe

desig designate

destn destination

det detach; detachment; detail; detective; determine

detd determined

detox detoxification

deu data exchange unit; digital evaluation unit

Deut Deuteronomy (Bible)

dev develop; developer; development; deviate; deviation

devs devotions

DEW distant early warning (DEW line)

DF damage free; direction finding

D.F.A. Doctor of Fine Arts

DFC Distinguished Flying Cross (medal)

dft draft

dg decigram

DG director general

DH designated hitter

D.H. Doctor of Humanities

dhe data-handling equipment

D.H.L. Doctor of Humane Letters

D.H.S. Doctor of Health Sciences

Di deterioration index; didymium (chem)

DI double indemnity

dia diagram; dialectic; diameter

DIA Defense Intelligence Agency

diag diagnose; diagonal; diagram

dial. dialect; dialectal; dialectic; dialectical; dialogue

diam diameter

dian digital anlog

diaph diaphragm

diast diastolic

dic defense identification code; dictionary; digital integrated circuit

di/do data input/data output

diet. dietary; dietetics; dietician

diff differ; difference; different; differential

diff calc differential calculus

diffr diffraction

diffu diffusion

dig. digest

digicom digital communications (system)

dil dilute; dilution

dim. dimension; diminish; diminutive

dimin diminuendo (mus); diminutive

DIN Data Identification Number

dink double income no kids

dio diode

dioc diocese; diocesan

dip. diploma; diplomat

diph tet diphtheria tetanus

diphth diphthong

dipl diplomacy; diplomat; diplomatic; diplomatist

dir direct; direction; director

Dir director

Dir-Gen director-general

dis discharge; disciple; discipline; disconnect; discontinue; discount; dispense; distance; distant; distribute or break up type

DIs Department Instructions

disb disbursement

disc. disciple; discipline; discount; discover; discoverer; discovery

disch discharge

disp dispensary; dispensation; dispense; disperse; dispersion

displ displacement

diss dissenter; dissertation; dissolve

dist distance; distant; distilled; distinguish; distributive

DISTAR Direct Instruction System for Teaching Arithmetic and Reading

Dist Ct District Court

distr distributor

div dividend, division; divorced

Div divine; divinity

divn division

DJ disc jockey; Dow Jones

DJIA Dow Jones Industrial Average

D.Jur. Doctor of Jurisprudence

dk dark; deck; dock; duck

dkg dekagram

dkl dekaliter

dkt docket

dl data link; dead load; demand loan; driver's license

dL deciliter

D.Lang. Doctor of Languages

dld deadline date; delivered

D.Lit(t). Doctor of Letters; Doctor of Literature

DLO Dead Letter Office

dlr dealer

dls dollars

D.L.S. Doctor of Library Science; Doctor of Library Service

dls/shr dollars per share

dly daily; delay

dm decimeter

DM Deutsche Mark

dm² square decimeter

dm³ cubic decimeter

D.Med. Doctor of Medicine

D.Met. Doctor of Metallurgy

dmg damage

D.M.J. Diploma in Medical Jurisprudence

D.M.L. Doctor of Modern Languages

dmn dimension; dimensional

D.M.Sc. Doctor of Medical Science

DMSO dimethyl sulfoxide

DMV Department of Motor Vehicles

DMZ demilitarized zone

dn deacon; down; dozen

D/N debit note

DNA deoxyribonucleic acid

DNB Dictionary of National Biography

DNC Democratic National Party

DND Department of National Defense

D.N.Ed. Doctor of Nursing Education

dnl do not load

D-Note $500 bill

do. (ditto), the same

d-o dropout

d/o delivery; direct order

D.O. Doctor of Ophthalmology

DOA dead on arrival; Department of the Army

dob date of birth

doc doctor; document

DOC Department of Commerce

dod date of death; died of disease

DOD Department of Defense

DoEn Department of Energy

dol dollar

Dom Rep Dominican Republic

D.O.M.S. Diploma in Ophthalmic Medicine and Surgery

Dom Sc Domestic Science

DON Department of the Navy

D.Oph. Doctor of Ophthalmology

D.Opt. Doctor of Optometry

Dor Doric

dorm dormitory

DOS disc operating system (computer)

DOT Department of Transportation; Department of the Treasury

dow dowager

doz dozen

dp damp proof; departure point; depreciation percentage (fin)

DP data processing; Democratic Party; displaced person

dpa deferred payment account

D.P.A. Doctor of Public Administration

D.Ph. Doctor of Philosophy

D.P.H. Doctor of Public Health

D.P.Hy. Doctor of Public Hygiene

dpi data processing installation

DPI Department of Public Information

D.P.M. Diploma in Psychological Medicine

dpob date and place of birth

D.Psych. Doctor of Psychology

dpt department; deponent; deposit; depot

dpt vaccines diphtheria, pertussis, tetanus vaccines

dpty deputy

dpu data processing unit

DPW Department of Public Works

dq direct question

dr debit; debtor; design requirements; door; drachma; dram; drama; draw; drawer; drawn; dresser; drive; drum; drummer

Dr director; doctor; Drive

D/R deposit receipt

dram. drama; dramatic; dramatist

Dr.Chem. Doctor of Chemistry

DRI Defense Research Institute

drn drawn

Dr.Nat.Sci. Doctor of Natural Science

ds date of service; document signed

d. & s. demand and supply

DSC Distinguished Service Cross

D.Sc. (Agric.) Doctor of Agricultural Science

dsgn design; designer

DSM Distinguished Service Medal

DSM-II Diagnostic Statistical Manual (of Mental Disorders)

DSO Distinguished Service Order

DST daylight saving time

dstn destination

d.t. (med) [L *delirium tremens*]

DT daylight time; Daily Telegraph; Department of the Treasury

D.T. Doctor of Theology

dta daily travel allowance; differential thermal analysis; distributing terminal assembly

dtd dated; direct to disc (recording system)

dte development testing, and evaluation; diagnostic test equipment

DTP diptheria, tetanus, pertussis (med test)

DTS Data Transmission System

DU died unmarried

dub. dubious

duo duodecimo

dup duplicate; duplex

dv dependent variable; dilute volume; double vision

d/v declared value

D.V.M. Doctor of Veterinary Medicine

D.V.Sc. Doctor of Veterinary Science

dwg drawing; dwelling

DWI driving while intoxicated

dwt pennyweight; deadweight tons

Dx diagnosis

Dy dysprosium (chem)

D/y delivery

dyn dyne

dz dozen

D.Zool. Doctor of Zoology

–E–

e base of natural system of logarithms (math); easterly; eastern; edition; elasticity; electro-motive force of cell; electron; engineer; engineering; error; wet air (met)

E earl; earth; east; Easter; engineer; England; English; English shilling (numis); equator; illumination

ea each

E/A enemy aircraft

EAA essential amino acid

E.A.A. Engineer in Aeronautics and Astronautics

ead error adjusted; estimated availability date; extended active duty

eaf emergency action file

eal electromagnetic amplifying lens; estimated average life

eam electronic accounting methods

eaon except as otherwise noted

eap equivalent air pressure

EAPG Eastern Atlantic Planning Guidance (NATO)

ear. electronic analog resolver

EAS equivalent air speed; estimated air speed

easl engineering analysis and simulation language

east. eastern

e/at. electrons per atom

EAT earliest arrival time; estimated arrival time; expected approach time

eax electronic automatic exchange

eb electron beam; emergency brake

e-b estate-bottled

e/b eastbound

EBAM Electron-Beam Addressed Memory

ebfa electron-beam fusion accelerator

EBCDIC extended binary coded decimal interchange code (computer)

EBICON electron bombardment induced conductivity

ebit earnings before interest and taxes

EBR electron-beam recorder; experimental breeder reactor

ec economics; electrical coding; electronic calculator; emergency capability; error correcting; extended coverage

Ec Ecuador

E & C engineering and construction

ecad error check analysis diagram

ECAFE Economic Commission for Asia and the Far East

ecal equipment calibration

ecam extended communications access method

ecat emission computerized axial tomography

Ecc. Hom. Behold the Man [L *Ecce Homo*]

eccl ecclesiastic; ecclesiastical

Eccles. Ecclesiastes (Bible)

Ecclus Ecclesiasticus (Bible/Apocrypha)

ecd estimated completion date

ECE Economic Commission for Europe

ecf extracellular fluid

ECG electrocardiogram

ech echelon; engine compartment heater

ecl eclipse; extended center line

ECL emitter-coupled logic

ecm electric coding machine; extended core memory

e/cm³ electroncs per cubic centimeter

ECME Economic Commission for the Middle East (UN)

eco ecology; economic; economics; electron-coupled oscillator

ECOA Equal Credit Opportunity Act

ecol ecology; ecological

E-COM electronic computer-originated mail

econ economical; economics; economist; economy

ecr electronic cash register; energy consumption rate

ECT electroconvulsive treatment

ecu ecumenism; electronic computing unit; environmental control unit; extreme closeup

ECV energy conservation vehicle

ed edited; edition; editor; educated; education

E.D. Doctor of Engineering

E & D exploration and development

Ed.B. Bachelor of Education

edc electronic digital computer; energy distribution curve; error detection and correction; estimated date of completion

EDC Eastern Defense Command; Economic Development Corporation; Educational Development Centers

edcn education

edd electronic data display; estimated delivery date

Ed.D. Doctor of Education

eddf error detection and decision feedback

edi electron-diffraction instrument

Edin Edinburgh

Ed in Ch Editor in Chief

edinet education instruction network

EDIP European Defense Improvement Program (NATO)

edit. edited; edition; editor; editorial

edm early diastolic murmur

Ed.M. Master of Education

Edn edition

edoc effective date of change

EDP electronic data processing

edpe electronic data processing equipment

edsac electronic delayed-storage automatic computer

EDSC Engineering Data Suppport Center (USAF)

Ed Spec educational specialist

edt effective date of training

EDT eastern daylight time

Educ educated

educom education communications

edv end-diastolic volume

e/e electrical/electronic

e-to-e end to end

EE errors excepted

E.E. Electrical Engineer

eeat end-of-evening astronomical twilight

EEB European Environmental Bureau

EEC European Economic Community (Common Market)

eed elastic energy density; electrical explosive device

EEG electroencephalogram

EE & MP Envoy Extraordinary and Minister Plenipotentiary

EENT eye, ear, nose, and throat

eeo equal employment opportunity

EEOC Equal Employment Opportunity Commission

eep emergency essential personnel

EEP Energy Emergency Planning

ees electronic environment simulator

eet estimated elapsed time

EET Eastern European Time

ef extra fine

efa essential fatty acids

e & fc examined and found correct

efi electronic flight instruments; electronic fuel injection

EFM electronic fetal monitoring

EFR Electronic Failure Report

EFTA European Free Trade Association

EFTS electronic funds transfer system

e.g. for example [L *exempli gratia*]; of a like kind [L *ejusdem generis*]

Eg Egypt

E Ger East Germany

eh educationally handicapped

e & h environment and heredity

eH oxidation-reduction potential

EHA Environmental Health Association

ehf extremely high frequency

ehl effective half life

eht extra-high tension

ehv extra-high voltage

e-i electromagnetic interference; electronic interference

EI East Indies

e-i children emotionally-impaired children

EIG Exchange Information Group

E-in-C engineer-in-chief

eit engineer in training

EKG electrocardiogram

ekv electron kilovolt

el elect; elected; electric; electricity; element; elevated; elevated railway; elevation; elongation

elec election; elector; electoral; electric; electrical; electrician; electricity; electron

elem element; elementary

elev elevation; elevator

ELIA English Language Institute of America

elim eliminate; eliminated; elimination

elint electronic intelligence

elong elongate; elongation

E Long. east longitude

elra electronic radar

elv extra-low voltage

e/m specific electronic mass

Em Eminence

EM electron microscope

E of M error of measurement

emb embargo

Emb Embassy

EMC electromagnetic control

emcee master of ceremony

emf electromotive force

EMG electromyography

emi electromagnetic interference

emic emergency maternity and infant care

emm electromagnetic measurement

Emp Emperor; Empire; Empress

emp agcy employment agency

emr electromagnetic resonance

EMS emergency medical services

emt emergency medical technique

emu electromagnetic unit

en enemy

enc enclosed; enclosure

encl enclosed; enclosure

ency encyclopedia; encyclopediac; encyclopediacal

encyc encyclopedia; encyclopediac; encyclopediacal

end. endorse; endorsement

endo endocrine; endocrinology

end wk end of week

end yr end of year

En1c engineman first class

eng electronic news gathering; engine; engineer; engineering; engrave; engraver; engraving

Eng Engineering; England; English

Eng.D. Doctor of Engineering

eng err engineering error

engl England; English

Eng Lit English Literature

eng rm engine room

engrv engraver; engraving

ENIAC electronic numerical integrator and calculator (computer)

enl enlist

Ens ensign

ent entomology

ENT ear, nose and throat

entr entrance

env envelope; environs

e.o. by virtue of office [L *ex officio*]

e & o errors and omissions

EO Eastern Orthodox; Executive Order

EOB Executive Office Building

eod every other day

e & oe errors and omissions excepted

EOF end of file

eom end of month

EOM end of message (data processing)

EOP employment ownership plan; Executive Office of the President

EOR end of record; end of run

eot end of transmission

e.p. first edition [L *editio princeps*]

EP European Plan (no meals) (travel); extended play; extraordinary and plenipotentiary (dipl)

EPA Environmental Protection Agency

EPG Economic Policy Group

Eph Ephesians (Bible)

epid epidemic

epig epigram

Epil epilogue

Epis Episcopal; Episcopalian

Episc Episcopal; Episcopalian

epit epitaph; epitome

eps earnings per share; emergency power supply

epsdt early and periodic screening, diagnosis, and treatment

EPT Early Pregnancy Test

epu emergency power unit

eq equal; equate; equation; equator; equatorial; equipment; equitable; equity; equivalent

EQ educational quotient

eqpmt equipment

Equat Gui Equatorial Guinea

equiv equivalent

Er erbium (chem)

ER emergency room

era earned run average

ERA Equal Rights Amendment

ERAP Economic Research and Action Project

ERB Educational Records Bureau

Ergon ergonomics

ERISA Employee Retirement Income Security Act

erom erasable read-only memory

EROS Earth Resources Observation Systems

ERP European Recovery Program

err. error

err & app error and appeals (legal)

erron erroneous; erroneously

ERS environmental research satellite

ERT estrogen replacement therapy

Es einsteinium (chem)

esc escalator; escape; escrow

ESC escape character (computer)

ESCO Educational, Scientific, and Cultural Organization (UN)

1 Esd 1 Esdras (Bible/Apocrypha)

2 Esd 2 Esdras (Bible/Apocrypha)

ESE east-southeast

esfc extended specific fuel consumption

esh equivalent solar hour

esi emergency stop indicator

Esk Eskimo

ESL English as a second language

esm electronic support measures

esot esoteric; esoterica

esp especially

ESP extrasensory perception

Esq esquire

esr electronic slide rule

ess essence

est establish; establishment; estate; estimate; estimation; estuary;

Est Esther (Bible/Apocrypha)

EST eastern standard time

estab establish; establishment

est wt estimated weight

esu electrostatic unit

ESU English-Speaking Union

et ethyl (chem)

ET eastern time

ETA estimated time of arrival

et al. and elsewhere [L *et alibi*]; and others [L *et alii*]

etc. and so forth [L *et cetera*]

ETD estimated time of departure

Eth Ethiopia

eti elapsed-time indicator

E-time execution time (computer)

etiol etiology

ETO European Theater of Operations

Et OH ethyl alcohol

ETP electron transfer particle

et seq. and the following [L *et sequentia*]

et ux. and wife [L *et uxor*]

ety etymological; etymologist; etymology

etym etymological; etymologist; etymology

eu electron unit

Eu europium (chem)

Eur Europe; European

Eurailpass European Railway Passenger (ticket)

Euratom European Atomic Energy Community

Eurodollars U.S. dollars used to finance foreign trade

Euromarket European Common Market (European Economic Community)

ev earned value; exposure value

eV electronvolt

evac evacuate; evacuation

eval evaluate; evaluation

evap evaporate; evaporation

evol evolution; evolutionary; evolutionist

EVT educational and vocational training

EW early warning

ewf equivalent weight factor

ex example; except; exception; exchange; exclude; exclusive; execute; executive; executor; exempt; export; express; extension; extra; extract

ex aq. out of water [L *ex aqua*]

Exc Excellency

exch exchange; exchecquer

excl exclusion; exclusive

ex div ex dividend

exec executive; execute; execution; executor;

exh exhaust

exhib exhibit; exhibitioner

ex int excluding interest (fin)

exist. existing

Exod Exodus (Bible)

ex off. by virtue of office [L *ex officio*]

exp exponential (math)

ex p. on one side only [L *ex parte*]

exp-imp export-import

expo exposition

exps expenses

expt experiment

expwy expressway

ext   extend; extension; extent; exterior; external; extinct; extra; extraction; extreme

ext.   extract (med) [L *extractum*]

extemp   extemporaneous

ext. liq.   liquid extract (med) [L *extractum liquidum*]

extn   extraction

extrem   extremity

e-z   easy

Ez   Ezra (Bible)

EZ   Eastern Zone

Ezek   Ezekiel (Bible)

–F–

f   engine (railway); facing; fair; father; fathom; feet; female; femto (prefix, one-quadrillionth); fluid; folio; following; foot; force; founded; frequency; function; furlong

F   Fahrenheit; farad; February; fellow; fluorine (chem); founded; franc; France; French; frequency; friar; Friday

F.   let it be made (med) [L *fiat*]

F₁   first filial offspring resulting from crossing animals/plants

F₂   second filial generation (biol)

FAA   Federal Aviation Administration

FAAAS   Fellow of the American Academy of Arts and Sciences

fab   fabric; fabricate; fabrication

fac   facsimile; factor; faculty

FAC   Federal Advisory Council; Federal Aviation Commission

FACC   Fellow of the American College of Cardiology

faccm   fast-access charge-coupled memory (computer)

FACD   Fellow of the American College of Dentistry

facet facetious

FACFP Fellow of the American College of Family Physicians

FACOG Fellow of the American College of Obstetricians and Gynecologists

FACP Fellow of the American College of Physicians

FACR Fellow of the American College of Radiology

FACS Family and Community Services

facsim facsimile

faf financial-aid form; forward air freight

FAG Finance and Accounting Group (USAF)

Fahr Fahrenheit

FAIA Fellow of the American Institute of Architects

Falk Is Falkland Islands

fam familiar; family

FAMA Fellow of the American Medical Association

FAO Food and Agriculture Organization (UN)

F & AO Finance and Accounts Office (US Army)

FAP Family Assistance Program; Foreign Assistance Program

FAPC Food and Agriculture Planning Committee (NATO)

FAPHA Fellow of the American Public Health Association

Far. Faraday

FAR Failure Analysis Report; Federal Aviation Regulations

FASB Financial Accounting Standards Board

FASCE Fellow of the American Society of Civil Engineers

fat. fatigue

fath fathom

fav favor; favorite

FAX facsimile transmission

fb freight bill; fringe benefits; fullback

f/b feedback

FBA Federal Bar Association

FBI Federal Bureau of Investigation

fbm board foot; board foot measure

FBN Federal Bureau of Narcotics

FBP Federal Bureau of Prisons

fbs fasting blood sugar

fc footcandle

f/c free and clear

f & c fire and casualty (ins)

fca frequency control and analysis

FCA Farm Credit Administration

FCAA Federal Clean Air Act

fcbu foreign currency banking unit

FCC Federal Communications Commission

fcd failure-correction coding

fcg facing

FCI Federal Correctional Institution

FCIC Federal Crop Insurance Corporation

FCIP Federal Crime Insurance Program

FCIS Foreign Counter-intelligence System (FBI)

FCMS Fellow of the College of Medicine and Surgery

FCPS Fellow of the College of Physicians and Surgeons

F/CS Flight-Control System

FCTC Fleet Combat Training Center (USN)

FCU Federal Credit Union

FD fire department

FDA Food and Drug Administration

FDEA Federal Drug Enforcement Administration

fdg funding

FDIC Federal Deposit Insurance Corporation

Fdr founder

FDR flight data recorder

Fe iron (chem)

FE Far East; format effective character (data processing)

FEA Federal Energy Administration

Feb February

FEC Federal Election Commission

Fed federal; Federal Reserve; federated; federation

Fell Fellow

f/e loader front-end loader

fem female; feminine

FEMA Federal Emergency Management Agency

F/Eng Flight Engineer

FEP Federal Employees Program

FEPC Fair Employment Practices Commission

FERA Federal Emergency Relief Administration

FERC Federal Energy Regulatory Commission

fert fertility; fertilizer

FET Federal Excise Tax

feud. feudal; feudalism

fev fever

ff following

f to f face to face

FF form feed (computer)

FFA Future Farmers of America

FFAS Fellow of the Faculty of Architects and Surveyors

FFCB Federal Farm Credit Board

FFPS Fellow of the Faculty of Physicians and Surgeons

FFV First Families of Virginia

FFZ Free Fire Zone

FG Federal Government

FGP Foster Grandparent Program

FGT Federal Gift Tax

FHA Federal Housing Administration

FHLBB Federal Home Loan Bank Board

FHLBS Federal Home Loan Bank System

FHLMC Federal Home Loan Mortgage Corporation (Freddie Mac)

fhr fetal heart rate

FHWA Federal Highway Administration

fi fade in

FIC Federal Insurance Corporation; Flight Information Center

FICA Federal Insurance Contributions Act

FICB Federal Intermediate Credit Bank

fict fiction; fictional; fictitious

fid fiduciary

FIDP Fellow of the Institute of Data Processing

FIFO first in, first out (system of inventory)

fig. figure

FIIN Federal Item Identification Number

FIJ Fellow of the Institute of Journalists

FILO first in, last out (system of inventory)

fin. at, or near, the end [L *ad finem*]; final; finance; financial; financier; the end [L *finis*]

Fin Finland

Fin Sec Financial Secretary

fio for information only

FIPS Federal Information Processing Standards

fitw federal income tax withholding

fix. fixture

Fj Fjord

fL footlambert

Fl Flanders; Flemish

FL Florida

Fla Florida

FLA Federal Loan Administration

Fld Field

Flem Flemish

FLEX Federal Licensing Examination

flex. flexible

fl/mtr flow meter

Fl O Flight Officer

fl oz fluid ounce(s)

FLPL fortran-compiled list-processing language

fl pt fluid pint

FLR Federal Law Reports

FLRA Federal Labor Relations Authority

FLSA Fair Labor Standards Act

Flt Adm Fleet Admiral

Flt Cmdr Flight Commander

Flt Lt Flight Lieutenant

flt/pg flight programmer

flt pln flight plan

FLTSATCOM Fleet Satellite Communications (DOD)

Flt Sgt Flight Sergeant/ Sergeant

fluor fluorescent; fluoridation; fluoride

fm femtometer

f/m feet per minute

Fm fermium (chem)

FM frequency modulation

FMA Federal Maritime Administration

FMC Federal Maritime Commission

fmcw frequency-modulated continuous wave

fmfb frequency-modulation feedback

FmHA Farmers Home Administration

fmrly formerly

fmu force measurement unit

FMVSS Federal Motor Vehicle Safety Standard

fn footnote

FNMA Federal National Mortgage Association (Fannie Mae)

fnp fusion point

FNS Food and Nutrition Service

f number lens focal length

fo folio

f/o for credit of

f.o.b. free on board

FOB Federal Office Building

f.o.c. free of charge

f.o.d. free of damage

FoIA Freedom of Information Act

fol folio; follow; following

forf forfeit

forg forgery

for. lang foreign language(s)

form. format; former

formn foreman

for. rts foreign rights

FORTRAN Formula Translation (computer language)

FOSDIC film optical sensing device (computer)

fp family plan; film pack; fine paper; first performance

FP family practitioner

F/P Fire Policy (ins)

FPA Family Planning Association; Foreign Policy Association; Foreign Press Association

FPC Family Planning Center; Federal Power Commission

FPCI Federal Penal and Correctional Institutions

fpdi flight path deviation indicator

fph feet per hour

FPHA Federal Public Housing Authority

F Pharm S Fellow of the Pharmaceutical Society

fplce fireplace

fpm feet per minute

FPO fleet post office; for position only

FPP Family Planning Program; Foster Parents Plan

fps foot/pound/second

fpsps feet per second per second

f/r fixed response; front to rear

fr from

f.r. right hand page [L *folio recto*]

Fr Father; France; francium (chem); French

FR frequency rate

fract fraction; fracture

frag fragile; fragment; fragmentation

Franc. Franciscan (religious order)

fraud. fraudulent

FRBs Federal Reserve Banks

FRC Federal Radiation Council; Federal Radio Commission; flight research center (NASA)

Fr Can French-Canadian

FR Dist Federal Reserve District

freq frequency; frequent; frequently

fresh. freshman; freshmen

FRG Federal Republic of Germany (West Germany)

frgt freight

Fri Friday

fric friction; frictional

front. frontispiece

frpb fireproof

FRS Federal Reserve System

frsc full range source code

frt freight

frt/fwd freight forward

fs facsimile

FS Forest Service

F/S financial statement

FSA Farm/Federal Security Administration

fsbo for sale by owner

FSCM Federal Supply Code for Manufacturers

FSE Federation of Stock Exchanges

FSIS Food Safety and Inspection Service (USDA)

FSLA Federal Savings and Loan Association

FSLIC Federal Savings and Loan Insurance Corporation

FSM Free Speech Movement

fss finite solution set (math)

FSS Federal Supply Service

ft foot

f/t freight ton

f & t fire and theft

ft² square foot

ft³ cubic foot

Ft Fort

FTC Federal Trade Commission

FTD florists telegraph delivery service

ftH₂O conventional foot of water

fti federal tax included

FT Index *Financial Times Index*

ft-lb foot-pound

ft-lbf foot pound-force

ft/min foot per minute

ft²/min square foot per minute

ft³/min cubic foot per minute

ft-pdl foot poundal

ft/s foot per second

ft²/s square foot per second

ft³/s cubic foot per second

ft/s² foot per second squared

ft/s³³ foot per second cubed

ft sec foot second

funct function; functional; functionally

fund. fundamental; fundamentalist

f/up follow up

fur. furlong; further

furl. furlough

furn furnace; furnish; furniture

fut future

fw formula weight

FWA Federal Works Agency

FWD four-wheel drive; front-wheel drive

fwd. forward

FWL Foundation for World Literacy

FWPCA Federal Water Pollution Control Administration

FWS Fish and Wildlife Service

fwy freeway

FX foreign exchange

FY fiscal year

fyi for your information

–G–

g acceleration of gravity; gauge; gelding; gender; general; general factor; genitive; gram; gravity; guilder; guinea

G conductance (elec); gauss; general (movie rating); German; Germany; giga (prefix, 1 billion) (phys); grand ($1,000); gravitation constant (phys); specific gravity

G-1, G-2, G-3, G-4 (mil) Each of the four sections of a general staff: personnel (G-1); intelligence (G-2); training and operation (G-3); supplies (G-4).

g/a general average (ins); ground to air

Ga gallium; Georgia

GA Gamblers Anonymous; general agent; general assembly; Georgia

GAA Gay Activists Alliance

GAAP Generally Accepted Accounting Principles

g/a con general average contribution

g/a dep general average deposit

Gael. Gaelic

gal   gallon

Gal   Galatians (Bible)

gal cap   gallon capacity

gall.   gallery

gal/min   gallons per minute

gal/s   gallons per second

galv   galvanic; galvanized

GAM   ground-to-air missile

GAO   General Accounting Office

GAP   gross agricultural product

GAPR   Grant Application Request

gar   garage

GAR   Grand Army of the Republic

Gara   Garamond (typo)

G.Arch.   Graduate in Architecture

gas   gasoline

gast   gastric

GATB   General Aptitude Test Battery

GATT   General Agreement on Tariffs and Trade

g at. wt   gram atomic weight

g/av   general average

GAW   guaranteed annual wage

gaz   gazette; gazetteer

gb   gall bladder

Gb   gilbert (phys)

GB   Great Britain

GBE   Knight (or Dame) Grand Cross Order of the British Empire

gb/l   government bill of lading

GBR   *Guiness Book of Records*

G-B s   Guillain-Barre syndrome

gc   good condition

GCA   Girls Clubs of America

g cal   gram calorie

GCC   Ground Control Center

gcd   greatest common divisor (math)

gcf greater common factor (math)

GCL ground-controlled landing

g/cm³ gram per cubic centimeter

gcr great circle route

gc/s gigacycles per second

GCT Greenwich civil time

gcu generator control unit; ground control unit

Gd gadolinium (chem)

GD General Delivery

gde gross domestic expenditure

gdn garden

gdp graphic display processor

GDP gross domestic product

GDR German Democratic Republic (East Germany)

gds goods

gdt graphic display terminal

gdu graphic display unit

Ge germanium (chem)

GE General Electric

GED General Education Diploma

GEDP General Educational Development Program

GEDT General Educational Development Test

Ge.Eng. Geological Engineer

gen gender; genealogy; general; generator; generic; genetic; genital; genuine, genus

Gen General; Genesis (Bible)

gen av general average

genl general

Gen Mgr general manager

gen prac general practice

gent gentleman

geod geodesy; geodetic

geog geographer; geographic; geography

geol geologic; geologist; geology

geom geometric; geometry

geophys geophysics

GEOS Geodetic Orbiting Satellite

gep gross energy product

ger gerund

Ger German; Germany

Ger Dem Rep German Democratic Republic (East Germany)

geriat geriatrics

gerontol gerontology

GeV Giga electron volt

gew gram equivalent weight

g-force gravity force

gg gamma globulin

GGM ground-to-ground missile

GH growth hormone

GHQ general headquarters

GHZ gigahertz (gigacycle per second)

gi gill

GI general issue; government issue; US military personnel (slang)

gia grant-in-aid

gigo garbage in, garbage out (computer)

g ion gram ion

GIS Government Information Service

gj gigajoule

Gk Greek

gl gill

g/l grams per liter

G.L. Graduate in Law

glac glacial

gloss. glossary

gly glycerine

gm gram; guinea (British currency)

g/m gallons per minute

gm² grams per square meter

GM General Motors

GMAC General Motors Acceptance Corporation

G-man a Federal Bureau of Investigation agent

GMAT Graduate Management Admissions Test; Greenwich mean astronomical time

GM counter geiger counter

gm mol gram-molecule; molecular weight in grams (phys)

gmp guaranteed minimum price

GMP General Medical Practice

gm & s general, medical, and surgical

GMT Greenwich mean time

G.N. Graduate Nurse

GNI gross national income

GNMA Government National Mortgage Association (Ginnie Mae)

GNP gross national product

GO General Office

GOC Ground Observer Corps

GOL general operating language (computer)

GOP Grand Old Party (Republican Party)

goth. gothic

Gov Governor

Gov Is Governor's Island

Govt government

g-p general purpose

Gp group

GP general practitioner

GPA grade point average

gpad gallons per acre per day

GPARM graduated-payment adjustable-rate mortgage

Gp Cmdr Group Commander

gpd gallons per day

GPFS General-Purpose Financial Statement

G.Ph. Graduate in Pharmacy

GPI general price index

gpm gross profit margin

GPM graduated payment mortgage

GPO General Post Office; Government Printing Office

gpu ground power unit

GQ general quarters

gr grade; grain; gram; grammar; gravity; gross; ground; group

g-r gamma ray

Gr Grecian; Greece; Greek

grad gradient; grading; graduate

gram. grammar; grammarian; grammatical

gran granite; granular

graph. graphology

Gre Greece

GRE Graduate Record Examination

GREB Graduate Records Examination Boards

grm gram

grnd ground

gro gross

groc grocery

Grp group

grt gross registered tonnage

gr tons gross tons

gr wt gross weight

gs gauss

GS Geological Survey; gold standard; grammar school

G & S Gilbert and Sullivan

GSA General Services Administration; Girl Scouts of America

GSFC Goddard Space Flight Center

GSL Guaranteed Student Loan

GSO general staff officer

Gt Great

GTA grand theft auto

Gt Br Great Britain

Gt Brit Great Britain

gtd guaranteed

gtr greater

GU Guam

guar guarantee

GULAG Soviet labor camp

GUO government use only

GV gigavolt

Gve Grove

GVP General Vice President

gvt government

GVW gross weight vehicle

gw gigawatt; green weight; ground wave; guerilla warfare

g/w gross weight

G + W Gulf and Western

gwh gigawatt hour

Gy gray

gym gymnasium; gymnastics

gyn gynecologist

gz ground zero

GZT Greenwich Zone Time

–H–

h hail (met); harbor; hardness; hearts (cards); heat; heavy; hecto (prefix, 100); height; hit; horizontal; hour; hundred; husband; Planck's constant

H Hamiltonian (phys); hardness (pencils); henry; horizontal force of earth's magnetism; hydrogen (chem); unit of inductance (H=Vs/A)

ha hectare

h.a. this year [L *hoc anno*]

Ha Haiti; Haitian; Hawaii; Hawaiian

hab habitat; habitation

Hab Habakkuk (Bible)

hab. corp. may you have the body (law) [L *habeas corpus*]

Hag Haggai (Bible)

hal halogen

Han Hanover; Hanoverian

hard. hardware

harm. harmonic; harmony

harp. harpoon; harpsichord

hAv hepatitis A virus

haz hazard; hazardous

hb halfback

h/b handbook

Hb hemoglobin

hbf hepatic blood flow

H-bomb hydrogen bomb

hbp high blood pressure

hBv hepatitis B virus

h.c. for the sake of the honor [L *honoris causa*]

HC hard copy; House of Commons

hcap handicap

hcb hard-covered book

hcd high current density

hcf highest common factor (math)

HCH hexachlorocyclohexane (insecticide)

hcl high cost of living

HCl hydrochloric acid (chem)

HCp heat of combustion of an element under constant pressure (chem)

hcptr helicopter

hcrit hematocrit

hcs high carbon steel

HCv heat of combustion of an element under constant volume

hd hand; head

h.d. at bedtime (med) [L *hora decubitus*]

h-d heavy-duty

HD Honorable Discharge

HDA High Duty Alloy

hdbk handbook

HDC Housing Development Corporation

hd cr hard chromium

hddr high-density digital recording

hdg heading

HDL high-density lipoproteins

hdlg handling

HDMR high-density moderated reaction

H Doc House Document

hdqrs headquarters

hdsp hardship

HDST high-density shock tube

h-duty heavy duty

hdv heavy-duty vehicle

hdwd hardwood

h.e. this is [L *hic est*]

h&e heredity and environment

He Hebraic; Hebrew; helium (chem)

HE His/Her Eminence; His/Her Excellency

Heb Hebrews (Bible); Hebraic; Hebrew

hect hectare

hectog hectogram

hectol hectoliter

hectom hectometer

HEH Her/His Exalted Highness

heir app heir apparent

heir pres heir presumptive

hel helicopter

Helv Helvetica (typo)

hem. hemoglobin; hemorrhage

HEPC Hydro-Electric Power Commission

her. heraldry

herb. herbalist; herbarium; herbaceous

hered heredity

HERMES heavy element and radioactive material electromagnetic separator

hero. hazards of electromagnetic radiation to ordnance; hot experimental reactor of 0 (zero power)

Herp herpetologist; herpetology

heu hydroelectric unit

hevr heavier

HEW Department of Health, Education and Welfare

hex. hexachord; hexagon; hexagonal

hexa hexamethylene tetramine

hf half

h/f held for

Hf hafnium (chem)

HF high frequency

H of F Hall of Fame

hf bd half-bound

hfc high frequency current

hf-df high-frequency direction finder

HFG high frequency gas

hfo high frequency oscillator

Hfx Halifax

hg hectogram

Hg mercury (chem) [L *hydrargyrum*]

HG Her(His) Grace; High German; Holy Ghost; Home Guard; Horse Guards

hga high gain antenna

hgb hemoglobin

HGH human growth hormone

hgt height

h/h hard of hearing

HH heavy hydrogen (chem); Her(His) Highness; His Holiness; His Honor

H.H.D. Doctor of Humanities (U.S.A.)

hhg household goods

H-hour the hour at which a military operation is to begin

HHS Health and Human Resources (Department of)

hi humidity index

Hi high; Hindi; humidity index

HI Hawaii; Hawaiian Islands

H.I. here lies [L *hic iacet*]

HIAA Health Insurance Association of America

hiac high accuracy

Hib Hibernia (Ireland); Hibernian

hicapcom high capacity communications

Hi Com high command; high commissioner

Hier hieroglyphics

hi fi high fidelity

HIH Her (His) Imperial Highness

hi-lo high-low

hi mi high mileage

Hind Hindi; Hindu; Hindustan; Hindustani

H-ion hydrogen ion

HIP Health Insurance Plan

hi pres high pressure

hist historian; historic; history

hi tech high technology

hi-temp high temperature

Hitt Hittite

HIUS Hispanic Institute of the United States

HIV human immunodeficiency virus

H.J. here lies [L *hic jacet*]; here lies buried [L *hic jacet sepultus*]

HK Hong Kong

h.l. in this place [L *hoc loco*]

hL hectoliter

HL House of Lords

hlw high-level waste

hlwn highest low-water neap tides

hm hallmark; hand made; headmaster; headmistress; hectometer

h.m. in this month [L *hoc mense*]

h & m hit and miss

H/m unit of magnetic permeability

HM Her(His) Majesty

hm² square hectometer

hm³ cubic hectometer

HMO Health Maintenance Organization

hms hours, minutes, seconds

HMS His (Her) Majesty's Ship

hmstd homestead

Hn Horn

hnbk handbook

HNP herniated nucleus pulposus (herniated disc)

ho hold over

Ho holmium (chem)

HO head/home office

Holl Holland

holo holograph

home ec home economics

homo homeopath; homeopathic; homosexual

hon honor; honorable; honorary

hons honors

hor horizon; horizontal; horology

hora decub. at bedtime [L *hora decubitus*]

hora som. at bedtime [L *hora somni*]

horiz horizontal

hort horticulture

Hos Hosea (Bible)

hosp hospital

Hou Houston

how. howitzer

hp horsepower

hpchd harpsichord

hp cyl high-pressure cylinder

hpf highest possible frequency

hph horsepower-hour

hpr high powered radar

HPS high protein supplement

hpt high point

hpu hydraulic pumping unit

HPV high-passage virus

HQ headquarters

hr home run; hour

HR House of Representatives

HRA Human Resources Administration

HRC Holy Roman Church

HRE Holy Roman Emperor/Empire

HRes House Resolution

HRH His (Her) Royal Highness

H.R.I.P. here rests in peace [L *hic requiescit in pace*]

HRWMC House of Representatives Ways and Means Committee

HS high school

H.S. here is buried [L *hic sepultus* or *situs*]

H Sch High School

hsda high-speed data acquisition

HSDE High-School Driver Education

Hse House

hskpg housekeeping

HSM Her/His Serene Majesty

hsp high-speed printer

hsr high-speed reader

HSV herpes simplex virus

ht heat; height

HT high temperature

hta heavier than air

htb high-tension battery

htd heated

htg heating

htl hotel

HTO high-temperature oxidation; horizontal takeoff

HTOL horizontal take off and land

htr heater

Hts Heights

HTT heavy tactical transport

HTU heat transfer unit

HUAC House Un-American Activities Committee

HUD Department of Housing and Urban Development

hugo highly unusual geophysical operations

HUKS hunter-killer submarine (USN)

hum. human; humanities; humanity; humorous

hund hundred

Hung Hungarian; Hungary

hur hurricane

hurevac hurricane evacuation

husb husband; husbandry

hustle. helium underwater speech translating equipment

hv high vacuum/velocity/voltage

h & v heating and ventilating

hvac high-voltage alternating current

hvf high viscosity fuel

hvi high viscosity index

hvps high-voltage power supply

hvy heavy

hwl high-water line

hwm high-water mark

HWMC House Ways and Means Committee

HWS Hurricane Warning System

hwvr however

hwy highway

hx hexode

hyb hybrid

hyd hydrate; hydraulic; hydrographic; hydrostatics

HYDAC hybrid digital-analog computer

hyg hygiene

hyp hypodermic; hypotenuse; hypothesis; hypothetical

hypoth hypothesis; hypothetical

hz haze

Hz hertz (cycles per second)

–I–

i current (elec); imaginary unit (math); interest; intermittent precipitation (met); intransitive; island; isle

I Independent; institute; instructor; intelligence; iodine (chem); Ireland; Irish; isopin; Italian; Italy

i.a. in the absence of [L *in absentia*]

Ia Iowa

IA Iowa

IAAE Institute of Automative and Aeronautical Engineers

IAAF International Amateur Athletic Federation

IAB Inter-America Bank

IABLA Inter-American Bank for Latin America

IAC Intelligence Advisory Committee (CIA)

IACB International Advisory Committee on Bibliography (UNESCO)

IACHR Inter-American Commission for Human Rights

IADB Inter-American Defense Board

iadt initial active duty training

iae integral absolute error

IAEA International Atomic Energy Agency

IAG Interagency Advisory Group

IAIAS Inter-American Institute of Agricultural Sciences

IAL International Algebraic Language

IAMP Inter-Agency Motor Pool

iao intermittent aortic occlusion

IAP Institution of Analysis & Programmers; International Academy of Pathology

IAPM International Academy of Preventive Medicine

IAR Institute for Air Research

I Arb Institute of Arbitrators

ias immediate access storage; indicated airspeed

iasd interatrial septal defect

iat inside air temperature

IAT Institute for Applied Technology

IATA International Air Transport Association

iatd is amended to delete

iatr is amended to read

iaw in accordance with

IAW International Alliance of Women

IBAA Investment Bankers Association of America

ibd interest-bearing deposit

IBEW International Brotherhood of Electrical Workers

ibid. in the same place [L *ibidem*]

IBM International Business Machines Corporation

IBOP international balance of payments

ibp initial boiling point

IBRD International Bank for Reconstruction and Development

ib test ink blot test

ibu imperial bushel

IBWM International Bureau of Weights and Measures

ic index/instrument correlation; integrated circuit; internal combustion

i.c. between meals [L *inter cibos*]

i/c in charge; intercom

ICA International Communication Agency

I of CA Institute of Chartered Accountants

icad integrated control and display

icade interactive computer-aided design evaluation

ICAO International Civil Aviation Organization

ICBM intercontinental ballistic missile

ICBP International Council for Bird Preservation

ICBR Institute for Child Behavior Research

ICC Interstate Commerce Commission

ICCAD International Center for Computer-Aided Design

Ice. Iceland; Icelandic

ICE Institute of Civil Engineers

ICED International Council for Educational Development

ICEF International Children's Emergency Fund

ICFA International Cystic Fibrosis Association

ich ichthyology

ichth ichthyology

ICIC International Copyrights Information Center

ICIP International Conference on Information Processing

icop imported crude oil processing

ICOR Intergovernmental Conference on Oceanic Research (UNESCO)

icp inventory control point

ICPO International Criminal Police Organization (Interpol)

ICRC International Committee of the Red Cross

ICSI International Conference on Scientific Information

ictus. counselor-at-law [L *Iurisconsultus*]

ICU intensive care unit

id inside diameter

id. the same [L *idem*]

ID Idaho; identification; industrial dynamics; infectious disease; information/intelligence department

Ida. Idaho

IDA Institute for Defense Analysis; International Development Association (UN)

idb integrated data base

IDB International Development Bank

IDC Industrial Design Council

ID card identification card

idcf indirect command file

i-d curve intensity-duration curve

IDD International Direct Dialing

IDEA International Drug Enforcement Association

ident identification; identify

IDF integrated data file

IDI Industrial Designers' Institute

IDL international date line

IDMS Integrated Database Management System

idp information data processing; integrated data processing

IDTS Instrumentation Data Transmission System

ie index error; inside edge; ion exchange

i.e. that is [L *id est*]

i-e internal-external

i/e ingress/egress

IE Indo-European

IEB International Energy Bank

ied individual effective dose

IEG Information Exchange Group

ieq index of environmental quality

i.f. he did it himself [L *ipse fecit*]

i-f in-flight

IF interferon; intermediate frequency

IFA Intercollegiate Fencing Association

IFAD International Fund for Agricultural Development

IFC International Finance Corporation (UN)

IFFA International Federation of Film Archives

if nec if necessary

ifo in front of; identified flying object

IFPA Institute for Foreign Policy Analysis

IFR instrument flight rules

IG Illustrators Guild; imperial gallon; Inspector General

igc intellectually gifted children

ign ignition

igr. therefore [L *igitur*]

IGS interactive graphics system

IHD ischemic heart disease

ihp indicated horsepower

IHQ International Headquarters

IIN item identification number

Il illinium (chem)

IL Illinois

ILA International Law Association; International Linguistic Association; International Longshoremen's Association

ILAS Institute of Latin American Studies

ILC International Law Commission (UN)

ILGWU International Ladies Garment Workers' Union

ill. illustrate; illustration; illustrator

Ill Illinois

illegit illegitimate

illit. illiterate

illus illustrate; illustration; illustrator

ILO International Labor Office (UN); International Labor Organization

ILP Independent Labor Party; Israel Labor Party

ILQ *International Law Quarterly*

im impulse modulation; installment mortgage; intensity modulation

IM intramuscular

imag imaginary; imagination; imagine

IMC International Maritime Committee

imcc item management control code

IMCC Integrated Mission Control Center

IMCO Intergovernmental Maritime Consultative Organization

I Meth Independent Methodist

IMF International Monetary Fund

im/fm intensity modulated/frequency modulated

imit imitate; imitation; imitative

immed immediate

immun immunity; immunization; immunology

IMO International Maritime Organization

imp. imperative; imperfect; imperial; impersonal; implement; import; important; importer; impression; let it be printed [L *imprimatur*]

IMP indeterminate mass particle; international match point

imper imperative

imperf imperfect; imperforate (stamps)

impers impersonal

imp-exp import-export

IMRADS Information Management, Retrieval, and Dissemination System

in inch

i/n item number

in² square inch

in³ cubic inch

In India; Indian; indium (chem)

IN Indiana

I & N Immigration and Naturalization

in. al. among other things [L *inter alia*]

inaug inaugurate

inc include; inclusive; income; increase

Inc incorporated

incl incline; include; inclusive

incog incognito

incompl incomplete

incorr incorrect

incr increase; increment

incun incunabula

ind independent; index; indicate; indication; indicative; indirect; indirectly

Ind Indiana; India

IND Independent Subway Line (NYC Subway); investigational new drug

indef indefinite

indic indicative; indicator

indiv individual

Ind L Independent Liberal

Ind Meth Independent Methodist

Indoc Indochina; Indochinese

Indo-Eur Indo-European

Indo-Ger Indo-German; Indo-Germanic

induc induction

indust industrial; industry

ined. unpublished [L *ineditus*]

in ex. at length [L *in extenso*]

inf infantry; inferior; infinitive; influence; information

INF Intermediate-range Nuclear Forces

infin infinitive

infirm. infirmary

info information

infra dig. undignified [L *infra dignitatem*]

in/h inch per hour

inhab inhabitant

inHg conventional inch of mercury

inH2O conventional inch of water

in init. in the beginning [L *in initio*]

in-lb inch-pound

inn. innings

in pr. in the beginning [L *in principio*]

in pro in proportion

inq inquiry

in ref in reference (to)

INRI Jesus of Nazareth, King of the Jews [L *Iesus Nazarenus Rex Iudaeorum*]

ins insurance

in s. in original place [L *in situ*]

in/s inch per second

INS Immigration and Naturalization Service; Institute of Naval Studies; Institute of Nuclear Sciences

in./sec. inch per second

inscr inscribe; inscription

insd val insured value

insep inseparable

insol insoluble

insolv insolvent

insp inspect; inspection; inspector

Insp Gen inspector general

inst instance; instant; institution; instruct; instruction; instructor; instrument

Inst Institute; Institution

Inst EE Institute of Electrical Engineers

Inst ME Institute of Mechanical Engineers

instn institution

Inst P Institute of Physics

Inst Plan & Res Institute for Planning and Research

int intake; integer; intelligence; interest; interior; interjection; intermediate; internal; international; intransitive

INTELSAT International Telecommunications Satellite Consortium

intens intensive

inter. intermediate; interrogative

intercom intercommunication

interj interjection

interp interpreter

Interpol International Criminal Police Organization

interrog interrogative

inter/w intersection with

INTIPS Integrated Information Processing System

Int J Theor Phys *International Journal of Theoretical Physics*

intl international

intr intransitive

in. trans. on the way [L *in transitu*]

Int Rev Internal Revenue

inv invent; invention; inventor; inversion; invert; invoice

Io ionium (chem)

I/O input/output

I O C International Olympic Committee

ioi internal operating instruction

Ion. Ionic

IOOF Independent Order of Odd Fellows

i & op in-and-out processing

IOS Institute of Oceanographic Science

IOU I owe you

i/p input

IPA *Information Please Almanac; International Pharmaceutical Abstracts;* international phonetic alphabet

iph impressions per hour;

IPL information processing language

ipo initial public offering

ipts international practical temperature scale

IPU input preparation unit (computer)

i.q. the same as [L *idem quod*]

IQ intelligence quotient

i.q.e.d. that which was to be proved [L *id quod erat demonstrandum*]

ir information retrieval; infrared; instrument reading

Ir Ireland; iridium (chem); Irish

IR incidence rate; index register; isoprene rubber

IRA individual retirement account; Irish Republican Army

irad independent research and development

Iran. Iranian

IRB Industrial Review Board; International Resources Bank

IRBM intermediate range ballistic missile

IRC infantry reserve corps; International Red Cross

IR & D International Research and Development

Ire Ireland

IRE Institute of Radio Engineers

irid iridescent

IRO International Refugee Organization

irr irredeemable (fin); irregular

irreg irregular

IRS Internal Revenue Service

IRT Interborough Rapid Transit (NYC Subway)

Is Isaiah (Bible); Islam; Islamic; island; isle; Israel; Israeli

Isa Isaiah (Bible)

isar information storage and retrieval

ISBD International Standard Book Description

ISBN International Standard Book Number

ISCO International Standard Classification of Occupations

ise integral square error

ISIC International Standard Industrial Classification

ISIS Integrated Scientific Information Service; Integrated Statistical Information Service

ISO International Standards Organization

ISODOC International Center for Standards in Information and Documentation

isol isolate; isolation

Isr Israel

iss issue

ISS Industry Standard Specifications

ISSN International Standard Serial Number

ISV International Scientific Vocabulary

It Italian; italic; Italy

ital italics

ITC International Trade Commission

itin itinerary

ITO International Trade Organization

ITT International Telephone and Telegraph Company

ITU International Telecommunication Union; International Typographical Union

ITWF International Transport Workers' Federation

IU international units

IUCD intrauterine contraceptive device

IUD intrauterine device

iv initial velocity; intravenous; invoice value

IWPA International Word Processing Association

IWW Industrial Workers of the World

I.X. Jesus Christ [L *Iesus Christus*]

IYHF International Youth Hostels Federation

–J–

j journal; judge; justice

J action variable; advance ratio; current density; Jacobian determinant (math); January; joule (phys); Jupiter

Ja January

JA Judge-Advocate; Justice of Appeal

J/A joint account

Jac Jacobean

JACS *Journal of the American Chemical Society*

JADA *Journal of the American Dental Association*

J Adv Gen Judge Advocate General

JAEIC Joint Atomic Energy Intelligence Committee

JAG Judge Advocate General

Jam James (Bible)

JAMA *Journal of the American Medical Association*

J Am Inst Electr Eng *Journal of the American Institute of Electrical Engineers*

Jan January

Jap Japan; Japanese

J Appl Phys *Journal of Applied Physics*

jar. jargon

jastop jet-assisted stop

jato jet-assisted takeoff

J.B. Bachelor of Laws [L *jurum baccalaureus*]

JBL *Journal of Business Law*

Jc Junction

JC Junior Chamber of Commerce (jaycee); juvenile court

J.C. Jesus Christ; Julius Caesar

JCA Joint Commission on Accreditation (college and university); Joint Communication Activity

JCAE Joint Committee on Atomic Energy

JCAH Joint Committee on Accreditation of Hospitals

J.C.B. Bachelor of Canon Law [L *juris canonici baccaulaureus*]

JCC Job Corps Center; Junior Chamber of Commerce

JC of C Junior Chamber of Commerce

J.C.D. Doctor of Civil Law

JCE *Journal of Chemical Education*

JCEE Joint Council on Economic Education

J Chem Soc *Journal of the Chemical Society*

JCL Job Control Language

jcm jettison control module

JCP Joint Committee on Printing (Congress)

JCS Joint Chiefs of Staff

Jct Junction

jct pt junction point

JD Justice Department; juvenile delinquent

J.D. Doctor of Jurisprudence [L *jurum doctor*]; Doctor of Law [L *juris doctor*]

J/deg joule per degree

JDL Jewish Defense League

J.D.S. Doctor of Juridical Science

JEC Joint Economic Committee (Congress)

J Ed *Journal of Education*

Jeep general purpose (GP) vehicle

jem jet engine modulation

Jer Jeremiah (Bible); Jersey; Jerusalem

JER *Japan Economic Review*

jerob jeroboam

Jes. Jesus

JETP *Journal of Experimental and Theoretical Physics* (USSR)

JFS *Jane's Fighting Ships*

JG junior grade

J Geophys Res *Journal of Geophysical Research*

JGS Joint General Staff (NATO)

JHS junior high school

J.H.S. Jesus Savior of Man [L *Jesus Hominum Salvator*]

JHVH Jehovah

JIC Joint Industrial Council

J Inor Nucl Chem *Journal of Inorganic and Nuclear Chemistry*

JIOA Joint Intelligence Objectives Agency

jkg joules per kilogram

jkt jacket

Jl journal; July

J/m² joules per meter squared

J Math Phys *Journal of Mathematical Physics; Journal of Mathematics and Physics*

Jn junction; June

Jnl *Journal*

JNM *Journal of Nuclear Medicine*

JOBS Job Opportunities in the Business Sector

Jon Jonah (Bible)

Josh Joshua (Bible)

jour journeyman

JP Justice of the Peace

JPB Joint Planning Board

JPL Jet Propulsion Laboratory (NASA)

J Prob Judge of Probate

JPRS Joint Publications Research Service

jpto jet-propelled take-off

Jr journal; junior; juror

JR Joint Resolution

Jr HS junior high school

JROTC Junior Reserve Officers' Training Corps

JSC Johnson Space Center (NASA)

J.Sc.D. Doctor of Juristic Science

J.S.D. Doctor of the Science of Laws

jt agt joint agent

jt auth joint author

Jth Judith (Bible/Apocrypha)

JTM&H *Journal of Tropical Medicine and Hygiene*

jto jump takeoff

JTPA Job Training Partnership Act

Ju June

jud judgment; judicial

Jud Judah; Judea; Judge

J.U.D. Doctor of Canon and Civil Law [L *Juris utriusque Doctor*]

Judg Judges (Bible)

Judge Adv Gen Judge Advocate General

junc junction

Jup Jupiter

jur juridical

Jur. D. Doctor of Law [L *juris doctor*]

juris jurisprudence

jurisd jurisdiction

jus justice

juv juvenile

jux juxtaposition

JV junior varsity

JW Jehovah's Witness

jwlry jewelry

Jy July; jury

–K–

k karat; kilo (prefix, 1,000); kilogram; kilometer; kilo-ohm; knot

K kayser; kelvin (phys); king (chess); knit; potassium [L *Kalium*]; strikeout (baseball); thousand

K² Mount Godwin Austen, Kashmir

K-12 kindergarten through 12th grade

ka kiloampere

Kans. Kansas

kb kilobyte (1024 bytes)

kbar kilobar

kbe keyboard entry

KBE Knight Commander of the Order of the British Empire

kbs kilobits per second

kbtu kilo British thermal unit

kc kilocycle

KC Kansas City; Knights of Columbus

K of C Knights of Columbus

kcal kilocalorie

kcas knots calibrated air speed

KCB Knight Commander of the Order of the Bath

kCi kiloCurie

kc/s kilocycles per second

kd knocked down

ke kinetic energy

keas knots equivalent airspeed

keV kiloelectronvolt

kg kilogram

kG kilogauss

KG Knight of the Order of the Garter

KGB Soviet Secret Police

kg cal kilogram calorie

kgf kilogram-force

kg/hr kilograms per hour

kgm kilogram meter

kg/s kilograms per second

kHz kilohertz (kilocycles per second)

ki kilo

KIA killed in action

kias knots indicated air speed

kilo kilogram

kind. kindergarten

KIPS Knowledge Information Processing System

KIQ key intelligence questions

KJ King James (version of the Bible)

KJV King James Version (Bible)

KKK Ku Klux Klan

K Kt king's knight (chess)

kL kiloliter

K of L Knights of Labor

klbf kilopound-force

klt kiloton

km kilometer

km² square kilometer

km³ cubic kilometer

kmc kilomegacycle

km/h kilometer per hour

kn knot (speed)

KO kick off; knock-out (boxing)

kOe kiloOersted

KOM Knight of the Order of Malta

Kor Koran; Korea

K of P Knights of Pythias

KP king's pawn (chess); kitchen patrol/police

kPa kilopascal (pressure unit)

kph kilometers per hour

KQ line squall (met)

Kr krypton (chem)

krad kilorad

KRC Knight of the Red Cross

KRP king's rook's pawn (chess)

ks storm of drifting snow (met)

Ks Kaposi's sarcoma

KS Kansas

KSC Kennedy Space Center

KSK ethyl iodoacetate (tear gas)

kt carat; kiloton; knot

Kt Knight

KT Knight Templar

kV kilovolt (elec)

kVA kilovolt-ampere

kVah kilovolt-amperehour

kvar kilovar

kVcp kilovolt constant potential

kW kilowatt

kWh kilowatthour

Ky Kentucky

KY Kentucky

kz dust/sand storm (met)

–L–

l lady; lake; lambda; land; large; late; lateral; latitude; law; leaf; left or port; legitimate; length; lignite; line; locus

L kinetic potential symbol; lactobacillus; lambert; Latin; left (in stage directions); Leo; lira; liter; lithium; London; Lord; Luxembourg; pound sterling

La lanthanum (chem); Louisiana

LA Latin America; legislative assembly; longacting; Los Angeles; Louisiana

L/A ledger account; letter of authority; law agent; Library Association; Lieutenant at Arms; Literate in Arts; low altitude

lab label; labor; laboratory

lac lacquer; lactation

LACE liquid air cycle engine

LADAR laser detection and ranging

laev. left [L *laevus*]

laf laminar air flow

LAFTA Latin American Free Trade Association

lag. lagoon

LAIS loan accounting information system

lam laminate

Lam Lamentations (Bible)

L.A.M. Master of Liberal Arts

LAMP Lunar Analysis and Mapping Program

lang language

L.A.O. Licentiate in Obstetric Science

lap. laparotomy; launch analysts; panel; left atrial pressure

Lap. Lapland

lapid. stony [L *lapideum*]

larg. width [F *largeur*]; broadly (music) [It *largamente*]; very slow (music) [It *largo*]

laryngol laryngology

LAS large astronomical satellite; League of Arab States; Legal Aid Society; low altitude satellite; lower airspace

laser light amplification by stimulated emission of radiation

LASRM low altitude short range missile

LASV low altitude surface vehicle; low altitude supersonic vehicle

lat lateral; latitude

lat. wide [L *latus*]

Lat Latin; Latvia

lav lavatory

Law-L Law-Latin

LAWRS limited airport weather reporting system

lax. laxative

lb landing barge; left back (sport); pound

LB Labrador; local board

L.B. Bachelor of Letters; to the kind reader [L *lectori benevolo*]

lb ap apothecary pound

lb avdp avoirdupois pound

lb cal pound calorie

lbd lower back disorder

lbf pound-force

lbf/ft pound-force foot

lbf/ft² pound-force per square foot

lbf/ft³ pound-force per cubic foot

lbf/in² pound-force per square inch

lb ft pound foot

lb/ft pound per foot

lb/ft² pound per square foot

lb/ft³ pound per cubic foot

LBH length, breadth, height

lbm lean body mass

lbp low blood pressure; lower back pain

Lbr librarian

lb t pound troy

lc lowercase

LC landing craft; left center (theater); legislative council; letter of credit; level crossing; Library of Congress

L of C Library of Congress

LCA Library Club of America; licensed company auditor; low cost automation

lcb longitudinal center of buoyancy

LCCC Library of Congress Catalogue Card

lcd lowest common denominator

L.C.E. Licentiate in Civil Engineering

lcf local cycle fatigue; longitudinal center of flotation; lowest common factor

lcg longitudinal center of gravity; liquid cooled garment

L.Ch. Licentiate in Surgery

lcm least/lowest common multiple; liquid curing media

LCP last complete program; low cost production; landing craft personnel

L.C.P. & S.A. Licentiate of the College of Physicians and Surgeons of America

lcu launch control unit; lower control unit

LCU large close-up (photo)

ld land; lead; lethal dose; lifeboard deck; light difference; line of departure/dutyload; low door; lower deck

LD Labor Department; low density

L.D. Doctor of Letters; Licentiate in Divinity; Praise be to God [L *Laus Deo*]

L/D Letter of Deposit

L&D loans and discounts; loss and damage

ldc less developed countries; long distance call; lower dead center

ldg lading; landing; leading; loading; lodging

L.Div. Licentiate in Divinity

ldl low density lipoprotein

ld lmt load limit

Ldp Ladyship; Lordship

LDS Latter-Day Saints (Mormons)

L.D.S. Licentiate in Dental Surgery

L.D.Sc. Licentiate in Dental Science

LDX long distance xerography

le leading edge; left eye; library/limited edition; low explosive; light equipment

LEAA Law Enforcement Assistance Administration

LEADS Law Enforcement Agencies Data System

L Ed Lawyer's Edition

LED light emitting diode

leg. legal; legate; legation; legislation; legislative; legislature smooth; sustained (mus) [It *legato*]

LEG Law Enforcement Group

legg. light; rapid (mus) [It *leggiero*]

legis. legislation; legislative

LEG (UN) Legal Affairs department of UN

leg. wt legal weight

L.E.L. Laureate in English Literature

LEM lunar excursion module

let. letter; linear energy transfer

leu leucine

Lev Levant; Leviticus (Bible)

lex lexicon

LEX land exercise

lf ledger folio; life float; light face (typo); line feed character (data processing); low frequency

LF low frequency

lfa local freight agent

l-fc lower frequency current

LFC Lutheran Free Church

lfd least fatal dose; low fat diet

lfl lower flammable limit

LFRD lot fraction reliability deviation

lft leaflet

l ft linear feet/force

L/ft² lumens per square foot (elec)

lg lagoon; large

lge large; league

lgth length

lg tn long ton

lg tpr long taper

lh left half/hand

LH left hand; luteinizing hormone

LH² liquid hydrogen

LHA landing helicopter assault; local health authority; local hour angle; lower hour angle

lhb left halfback (sport)

L.H.B. Bachelor of Humane Letters

L.H.D. Doctor of Humane Letters

L Heb Late Hebrew

l hr lumen hour (phys)

LHS left hand side

lh th left hand thread

li letter of introduction; link; lithograph; lithography; longitudinal interval

Li lithium (chem)

LI Long Island

lib liberal; liberation; liberty; librarian; library; libretto

Lib Liberal Party; Liberia

lib cat. library catalogue

Lib Cong Library of Congress

Lic.Econ. Licentiate in Economic Sciences

Lic.Jur. Licentiate in Law

Lic.Med. Licentiate in Medicine

lidoc lidocaine (xylocain)

Lieut lieutenant

LIFO last in, first out (system of inventory)

lig ligament; ligature

LILO last in, last out (system of inventory)

lim limit; linear induction motors

lin lineal; linear; linear accelerator; lines; liniment

lin ft linear foot

ling linguistics

lino linotype; linoleum

L.Inst.P. Licentiate of the Institute of Physics

liq liquid

lisp. list processor (computer)

lit literal; literary; literature; litter; little

Lit letters

litho lithograph; lithographic; lithography

Litt.D. Doctor of Letters

LJ *Library Journal*; long jump

Lk Luke (Bible)

lkg & bkg leakage and breakage

lkr locker

ll laws; leaves; lines; live load; lower left/limit;

l.l. in the place quoted [L *loco laudato*]

l & l leave and liberty

LL Law List; lending library; lend lease

L Lat Late Latin

LLB Little League Baseball

LL.B. Bachelor of Laws

LL.D. Doctor of Laws

L.Lett. Licentiate of Letters

lli latitude and longitude indicator

LLL low level logic

llm localized leucocyte mobilization

LL.M. Master of Laws

LL.M.Com. Master of Laws in Commercial Law

LLU lending library unit

llw low level waste

lm land mine; liquid/light metal; longitudinal muscle; lumen

l/m lines per minute

LM Legion of Merit; lunar module (space)

L.M. Licentiate in Medicine/Music

lm/ft² lumen per square foot

lm hr lumen hour (phys)

lm/m² lumen per square meter

lm-s lumen second

Lmtd logarithmic mean temperature difference

L.Mus. Licentiate in Music

lm/W lumen per watt

ln Napierian logarithm (math)

Ln lane

LNG liquified natural gas

lo launch operator; liaison officer; local oscillator

LO² liquid oxygen

loa length over all (shipping)

LOA leave of absence; Life Officers Association

LOB line of balance

loc letter of credit; lines of communication; local; location; locative

LOC launch operations center/complex

loc. cit. in the place cited [L *loco citato*]

loc. laud. in the place cited with approval [L *loco laudato*]

locn location

loco locomotion; locomotive

loc. primo. cit. in the place first cited [L *loco primo citato*]

lod line of duty

lof lowest operating frequency

log logarithm (math); logic; logical; logistic

loglan logical language

LOH light observation helicopter

LOI lunar orbit insertion; loss on ignition

lom locator at outer marker (compass)

long. longitude

longl longitudinal

LOOM Loyal Order of Moose

lop line of power

loq. he/she speaks [L *loquitur*]

LOR light output ratio; lunar orbit rendezvous

Lt jg Lieutenant Junior Grade

lto landing take off

LTPD lot tolerance percent defective

ltr letter; lighter

ltrs letters shift (data processing)

lu. syphilis [L *lues*]

Lu lutetium (chem)

lub lubricant; lubricate; lubrication

Luc Lucifer

LUCOM lunar communication system (space)

lud liftup door

lue left upper entrance (theater); left upper extremity

lu h lumen hour (phys)

LUHF lower useful high frequency (elec)

lum lumbago; lumber; luminous; lumbar

LUM lunar excursion module

LUS land utilization survey

lust. lustrous

Luth Lutheran

lux luxurious

lv leave

LV largest vessel

lved left ventricular end diastolic (med)

LVI low viscosity index

LVN Licensed Visiting Nurse; Licensed Vocational Nurse

lw lumens per watt (elec)

LW light weight; low wave; low water

lwb long wheel base

LWF Lutheran World Federation

LWM low water mark

LWV League of Women Voters

lx lux

lym last year's model; lymph; lymphatic

lyr lyric; lyrical

LZ landing zone

LZOA Labor Zionist Organization of America

–M–

m male; manual; mark; married; masculine; mass (phys); mate; measure; medical; medium; meridian; meter; midday; middle; mile; milli (prefix, one-thousandth); million; minim; minimum; minute; missing; mixture; moderate; molar (dental)

m² square meter

m³ cubic meter

m. noon [L *meridies*]

M gram molecule; Mach number (phys); mega (prefix, 1 million); metal (chem); middle term of a syllogism (logic); million; modulus (phys); molar (chem); moment (phys); money supply; mutual inductance (phys); thousand

M₁ monetary aggregate

mA milliampere

MA Maritime Administration; Massachusetts;

mental age; middle ages; military academy

M.A. Master of Arts

MAA methacrylic acid; master army aviator; master at arms

M.A.A. Master of Applied Arts

mabp mean arterial blood pressure (med)

M.Acc. Master of Accountancy

1 Macc 1 Maccabees (Bible/Apocrypha)

2 Macc 2 Maccabees (Bible/Apocrypha)

MACE Machine Aided Composition and Editing

mach machine; machinery; machinist

MACS Marine Air Control Squadron

MAD magnetic anomaly detection; maintenance, assembly and disassembly; mean absolute deviation; Michigan algorithm decoder; mutual assured destruction

MADD mothers against drunk driving

M. Admin. Master of Administration

mae mean absolute error

Ma.E. Master of Engineering

M.A.E. Master of Aeronautical Engineering; Master of Art Education

M.A. Ed. Master of Arts in Education

mag magazine; magnesium; magnet; magnetic; magnetism; magnitude; magnum

M.Ag. Master of Agriculture

M.Ag. Ec. Master of Agricultural Economics

mai minimum annual income

maint maintenance

maj major; majority

Maj major

Maj Gen major general

Mal Malay; Malayan; Malaysia; Malta; Malachi (Bible)

man. management; manager; manual; manufacture; manufacturer

Man Manitoba

manf manufacturer

manuf manufacture; manufacturer

MAP maximum average price; medical aid post; minimum association price; modified American plan (travel)

M.App.Sc. Master of Applied Science

mar. marine; maritime; married

Mar March

MARAD Maritime Administration

M.Arch. Master of Architecture

marg margin; marginal

marit maritime

marit admin maritime adminstration

mar lic marriage license

Mart Martinique

M.A.S. Master of Applied Science

masc masculine

MASER microwave amplification by stimulated emission of radiation

MASH mobile army surgical hospital

Mass Massachusetts

M.A.S.S. Master of Arts in Social Science

mat. maternity; matins; maturity

M.A.T. Master of Arts in Teaching

matern maternity; maternal

math mathematical; mathematically; mathematician; mathematics

mat.med. materia medica

matric matriculate; matriculation

Matt Matthew (Bible)

Maur Mauritania

MAUS metric association of the United States

max maxima; maximum

MAYDAY help me (international distress signal) [Fr *m'aidez*]

mb magnetic bearing; main battery; medium bomber; millibar; motor boat

MB Manitoba

M.B. Bachelor of Medicine; Bachelor of Music

M.B.A. Master of Business Administration

mbar millibar

M.Bdg.Sc. Master of Building Science

MBE Member of the Order of the British Empire

MBL marine biological laboratory

M.B.M. Master of Business Management

mbp mean blood pressure

mbt mean body temperature; mechanical bathythermograph; mobile boarding team

mc millicycle; millicuries

Mc megacycle

MC magistrate's court; magnetic course; marine corps; master of ceremonies; master of surgery; medical certificate; medical corps; member of Congress; Methodist Church; Military Cross

MCAT medical college admission test

mcb miniature circuit breaker

MCDS management control data system

M.C.E. Master of Civil Engineering

M.Ch. Master of Surgery

M.Ch.D. Master of Dental Surgery

M.Ch.E. Master of Chemical Engineering

mc hr millicurie hour

M.C.L. Master of Civil Law

M.Cl.Sc Master of Clinical Science

M.Comm. Master of Commerce

M.C.P.S. Member of the College of Physicians and Surgeons

mc/s megacycles per second

M.C.S. Master of Commercial Science

MCT mechanical comprehension test

MCU median control unit; medium close up

mcw modulated continuous wave

MCW maternity and child welfare

Md Maryland; mendelevium (chem)

MD Maryland; mentally deficient; military district; muscular dystrophy; musical director

M.D. Doctor of Medicine

M/D memorandum of deposit; months after date

MDA Muscular Dystrophy Association; multiple docking adaptor

M.Dent.Sc. Master of Dental Science

mdf main distributing frame (data processing)

M.Dip. Master of Diplomacy

M.Div. Master of Divinity

mdr minimum daily requirement

M.D.S. Master of Dental Surgery

M.D.Sc. Master of Dental Science

mdse merchandise

MDST mountain daylight saving time

MDTA Manpower Development and Training Act; modular data transaction system

M.D.V. Doctor of Veterinary Medicine

Me Maine

ME Maine; managing editor; marine engineer; master of engineering; mechanical engineer; memory error; Methodist Episcopal; Middle East; military engineer

meas measurable; measure; measurement

M.Ec. Master of Économics

MEC Methodist Episcopal Church

M.E.C. Master of Engineering Chemistry

mech mechanic; mechanical; mechanically; mechanism; mechanize

M.Econ. Master of Economics

med median; medical; medicine; medieval; medium; minimal effective dose

Med Mediterranean

M.Ed. Master of Education

MED minimum effective dose

medevac medical evacuation

M.Ed.L.Sc. Master of Education in Library Science

MedRC medical reserve corps

Med.Sc.D. Doctor of Medical Science

Med Tech medical technician

M.E.E. Master of Electrical Engineering

meg megacycle; megaton; megawatt

M.E.L. Master of English Literature

mem member; memorandum; memorial

memo memorandum

mep mean effective pressure

mer mercantile; merchandise; meridian

Mer mercurial; mercury

M.E.Sc. Master of Engineering Science

Messrs. Messieurs (plural of Mr.)

met. metallurgical; metaphor; metaphysical; meteorological; metronome (mus); metropolitan

metal. metallurgical; metallurgy

metaph metaphor; metaphorical

metas metastasis; metastasize

Met.E. Metallurgical Engineer

Meth Methodist

METO Middle East Treaty Organization

metrop metropol; metropolis; metropolitan

MEU marine expeditionary unit; modern English usage

MeV mega/million electron volts

Mex Mexico

mf machine finish; male to female; manufactured; medium frequency multiplying factor

mF millifarad

M.F.A. Master of Fine Arts

M.F.A.Mus. Master of Fine Arts in Music

mfd manufactured

MFD minimum fatal dose

Mfg manufacturing

MFH mobile field hospital

MFN most favored nation

Mfr manufacturer

M.F.S. Master of Food Science

mg milligram; morning

Mg magnesium (chem)

mgmt management

Mgr manager; monsignor

mgt management

mgw maximum gross weight

MH megahertz

M.H. Master of Horticulture/Hygiene

M.H.A. Master of Hosptial Administration

mhf medium high frequency

MHRI Mental Health Research Institute

mHz millihertz

MHz megahertz

mi mile (statute)

mi² square mile

MI Michigan; military intelligence

MIA missing in action

Mic Micah (Bible)

Mich Michaelmas; Michigan

micro microscope

microbiol microbiology

mid middle; midnight

mi/gal mile(s) per gallon

mi/h mile per hour

mil mileage; military; militia

mi min miles per minute

min mineralogical; minim; minima; mining; ministry; minor; minute; minute (time)

Min minister; ministry

Min B/L minimum bill of lading

minelco miniature electronic component

Minn Minnesota

Min Plen minister plenipotentiary

min wt minimum weight

mip mean indicated pressure

mirad monostatic infrared intrusion detector

MIRD medium internal radiation dose

MIRV multiple independently targetable reentry vehicle

misc miscellaneous; miscellany

Miss Mississippi

MIT Massachusetts Institute of Technology

MITI Ministry of International Trade and Industry (Japan)

mixt mixture

MJD management job description

mkt market

ml machine language; maintained load; mean level; middle left; mine layer

mL millilambert; milliliter

M.L. Licentiate in Midwifery; Master of Laws/ Letters

MLA Medical Library Association; Modern Language Association

M.L.A. Master of Landscape Architecture; Master of Liberal Arts

MLAT Modern Language Aptitude Test

MLBPA Major League Baseball Players Association

MLF multilateral (nuclear) force

M.Lib. Master of Librarianship/Library Science

M.Litt. Master of Letters/Literature

Mlle mademoiselle

MLR *Modern Law Review*

M.L.S. Master of Library Science

mlw mean low water (tides)

mm millimeter; mucous membrane

mm² square millimeter

mm³ cubic millimeter

m.m. with the necessary changes [L *mutatis mutandis*]

MM maintenance manual; Mariner Mars Project; memory module; merchant marine; messieurs

Mme madam

M.Med. Master of Medicine; Master of Medical Sciences

Mmes mesdames

mmHg conventional millimeter of mercury

MMU million monetary units

Mn manganese (chem)

MN magnetic north;

merchant navy; Minnesota

mnm minimum

M.Nurs. Master of Nursing

mo month

Mo molybdenum (chem); Missouri

MO Missouri; money order; method of operation [L *modus operandi*]

M.O. Master of Obstetrics/Oratory

mod moderate; modern; modification; modified; modulus (math)

MODEM modulator/demodulator

mof maximum observed frequency

M.O.G. Master of Obstetrics and Gynecology

mohms milliohms

mol mole (unit of substance)

mol wt molecular weight

Mon Monaco; Monday; Montana

Mong Mongol; Mongolia; Mongolian

mono mononucleosis; monorail

Mono monotype (typo)

monog monograph

Mont Montana

Montr Montreal

MOPAR master oscillator power amplifier radar

MOPS missile operations system

Mor Moroccan; Morocco

MOR middle-of-the-road (mus)

MORC medical officers reserve corps

Morm Mormon

morph morphological; morphology; morphine

mort mortal; mortality; mortgage; mortuary

mos metal oxide semiconductor; months; mosaic

MOs military observers

Moz Mozambique

mp melting point

MP Member of Parliament; military police

MPAA Motion Picture Association of America

MPB Missing Persons Bureau

MPC maximum permissible concentration

MPD maximum permissible dose

MPE maximum permissible exposure (radiation)

mpg miles per gallon

mph miles per hour

M.Ph. Master of Philosophy

mps megacycle/meters per second

Mqe Martinique

MQF mobile quarantine facility

Mr. mister

M & R maintenance and repairs

MRBM medium range ballistic missile

mre mean radial error

MRI magnetic resonance imaging

Mrs. mistress

ms manuscript; millisecond

m/s meter per second

Ms. coined feminine title (plural, **Mses.**)

MS Mississippi; motor ship; multiple sclerosis

M.S. Master of Sciences; Master of Surgery

M & S maintenance and supply

MSA metropolitan statistical area

M.S.Arch. Master of Science in Architecture

msc miscellaneous

M.Sc. Master of Science

mse mean square error

msg message

MSG monosodium glutamate; Madison Square Garden

msgr messenger

Msgr monsignor

M Sgt master sergeant

M.S.J. Master of Science in Journalism

msl mean sea level; missile

M.S.L.S. Master of Science in Library Science

M.S.M. Master of Medical Science

M.S.M.E. Master of Science in Mechanical Engineering

M.S.Med. Master of Medical Science

M.S.Mus. Master of Science in Music

M.S.N. Master of Science in Nursing

M.Soc.Sc. Master of Social Science

MST mountain standard time

Mt megaton; Mount

MT Montana; mountain time

M.T. Master of Teaching

mtd mounted

mtg mortgage

M.Th. Master of Theology

mtn motion; mountain

MTN multilateral trade negotiations

mtt mean transit time

mu maintenance/mass/monetary unit

mult multiplication

mun municipal; municipality

Mus.B. Bachelor of Music

Mus.D. Doctor of Music

Mus.M. Master of Music

mut mutual

mv market value; mean variation; medium voltage; monochromatic vision; muzzle velocity

mV millivolt

Mv mendelevium (chem)

MV motor vessel/vehicle

MVD motor vehicle department

M.V.D. Doctor of Veterinary Medicine

MVP most valuable player

mvt movement

mW milliwatt

MW medium wave; megawatt; molecular weight

MWH megawatt hour

mwp maximum working pressure

Mx maxwell (phys)

mxd mixed

myc mycological; mycology

myst mystery

myth. mythological; mythology

"mu" micro (prefix, one-millionth)

"mu" micron; millimicron

"mu"A microampere

"mu"bar microbar

"mu"F microfarad

"**mu**"g   microgram

"**mu**"H   microhenry

"**mu**"in   microinch

"**mu**"m   micrometer

"**mu**"m²   square micrometer

"**mu**"m³   cubic micrometer

"**mu**"s   microsecond

"**mu**"V   microvolt

"**mu**"W   microwatt

–N–

n   en (typo); indefinite number (math); load factor; name; nano (prefix, one-billionth); nasal; negative; net; neuter; neutral; neutron; new; night; nominative; noon; norm; normal; north; northern; notative speed; note; noun; number

n/30   net payment in 30 days

N   Avogadro's number (chem); knight (chess); magnetic flux; national; navigation; near (optics); net; newton; nitrogen (chem); north; nullity (legal)

nA   nanoampere

Na   sodium (chem) [L *Natrium*]

NA   North America; not available; not applicable

NAACP   National Association for the Advancement of Colored People

NAADC   North American Area Defense Command

NAAFI   Navy Army and Air Force Institutes

NAB   National Alliance of Businessmen; National Association of Broadcasters

NABC   National Association of Boys' Clubs

NABE   National Association of Book Editors

NAC   National Association of Counties; National Advisory Council

NaCl   sodium chloride (chem)

nad nadir

NAD National Academy of Design

NADC naval aide de camp; Naval Air Development Center

NADOP North American Defense Operational Plan

NAE National Academy of Engineering

N Afr North Africa

NAFTA North Atlantic Free Trade Area

nag net annual gain

Nah Nahum (Bible)

N Am North America

NAMFI NATO Missile Firing Installation

NAMH National Association for Mental Health

NANA North American Newspaper Alliance, Inc

NAO Noise Abatement Office

NAPA National Association of Performing Artists

napalm naphthenate palmitate

NAPAN National Association for the Prevention of Addiction to Narcotics

NAPO National Association of Property Owners

nar narrow; net assimilation rate

narc narcotic

Narconon Narcotics Anonymous

NARI National Agriculture Research Institute

NARTB National Association of Radio and Television Broadcasters

NARTU naval air reserve training unit

nas nasal; nasology

NAS National Academy of Science; Noise Abatement Society; National Academy of Sciences; naval air station; National Adoption Society

NASA National Aeronautics and Space Administration

NASD National Association of Securities Dealers

NASDAQ National Association of Securities Dealers Automated Quotations

NASM National Air and Space Museum

NASULGG National Association of State Universities and Land Grant Colleges

nat national; nationalist; native; natural; naturalize; naturist; normal allowed time

N At North Atlantic

NATB National Automobile Theft Bureau

NatBurEconRes National Bureau of Economic Research

NATCS National Air Traffic Control Service

Nat Dem National Democratic

Nat Gal National Gallery

Nat Hist Natural History

natl national

NatMon National Monument

NATO North Atlantic Treaty Organization

NATS Naval Air Transport Services

Nat Sc Natural Sciences

Nat.Sc.D. Doctor of Natural Science

NATSPG North Atlantic Systems Planning Group

N Att naval attache

natur naturalist

naut nautical

nav naval; navigable; navigate; navigation; navigator; net asset value (fin)

NAVAIR Naval Air Systems Command

navdac navigation data assimilation computer

NAVIC Navy Information Center

NAVOCEANO Naval Oceanographic Office

NAVOCS Naval Officer Candidate School

NAVS National Anti Vivisection Society

NAVSAT navigational satellite

NAYC National Association of Youth Clubs

n.b. note well [L *nota bene*]

Nb niobium (chem)

NB naval base; New Brunswick

NBA National Basketball Association; National Boxing Association

NBC National Boys' Club; National Book Council; National Broadcasting Company

NBER National Bureau of Economic Research

NBL National Book League

NBRMP National Board of Review of Motion Pictures

NBS National Bureau of Standards; National Broadcasting Service; National Bureau of Standards

nbv net book value

NC national certificate; Nature Conservancy; North Carolina

N/C no charge; no credit

NCAA National Collegiate Athletic Association

NCAI National Congress of American Indians

NCAPC National Center for Air Pollution Control

NCAR National Center for Atmospheric Research

NCARB National Council of Architectural Registration Boards

NCCH National Council to Control Handguns

NCCJ National Conference of Christians and Jews

NCCL National Council for Civil Liberties

NCCW National Council of Catholic Women

NCDC National Center for Disease Control; National Communicable Disease Center

NCET National Council for Educational Technology

NCERT National Council for Educational Research and Training

NCHS National Center for Health Statistics

NCI National Cancer Institute; National Cheese Institute

NCIC National Crime Information Center

NCO non-commissioned officer

NCOIC non-commissioned officer in charge

NCPT National Congress of Parents and Teachers

NCTA National Community Television/Cable Television Association

NCUA National Credit Union Administration

NCWUS National Council of Women, US

Nd neodymium (chem)

ND National Debt; no date; North Dakota; *Notre Dame* [Fr]

N.D. Doctor of Naturopathy

NDAC Nuclear Defense Affairs Committee (NATO)

N Dak North Dakota

NDC Natural Distribution Certificate; Nato Defense College; National Democratic Club; Nuclear Development Corporation

NDEA National Defense Education Act

NDMB National Defense Mediation Board

NDPS National Data Processing Service

NDRC National Defense Research Committee

Ne neon (chem)

NE Nebraska; New England; northeast

NEA National Education Association

NEB New English Bible

Nebr Nebraska

nec necessary; not elsewhere classified

NECM New England Conservatory of Music

necrol necrology

NECS National Electrical Code Standards

necy necessary; necessity

NEDO National Economic Development Office

neg negation; negative; negotiate

Neh Nehemiah (Bible)

N Eng New England

neol neologism

Nep Nepal

NEP New Economic Policy

Nept Neptune

NERA National Emergency Relief Administration

NERC Natural Environment Research Council

NET National Education Television

Neth Netherlands

net wt net weight

neurol neurological; neurology

neut neuter

Nev Nevada

New Test. New Testament (Bible)

nF nanofarad

N/f no funds

NF Newfoundland; nouveau (new) franc

NFAH National Foundation on the Arts and the Humanities

NFAL National Foundation of Arts and Letters

Nfd Newfoundland

NFL National Football League; National Forensic League

NFPA National Fire Protection Association

NFU National Farmers Union

NFWI National Federation of Women's Institutes

NGAC National Guard Air Corps

NGC New General Catalogue (astron)

NGS National Geographic Society

N Gui New Guinea Territory

NH New Hampshire

N.H.D. Doctor of Natural History

NHI National Health Insurance

NHL National Hockey League

nhp nominal horse power

NHSB National Highway Safety Bureau

Ni nickel (chem)

NI Northern Ireland

NIB National Institute for the Blind

Nic Nicaragua

NID National Institute for the Deaf

NIE National Institute of Education

Nig Nigeria

NIH National Institutes of Health

NIMR National Institute for Medical Research

NIN national information network

NINB National Institute of Neurology and Blindness

NIO National Institute of Oceanography

NIRA National Industrial Recovery Act; National Industrial Recovery Administration (U.S.A.)

NISCON National Industrial Safety Conference

nitro nitrocellulose; nitroglycerine

NJ New Jersey

NK not known

nl natural log or logarithm

NL National League; Navy Library; Netherlands; New Latin

NLB National Labor Board; National Library for the Blind

NLF National Liberation Front

NLM National Library for Medicine

NLRB National Labor Relations Board

NLTA National Lawn Tennis Association; National League of Teachers Associations

N-m newton meter

N/m2 newton per square meter

NM New Mexico

NMB National Maritime Board; National Mediation Board

N Mex New Mexico

NMHA National Mental Health Association

nmi nautical mile

NMU National Maritime Union

NNW north-northwest

No nobelium (chem); number

NOAA National Oceanic and Atmospheric Administration

NOB naval operating base

NOD naval ordinance department; night observation device

NODC National Oceanographic Data Center

noibn not otherwise indexed by name

nok next of kin

nom nominative

NOMAD navy oceanographic meteorological automatic device

nomin nominative

non com noncommissioned

non res non resident

non seq. it does not follow logically [L *non sequitur*]

nonstand nonstandard

NORAD North American Air Defense Command

NORC National Opinion Research Center; naval ordinance research computer

norm. normal; normalized

Norw Norway; Norwegian

nos not otherwise specified

NOS National Ocean Service

not. notary; notice

Nov November

NOVS National Office of Vital Statistics

NOW National Organization of Women

NOWC National Association of Women's Clubs

NOx nitrous oxide

np net proceeds; new paragraph; nursing procedure

Np neptunium (chem)

NP notary public

NPC National Peace Council; National Press Club

n pl noun plural

NPR National Public Radio

NPS National Park Service

npv net present value (fin); no par value (fin)

nqa net quick assets (fin)

NRA National Recovery Administration; National Rifle Association

NRC National Research Corporation; Nuclear Regulatory Commission

NRCA National Retail Credit Association

NRCC National Republican Congressional Committee

NRD naval recruiting department

NRDO National Research and Development Organization

NRT net registered tonnage

ns nanosecond

NS Nova Scotia; nuclear ship

NSC National Security Council

NSF National Science Foundation

n-s/m² newton second per square meter

NSMR National Society for Medical Research

NSP Navy Standard part

NSPA Navy Shore Patrol Administration; National Scholastic Press Association National Society of Public Accountants

NSPC National Security Planning Commission

nspf not specifically provided for

NSR National Scientific Register

NSRB National Security Resources Board

NSRDC National Standards Reference Data System

NSSCC National Space Surveillance Control Center

NSSE National Society for the Study of Education

NSSU National Sunday School Union

NSVP National Student Volunteer Program

NSW New South Wales

NSY New Scotland Yard

nt net

n/t net tonnage

NT New Testament; Northern Territory; Northwest Territories

NTA National Tax/Tuberculosis Association

NTAA National Travelers Aid Association

NTAs Nielsen Television Areas

NtBurStnds National Bureau of Standards

NTC National Teacher Corps; National Theater Conference

NTDA National Trade Development Association

NTE National Teacher Examination

N-test nuclear testing

NTHP National Trust for Historic Preservation

NTI Nielsen Television Index

NTID National Technical Institute for the Deaf

NTIS National Technical Information Service

NTO National Tenants Organization

ntp normal temperature and pressure; no title page

NTR National Tape Repository

NTRL Naval Training Research Laboratory

NTS Nevada Test Site

NTSB National Transportation Safety Board

NTSC National Televi-

sion Standards Committee

nt wt net weight

nu name unknown

nuc nuclear; nucleus

NUC National Urban Coalition; Naval Undersea Center

Nuc. E. Nuclear Engineer

nuc phy nuclear physics

NUJ National Union of Journalists

num number; numerical; numerology

Num Numbers (Bible)

NUMEC Nuclear Materials and Equipment Corporation

numis numismatic; numismatology

nu-tec nuclear detection (radiation monitoring device)

NV Nevada

NVB National Volunteer Brigade

NVF National Volunteer Force

nvm non volatile matter

NVMA National Veterinary Medical Association

NVTS National Vocational Training Service

NW northwest

NWC National War College; National Water Commission; National Writer's Club

NWCTU National Woman's Christian Temperance Union

NWF National Welfare Fund; National Wildlife Federation

NWPC National Women's Political Caucus

NWR National Welfare Rights; National Wildlife Refuge; Nuclear Weapon Report

NWRC National Weather Records Center

NWRF Naval Weather Research Facility

NWRO National Welfare Rights Organization

NWRS National Wildlife Refuge System

NWS National Weather Service; Naval Weapons Station; Nimbus Weather Satellite

NWSA National Women's Suffrage Association

NWSC National Weather Satellite Center

n wt net weight

NWT Northwest Territories

NY New York

NYC New York City

NYSBB New York State Banking Board

NYSE New York Stock Exchange

NYT National Youth Theater; New York Times

NZ New Zealand

–O–

o occasional; octavo; ohm (elec); overcast sky (met)

O octave; Ohio ; oxygen (chem)

OA office address; officers' association; old account; operation analysis; over all

O/A on account; on or about

O of A Office of Administration

OAB Old Age Benefits

oad overall depth

OAD ordered, adjudged, and decreed

OADAP Office of Alcoholism and Drug Abuse Prevention

oah overall height

OAH Organization of American Historians

oal overall length

O.A.M.D.G. All to the Greater Glory of God [L *Omnia ad Majorem Dei Gloriam*]

OAO Orbiting Astronomical Observatory

OAP old age pensioner

OAR Office of Aerospace Research

OART Office of Advanced Research and Technology (NASA)

OAS on active service; Organization of American States

OASDHI Old-Age, Survivors, Disability, and Health Insurance

OASI Old-Age and Survivors Insurance

OAU Organization of African Unity

oaw old abandoned well; overall width

ob obstetric; obstetrician; obstetrics; on board; outbound

ob. died [L *obit*]

OB obstetrical; obstetrician; obstetrics; off Broadway

Obad Obadiah (Bible)

ob dk observation deck

OBE Officer of the Order of the British Empire

Ob-Gyn obstetrician gynecologist

obit obituary

obj object; objection; objective

obl obligation; oblige; oblique; oblong

Ob Ph oblique photography

OBS Organic Brain Syndrome

obs oscure; observation; observatory; obsolete; obstetric; obstetrician

ob. s.p. died without issue [L *oblit sine prole*]

obv obverse

oc office copy; official classification; on center; only child; open charter

o.c. in the work cited [L *opere citato*]

o/c overcharge

OC Observer Corps, Office of Censorship; officer commanding; operating characteristic; overseas command

OCAS Organization of Central American States

OCAT Optometric College Aptitude Test; Optometry College Admissions Test

OCAW Oil, Chemical and Atomic Workers (union)

Oc B/L ocean bill of lading

occ occupation

occip occipital; occiput

OCD obsessive compulsive disorder; Office of Civil Defense; online communications drive

OCDM Office of Civil Defense Mobilization

O/Cdt officer cadet

ocg omnicardiogram

och ochre

OCI Office of Computer Information (U.S. Department of Commerce); Office of Current Information (CIA)

OCIS Organized Crime Information System (FBI)

OCONUS outside continental United States

OCP Office of Consumer Protection

ocr optical character reader; optical character recognition

OCR optical character recognition (computer); Office of Civilian Requirements

OCS Officer Candidate School

OCSA Office, Chief of Staff, Army

oct octave (music); octavo

Oct Octavius; October

ocul. to the eyes [L *oculis*]

od olive drab; on demand; optical density; outside diameter

OD officer of the day; overdose

O.D. Doctor of Ophthalmology/Optometry/Osteopathy

O/D on demand; overdraft; overdrawn

o & d origin and destination

ODA Overseas Development Administration

ODESSA Ocean Data Environmental Sciences Services Acquisition

ODESY On-Line Data Entry System

ODRC Office of Disaster Relief Coordinator (UN)

ODS Ocean Data Station

oe open end

OE Office of Education; Old English; Old Etonian; omissions excepted; original error

O & E operations and engineering

OEA Office of Economic Adjustment (USA); Overseas Education Association

OECD Organization for Economic Cooperation and Development

OECF Overseas Economic Cooperation Fund

OED *Oxford English Dictionary*

OEDA Office of Energy Data and Analysis

OEM optical electronic microscope

OEO Office of Economic Opportunity

OEP Office of Emergency Planning; Office of Emergency Preparedness

OER Office of Aerospace Research (USAF); Office of Energy Research; Officer Effectiveness Report

OERC optimum earth re-entry corridor (space)

o/f oxidation/fermentation; oxidizer to fuel ratio

OF oceanographic facility; Odd Fellows; old face type; Old French; operating/operational forces

ofc office

off. offer; office; officer

offic official; officially

ofh oxygen-free high conductivity

OFM Order of Friars Minor

OFPA Order of the Founders & Patriots of America

O Fr Old French

OFS Orange Free State

oge operational ground equipment

OGE Office of Government Ethics

OGO Orbiting Geophysical Observatory

oh observation helicopter; office hours; on hand

o.h. hourly (med) [L *omni hora*]

OH Ohio

OHD organic heart disease

OHDETS over horizon detection system

OHDS Office of Human Development Services (HEW)

OHMS On Her (His) Majesty's Service

ohv overhead valve; overhead vent

OI Office of Information

OIAA Office of Inter-American Affairs; Office of International Aviation Affairs

OIAS Occupational Information Access System

O-i-C Officer in Charge

oj orange juice

ojt on job training

OK Oklahoma; all correct

Okla Oklahoma

ol overflow level; overhead line

o.l. left eye [L *oculus laevus*]

OL Olympiad; Olympic

OLBM orbital launched ballistic missile

olc on-line computer

OLC oak leaf cluster (mil); online computer

Old Test. Old Testament

OLIVER on-line instrumentation via energetic radioisotopes

OLPS on line programming system

olr overload relay

OLRT on line real time (computer)

OLS Optical Landing System

o.m. every morning [L *omni mane*]

OM Order of Merit

O & M operations and management; organization and method

OMBE Office of Minority Business Enterprise

omr office methods research; optical mark reader; optical mark recognition

oms output per man shift

OMS Office of Management Studies

OMSF office of manned space flight

o.n. every night [L *omni nocte*]

o/n own name

ON octane number; Ontario

ONA optical navigation attachment

ONI Office of Naval Intelligence

ONP Office of National Programs

ont ordinary neap tide

Ont Ontario

o/o on order; order of

o & o owned and operated

ooa on or about

oob opening of business; out of bed

oobe out of body experience

OOD officer of the day/deck

o/o/o out of order

OO/USA out of stock but on order from (e.g.) U.S.A.

OOW Officer of the watch

op. excellent [L *opti-*

mus]; work [L *opus*]; works [L *opera*]

o/p off peak; output; overpriced

OP old prices; open policy (ins); other people's; out of print

opa optical plotting attachment; optoelectric pulse amplifier

OPA Office of Price Administration/Public Affairs

OPAL optical platform alignment linkage

OPCA Overseas Press Club of America

op. cit. in the work cited [L *opere citato*]

OPDAR optical detection and ranging

OPEC Organization of Petroleum Exporting Countries

op ed opposite the editorials (newspaper page)

OPER Office of Policy, Evaluation, and Research

OPEX operational, executive, and administrative personnel

ophth ophthalmologist; ophthalmology

OPIC Overseas Private Investment Corporation

opm operations per minute

OPM Office of Personnel Management; other people's money

opn operation; opinion; option

o.p.n. pray for us [L *ora pro nobis*]

opo one price only

OPO Office of Personnel Operations (US Army)

OPOR Office of Public Opinion Research

opp opportunity; oppose; opposite; opposition

oppy opportunity

ops operations

OPS Office of Price Stabilization; Office of Product Standards

opscan optical scanning

opstat operational status

opt. optics; optimal; optimum; option; optional

Opt. D. Doctor of Optometry

opv oral polio virus

OPW Office of Public Works

OQ Officers Quarters

or. out of range; overhaul and repair

o/r on request; other ranks

OR official receiver/referee; operating room; Oregon; other ranks (mil); outside right (sport); owner's risk

ORACLE Optimum Record Automation for Courts and Law Enforcement

Orat. Oratorio

ORB oceanographic research buoy; owner's risk of breakage

ORBIS orbiting radio beacon ionospheric satellite

ORBIT on line retrieval of bibliographic information

ORC Order of the Red Cross; Overseas Research Council

ORCA Ocean Resources Conservation Association

orch orchestra; orchestral; orchestrate; orchestration (mus)

ord ordain; order; ordinal; ordinance; ordinary; ordnance

ORD owner's risk of damage

Ord Bd ordnance board

Ord Dept ordnance department

ordn ordnance

ords ordinary shares

OR & E Office of Research and Engineering

Oreg Oregon

org organ; organic; organism; organization; organize

ORI Ocean Research Institute

orig origin; original; originator

orn ornament; ornithology

ORN Operating Room Nurse

ORNL Oak Ridge National Laboratory

orph orphan; orphanage

ORS Office of Research and Statistics; Operational Research Society

ORT Operational Readiness Test

orth orthography; orthopedic; orthopedics

os ocean station; only son; outside

o/s on sale; out of service/stock; outsize; outstanding

Os osmium (chem)

OS old school; Old Style; ordinary seaman; Ordnance Survey; output secondary

OSA Office of the Secretary of the Army; Official Secrets Act; old style antique; Optical Society of America

OSAHRC Occupational Safety and Health Review Commission

osc oscillator

OSD Office of the Secretary of Defense; on line system driver (computer)

osdp on-site data processing

osf operational service fee; ordinary shareholders funds

O.S.F. Order of St. Francis

OSG Office of the Secretary General (UN)

OSH Office on Smoking and Health

OSHA Occupational Safety and Health Administration

OSI Office of Special Investigation (USAF)

OSIP Operational and Safety Improvement Program

OSIS Office of Science Information Service

OSL Old Style Latin;

ordnance sub lieutenant

osm osmosis; osmotic

OSN Office of the Secretary of the Navy

OSO orbiting solar observatory

osp outside purchase

o-sp off-street parking

o.s.p. died without issue [L *oblit sine prole*]

O.S.P. Order of Saint Paul

OSR Office of Scientific Research; Office of Security Review

OSRD Office of Scientific Research and Development; Office of Standard Reference Data

oss orbiting space station

OSS Office of Strategic Services

OSSA Office of Space Sciences and Applications (NASA)

ost objectives, strategics, tactics; on same terms; ordinary spring tides

osteo osteopath; osteopathic; osteopathy

OSTS official seed testing station

OSV ocean station vessel

o/t on truck; overtime

OT occupational therapy; ocean transportation; off time; Old Testament (Bible); overseas trade; overtime

OTA Office of Technology Assessment

OTAR Overseas Tariffs and Regulations

otb off-track betting

otc over the counter

OTC Organization for Trade Cooperation

otdc optical target designation computer

otf optical transfer function

oth over the horizon

OTID Office of Talented Identification and Development (Johns Hopkins)

otj on the job

otl out to lunch; over the line

OTM Office of Telecommunications Management

OTS officers' training school

OTSG Office of the Surgeon General

Ott Ottawa

OTT Ocean Transport and Trading; Office of Traffic and Transportation

OTU operational training unit

OTUS Office of the Treasurer of the United States

OU official use

ov observed vehicle; orbiting vehicle

OVH overhead projector

ovhd overhead

ovrd overrride

ow one way; out of wed-lock; over water

O/W oil in water

OWC ordnance weapons command

OWF optimum working frequency

OWRR Office of Water Resources Research

OWWS Office of World Weather Systems

ow/ym older woman/younger man

Ox. Oxford

Oxon. Oxford [L *Oxonia*]

OXFAM Oxford Committee for Famine Relief

OY optimum yield

OYD Office of Youth Development

oz ounce (avoirdupois)

oz ap apothecaries' ounce

OZONE International Bureau of Atmospheric Ozone

oz t troy ounce

–P–

p absolute humidity; fluid density; momentum; page; paragraph; part; participle; particle; past; per; pico (prefix, one-trillionth); pint; proton

p- para (chem)

P parity (phys); pawn (chess); pedestrian; phosphorus (chem); Portugal; postage; posterior; Presbyterian; pressure (phys); Protestant; purl

pa participial adjective; permanent address; personal appearance; power amplifier

p/a personal account

pA picoampere

Pa pascal; Pennsylvania; protactinium (chem)

PA Pennsylvania; police agent; public address system

P/A power of attorney

PAA per acetic acid (chem); polyacrylic acid (chem)

PAAC program analysis adaptable control

PABA para-aminobenzoic acid

PABX private automatic branch exchange

pac phenacetin-aspirin-caffeine

Pac Pacific

PAC Pacific Air Command; Pan African Congress; Pan American Congress; political action committee

PACAF Pacific Air Forces

PACCS post attack command and control system

PACE precision analog computing equipment

PACS Pacific Area Communications System

PADAR passive detection and ranging

p.ae. equal parts [L *partes aequales*]

PAF peripheral address field

PAHO Pan American Health Organization

Pak Pakistan

pam pulse amplitude modulation

PAM pledged-account mortgage

PAMA Pan American Medical Association

Pan Panama

PAO public affairs officer

PaO2 arterial oxygen pressure

PAO2 alveolar oxygen pressure

Pap smear Papanicolaou Test (for cervical cancer)

par. paragraph; parallel; per acre rental; precision approach radar

Par Parish

PAR perimeter acquisition radar

para parachute; paragraph; parallel

Para Paraguay

paradrop parachute air-drop

Parag Paraguay; Paraguayan

paramp parametric amplifier

PARCA Pan American Railway Congress Association

paren parenthesis

Parl Parliament

PARL Palo Alto Research Laboratory

PARS passenger/programmed airlines reservation system

parsec parallax second

part. partial; participate; participle; particle; partition; partnership

pas passive; power assisted steering; public address system

pass. here and there, throughout [L *passim*]; passage; passenger; passive

pat. patent

patd patented

path. pathological; pathology

PATH Port Authority Trans-Hudson line (NYC/NJ transit)

pat. med patent medicine

Pat. Off. patent office

pat. pend. patent pending

PAU Pan American Union

Pav pavilion

PAW powered all the way

pax peace be with you [L *pax vobiscum*]

PAX private automatic exchange (telephone)

PAYE pay as you earn

paymr paymaster

payt payment

Pb lead (chem) [L *plumbum*]

PB pass book; Plymouth Brethren; prayer book; Primitive Baptists; provisional battalion; purl into back of stitch (knit); push button

P.B. Bachelor of Philosophy

PBA Public Buildings Administration

PBK Phi Beta Kappa

P boat patrol boat

PBR power breeder reactor; precision bombing range

PBS Public Building Service; Public Broadcasting Service

pbt profit before tax (fin)

pbwt parts by weight

pc pica; percentage; piece; postcard

p.c. after meals (med) [L *post cibum*]

PC Panama Canal; peace commissioner; personal computer; port of call

P/C petty cash; price current

pcc precipitated calcium carbonate

PCC Communist Party of Cuba

pcf pounds/power per cubic foot

PCF Parti Communiste Francais (French Communist Party)

pcl parcel

pcm pulse code modulation

PCP phencyclidine (angel dust)

PCSP Permanent Commission for the South Pacific

pct percent; precinct

pcu power/pressurization control unit

PCV passenger control vehicle; peace corps volunteers

PCZ Panama Canal Zone

pd paid; pitch diameter; postage due; post dated; potential difference (elec); pound; preliminary design

p.d. by the day [L *per diem*]

p/d post dated

p & d pick-up and deliver

Pd palladium (chem)

PD police department; postal district; pulse duration

P.D. Doctor of Pharmacy; Doctor of Philosophy

Pd.B. Bachelor of Pedagogy

Pd.D. Doctor of Pedagogy

pdi pre-delivery inspection

pdm pulse duration modulation

Pd.M. Master of Pedagogy

pdn production

p/doz per dozen

PDP program development plan; programmed data processor

PDQ ("pretty damned quick") immediately

PDR Physician's Desk Reference

PDS programming documentation standards

PDST Pacific daylight saving time

PDT Pacific daylight time

PE permissible error; physical education; pocket edition; probable error (math); Protestant Episcopal

P/E price-earnings ratio (fin); port of embarkation

PEC photoelectric cell; Protestant Episcopal Church

ped pedal; pedestrian

Ped. B. Bachelor of Pediatrics

Ped. D. Doctor of Pedagogy

PEI Prince Edward Island

Pen. penitentiary

PEN Poets, Playwrights, Essayists, Editors and Novelists (Club)

Pent. Pentateuch; Pentecost; Pentagon

per. period; periodic; periodicity; person

per an. yearly [L *per annum*]

per cent. by the hundred [L *per centum*]

per con. on the other side [L *per contra*]

perf perfect; perforated; perforation; performance

perk perquisite

PERK perchlorethylene

perm permanent; permission; permutation

PERO President's Emergency Relief Organization

perp perpendicular; perpetual; perpetrator

per pro. on behalf of [L *per procurationem*]

pers person; personal; personally; perspective

pert. pertain

PERT performance/program evaluation review technique

PET positron emission tomography

1 Pet 1 Peter (Bible)

2 Pet 2 Peter (Bible)

pf prefer; proof

pF picofarad; water-holding energy

PF panchromatic film; pianoforte (music); power factor; public funding (fin)

P/F Peace and Freedom (political party)

Pfc private first class

pfd preferred (fin)

pfd sp preferred spelling

pfm power factor meter; pulse frequency modulation

PFN pulse forming network

PFR prototype fast reactor

pfx prefix

pg pay group; paying guest; proving ground

PGA Professional Golfers Association

pgt per gross ton

ph past history (med); pharmacopoeia; phase

pH hydrogen-ion concentration; measure of acidity/alkalinity of a liquid

Ph phenyl; Philosophy

PH Pearl Harbor; Public Health; public house; Purple Heart

PHA Public Health Act; Public Housing Administration

phal phalange; phalanx

phar pharmaceutical; pharmacist; pharmacology; pharmacy

Phar.B. Bachelor of Pharmacy

Phar.D. Doctor of Pharmacy

Phar. M. Master of Pharmacy

Pharm Chem pharmaceutical chemistry

Ph.B. Bachelor of Philosophy

Ph.D. Doctor of Philosophy

P.H.D. Doctor of Public Health

Ph.D.Ed. Doctor of Philosophy of Education

Ph.G. Graduate in Pharmacy

phil philosopher; philosophical; philosophy

Phil Philippians (Bible)

Philem Philemon (Bible)

Phil I Philippine Islands

Phil Soc Philharmonic Society

Ph. M. Master of Philosophy

PHN Public Health Nursing

phon phonetic; phonetics; phonology

photo photograph

photog photographer

php pound horsepower; pounds per horsepower

phys physical; physician; physics; physiology

PHS Pennsylvania Historical Society; Printing House Square; Public Health Service

Phys Ed physical education

Phys Sc physical science

p & i principal and interest

P.I. International Pharmacopeia

Pic pictorial

PIM pulse interval modulation

PIN personal identification number

PINS person in need of supervision

pinx. he/she painted it [L *pinxit*]

p in² parts per square inch

p in³ parts per cubic inch

PIRG Public Interest Research Group

pix motion pictures

pk pack; park; peak; peck

pkg package; packing

pkt packet; pocket

Pkwy parkway

pl place; plate; plural

Pl Place

PL partial loss; poet laureate; public library

P & L profit and loss

PLA People's Liberation Army

Plen plenipotentiary

plm pulse length modulation

PLO Palestine Liberation Organization

plup pluperfect

p.m. afternoon [L *post meridiem*]; post mortem

p/m parts per million; pounds per minute

Pm promethium (chem)

PM postmaster; Prime Minister; provost marshal

PMG post master general

pmh past medical history; per man hour

pms pre-menstrual syndrome

pn percussion/percussive note; please note; positive negative

P/N part number; promissory note

pneum pneumatic; pneumonia

p.n.g. undesirable person [L *persona non grata*]

PNP positive negative positive (transistor)

pnr prior notice required

pnxt he/she painted it [L *pinxit*]

Po polonium (chem)

PO parole officer; passport/patent office; personnel/petty/pilot officer; post office; postal order; public office; purchase order

poc port of call

POE Pacific Orient Express; port of embarkation/entry

poet. poetic; poetical; poetry

Pol Poland; political

pol ind pollen index

poli sci political science

POLS Problem Oriented Languages (computer)

Pol Sci Political Science

pop. popular; population

POP point of purchase

Port. Portugal

pos position; positive

POS point of sale

POSH port side out, starboard home

posn position

poss possessive; possible

POW prisoner of war

powd powder

pp partial paid; passive participle; past participle; post paid; privately printed

ppd postage paid in advance; postpaid

PPFA Planned Parenthood Federation of America

ppi parcel post insured

P-plane pilotless plane

ppm parts per million; pulse position modulation

PPM pulse mode multiplex

ppo prior permission only

pps pictures per second; pounds per second; pulses per second

P.P.S. additional postscript

pptn precipitation

PQ Province of Quebec

Pr praseodymium (chem); provost

PR public relations; Puerto Rico

P/R payroll

PRC price regulation committee

preemie premature baby

pref preface; preference; prefix

prefab prefabricated

prefd preferred

preg pregnancy; pregnant

prehist prehistory; prehistoric

prelim preliminaries; preliminary

prem premium

premed premedical student

pre-op preparation for operation

prep preparatory; preposition; preparation

pres present

Pres Presbyterian; president

pres part. present participle

prev previous

pro-am professional-amateur

prob probate

prod product; production

prof professional; professor

prole proletarian

promo promotional

pron pronoun; pronunciation

prop wash propellor wash

props theatrical properties

prosc proscenium

Prot protestant

pro tem temporarily [L *pro tempore*]

prov provisional

Prov Proverbs (Bible)

prox proximal; proximity

prp pulse repetition period

prr pulse repetition rate

prt parachute radio transmitter; personnel research test; pulse repetition time

ps picosecond

Ps Psalms (Bible)

PS public school (with number)

P.S. postscript [L *post scriptum*]

P sac pericardial cavity

p's and q's pints and quarts (on your best behavior)

PSAT Preliminary Scholastic Aptitude Test

psc per standard compass

PSC public service commission

PSD pay supply depot; personal services department

PSE Pacific Stock Exchange

pseud pseudonym

psf pounds per square foot

psi pounds per square inch

psia pounds per square inch absolute

psig pounds per square inch gauge

psm presystolic murmur

PST Pacific standard time

PSW psychiatric social worker

psych psychology

pt part; pint

Pt platinum (chem)

PT Pacific time; physical therapist

PTA parent-teachers' association; plasma thromboplastin antecedent (med); posttraumatic amnesia (med)

ptc positive temperature coefficient

pt ex part exchange

ptg printing

PTM pulse time modulation/multiplex

pw prisoner of war; psychological warfare; public works

pW picowatt

PW pulse width

P W A public works administration

PWD public works department

pwr power

pwt pennyweight

PWU Postal Workers Union

PX post exchange; private examination

pyro pyromaniac; pyrotechnics

Pu plutonium (chem)

pvt private

–Q–

q coefficient of association (math); electrical charge; quartile deviation; stagnation pressure

Q Coulomb, unit of quality (elec); quantity; quartermaster; quarto; quartoquadrillion; queen (chess); query, question

QA qualification approval; quality assurance; quarters allowance

Q & A question and answer

QAC quality assurance check; quality assurance code

QADS quality assurance data system

QAE quality assurance engineering

QAG Quaker Action Group

QAO Quality Assurance Office

qar quick-access recording

QAS question answering system

QASAR Quality Assurance Systems Analysis Review

QAT Qualification Approval Test; Quantitative Assessment and Training Center

QAVT Qualification Acceptance Vibration Test

qb quarterback

QB Queen's bench; queen's bishop (chess)

Qbc Quebec

QBP queen's bishop's pawn (chess)

q/c quick change

Qc impact pressure (symbol)

QC quality control; quartermaster corps; Queen's College/Counsel; quit claim

Qcc qualification correlation certification; quick-connect coupling

qcd quality-control data; quantum chromodynamics

QCE Quality Control Engineering

qci quality-control information

qcl quality-control level

QCOP Quality Control Operating Procedure

Qc/Ps impact/static pressure ratio (symbol)

qcr quick-change response

qcrt quick-change real time

qct quiescent carrier telephony

QCT quality control technology

qcu quartz crystal unit; quick-change unit

qd quarterdeck; quartile deviation; questioned document; quick delivery

q & d quick and dirty

qdrnt quadrant

qdta quantitative differential thermal analysis

qdv quick disconnect valve

QE quantum electronics

QE2 Queen Elizabeth the second (Cunard liner)

qed quantitative evaluative device; quantum electrodynamics; quick-reaction dome

q.e.d. which was to be demonstrated [L *quod erat demonstrandum*]

q.e.f. which was to be done [L *quod erat faciendum*]

q.e.i. which was to be discovered [L *quod erat inveniendo*]

QEST Quality Evaluation System Test

qev quick exhaust valve

qf quality factor; quick freeze; quick frozen

qfc quantitative flight characteristics

qfe quartz fiber electrometer

QFI Qualified Flight Instructor

qfm quantized frequency modulation

QFP Quick-Fix Program

qft quantized field theory

QG Quartermaster General

qh quartz helix

q.h. every hour [L *quaque hora*]

q-h quartz-halogen (lights)

qi quality indices

qil quartz incandescent lamp; quartz iodine lamp

QIP quality inspection point

QITS Quality Information and Test System

QKt queen's knight (chess)

QKtP queen's knight's pawn (chess)

QL quantum leap

Qld Queensland

qli quality of life index

qlt quantitative leak test

qlty quality

QM quantum mechanics; query message

qmao qualified for mobilization ashore only

QMC quartermaster corps

QMG quartermaster-general

QM Gen quartermaster-general

qmo qualitative material objective

QMS quartermaster-sergeant

QM Sgt quartermaster-sergeant

qn question; quotation

Qn Queen

QNS quantity not sufficient

qnty quantity

qo quick opening; quick outlet

qod quick-opening device

qpa qualitative point average

qpf quantitative precipitation forecast

qpi quadratic performance index

qpit quiet propulsion lift technology

QPRI Qualitative Personnel Requirements Information

qps quantitative physical science

QPS Quick Program Search

qq quartos; questions

q/qy question/query

qr qualifications record; quick reaction; quire

QR Quotation Request

qri qualitative requirements information

QRMF Quick-Reacting Mobile Force

QRO Quick Reaction Operation; Quick Reaction Organization

qs quarter section; quarter session

q.s. a sufficient quantity [L *quantum sufficit*]

QS quadraphonic stereo; Quarantine Station; quarter section

qsam queued sequential access method

qse qualified scientists and engineers

qsf quasi-static field; quasi-stationary front

qsic quality standard inspection criteria

Q & SL Qualifications and Standards Laboratory

QSO quasi-stellar object (astron)

qsr quick-strike reconnaissance

QSS Quota Sample Survey

qstn question

Q-switch quantum switch

qt quantity; quart

QT on the quiet

qtam queued telecommunication access method

qted quick text editor; quoted

qtly quarterly

qtn quotation

qto quarto

QTP Qualification Test Procedure

qtr quarter

qty quantity

qu as it were [L *quasi*]

quad quadrangle; quadrant; quadrat (typo); quadrilateral; quadrillion (10^{15}); quadruplicate

qual qualification; qualitative; quality

qual anal. qualitative anlysis

quam quadrature-amplitude modulation

quantras question analysis transformation and search (data processing)

quant suff a sufficient quantity

quar quarter; quarterly; quarantine

Que Quebec

QUIDS Quick Interactive Documentation System

quint quintuplicate; quintet

quor quorum

quot quotation

qv quality verification

q.v. which see [L *quod vide*]

qvt quality verification test

qw quarter wave

qwl quick weight loss

qwot quarter-wave optical thickness

qy quantum yield; query

Qz quartz

–R–

r correlation coefficient (ps); radius; rain (met); recto; red; registered; resistance ohm (electronics); right; rises; river; rubber (cards)

R gas constant (chem); Rankine; Reamur; regular; roentgen; rook (chess)

R' radius of circle

ra radio; radioactive; right angle; right atrium; right auricle

Ra radium (chem)

RA rear admiral; regular army

R.A. right ascension (astron); Royal Academy

RAA Royal Academy of Arts

RABAR Raytheon advanced battery acquisition radar

RACON radar beacon

RACS remote access computing system

rad radiation; radiation absorbed dose; radical; radio; radius; random access disc; rapid automatic drill

rad. root [L *radix*]

radal radio-detection and location (system)

RADAR radio detection and ranging

RADAS random access discrete address system

RADATS Radar Data-Transmission System

RADCM radar countermeasures and deception

radiog radiography

radiol radiology

radir random access document indexing and retrieval

rad lab radiation laboratory

rad op radio operator

rad/s radians per second

radu radar analysis and detection unit

Ra Em radium emanation

RAF Royal Air Force

rai radioactive interference; random access and inquiry

rair remote access/immediate response

RAIR ram-augmented interstellar rocket

ralu register and arithmetic logic unit

RAM radio attenuation measurement; random access memory (computer); random access method; rocket assisted motor

ramac random access memory accounting

RAMIS Rapid-Access Management Information System

RAMP Raytheon Airborne Microwave Platform (sky station)

ran. reconnaissance-attack navigator; request for authority to negotiate

RANCOM random communication satellite

randid rapid alphanumeric digital indicating device

rao radio astronomical observatory

rar radio acoustic ranging; rapid-access recording

RASER radio frequency amplification by stimulated emission of radiation

rastac random access storage and control

rat. rate; rations; rating

ratc radar-aided tracking computer

ratcon radar terminal control

rato rocket-assisted takeoff

RAVE research aircraft for visual environment

RAVES Rapid Aerospace Vehicle Evaluation System

ravir radar video recorder; radar video recording

RAW Reconnaissance Attack Wing (USN)

rawarc radar and warning coordination

rax random access (computing system)

RAYCI Raytheon Controlled Inventory

razel range, azimuth, elevation

razon range and azimuth only

rb read backward; relative bearing

Rb rubidium (chem)

R B reconnaissance bomber

R_B Rockwell hardness (B-scale)

R&B rhythm and blues (mus)

r.b.c. red blood cell/corpuscle

RBD rapid beam deflector

RBF read bit feedback (computer)

rbi runs batted in

rc radio code/coding; red corpuscle; reinforced concrete; reverse course; right center; rotary combustion; rubber cushioned;

r/c reconsigned; recredited

RC Roman Catholic; Red Cross

R_C Rockwell hardness (C-scale)

RCA Rabbinical Council of America; Radio Club of America; Radio Corporation of America

RCAF Royal Canadian Air Force

RCC Radiological Control Center; Rescue Coordination Center; Roman Catholic Church

rcd received

rce remote-controlled equipment; right center entrance

rcf relative centrifugal force

rcfm radiocommunication failure message

RCMP Royal Canadian Mounted Police

RCSS random communication satellite system

RCU remote control unit; rocket countermeasure unit

rcv receive

RCV remote-controlled vehicle

rd rad; rod, unit of measurement; round

Rd Road

R&D research and development

RDA recommended daily allowance

rdd required delivery date

rd & e research, development, and engineering

rdi recommended daily intake

RDT&E research, development, testing, and evaluation

RDZ radiation danger zone

re rate of exchange; with reference to

Re rhenium (chem)

RE revised edition

R & E research and engineering

Rear Adm rear admiral

rec receipt; receive; receipt; recent; record; recreation

recid recidivism; recidivist

Rec Sec recording secretary

recap recapitulate

recd recorded

recip reciprocal

recir recirculate; recirculation

recom recommend

recon reconcentration; reconciliation; recondition; reconnaissance; reconnoitre; reconsignment

RECON retrospective conversion of bibliographic records (Library of Congress)

ref reference

refl reflexive

reg regent; regiment; registered; registry; regulator; regular; regulation; regulatory

Reg. queen [L *regina*]

regd registered

Regt regiment

Reg TM registered trade mark

rehab rehabilitate

REIC Radiation Effects Information Center; Rare Earth Information Center

reinf reinforce

REIT real estate investment trust

rej reject; rejected; rejection

rel relative

REL Radio Engineering Laboratories; rate of energy loss

rel hum relative humidity

rel pron relative pronoun

rem roentgen equivalent man

REM rapid-eye movement (in sleep)

rep repair; repertory; reporter; representative; reprint; republican; Roentgen equivalent physical (phys)

Rep representative

REP recovery and evacuation program

repo repossession

repop repetitive operation

repr represent; representative

repro reproduced

req request; require; requisition

reqd required

res rescue; research; residence; resign; resolution

resc rescue

resid residual

resist. resistance; resistor

resp respective; respectively; respiration; responsibility

Res Phys Resident Physician

REST routine execution selection table (computer)

ret retain; retired

Ret retired

RETP Reliability Evaluation Test Procedure

rev revenue; reverse; revise; revolve

Rev Revelation (Bible); reverend

REV re-entry vehicle (space)

rev a/c revenue account

rev ed revised edition

rev/min revolutions per minute

rev/s revolutions per second

Rev Ver Revised Version

rf rheumatic fever; right field/fielder

RF radio frequency

rfa radio frequency authorization

rfd refund; reporting for duty

RFD rural free delivery

RFE Radio Free Europe

rfm radio frequency management

rfp retired on full pay

RFQ request for quotation

rgl regulate; regulation; regulatory

Rgt Regiment

rh relative humidity; rheumatic; rheumatism; rheumatoid; right hand

r/h relative humidity; roentgens per hour

Rh Rhesus (blood factor); Rhodesia; rhodium (chem)

Rh+ Rhesus positive

Rh− Rhesus negative

rhd radioactive health data; rheumatic heart disease

rheo rheostat

rhet rhetoric

Rh Factor Rhesus Factor

RHI range height indicator

rhom rhombic; rhomboid; rhombus

rhp rated horsepower

RI Rhode Island; Rotary International

RICO Racketeer-Influenced Corrupt Organization (statute)

RIF resistance-inducing factor

rifl random item file locator

RIN report identification number

RIO reporting in and out

R.I.P. Rest in Peace

RIPPLE radioactive isotope powered pulsed light equipment

RIPS Radar-Impact Prediction System; Range-Instrumentation Planning System

RIQS Remote Information Query System

RIS Radio Information Service; Regulatory Information System

RIT Radio Information Test; Rochester Institute of Technology

RITE rapid information technique for evaluation

RITS Rapid Information Transmission System; Reconnaissance Intelligence Technical Squadraon

r/l radio location

rly relay

rm radio monitoring; range mark; raw material; ream; research memorandum; ring micrometer; room

r & m redistribution and marketing; reliability and marketing; reports and memoranda

RM Registered Magistrate; Registered Mail; research memorandum

r/min revolutions per minute

rms root mean square

rmsd root-mean-square deviation

rmse root-mean-square error

Rn radon (chem)

RN registered nurse

RNA ribonucleic acid (chem)

RNC Republican National Committee

RNW Radio Navigational Warning

ro recto; right opening; right orifice; rood; rough opening; rowed over; run out

r/o roll out; rule out

RO radar observer; radar operator; receiving office; receiving order; record office; registered office

RoA Record of Acquisition

ROB remaining on board (ship)

Roch Rochester

RoD Record of Decision

ROGER your message received and understood

ROI return on investment

ROK Republic of Korea

rom radar operator mechanic; range of movement; roman type

Rom Romans (Bible)

ROM read only memory (computer)

romv return on market value

rop run of press

ROR release on recognizance

ROTC Reserve Officers' Training Corps

ROT remedial occupational therapy

ROW right of way

rp reply paid

RP remote pickup (broadcast); Rules of Procedure

RPA Regional Planning Association

rpd radar planning device

RPD rocket propulsion department

rpe range probable error; related payroll expense

RPG Regional Planning Group

rph revolutions per hour

RPh Registered Pharmacist

rpi random procedure information; rated position identifier

RPI radar precipitation integrator

rpm revolutions per minute

RPM revolutions per minute

RP/ND reprinting, no date

RPO railway post office

rps revolutions per second

rpt repeat

RPT Registered Physical Therapist

R/Q Request for Quotation

rqr require; requirement

rr radiation resistance; radiation response; radio ranging; rendezvous radar; respiratory rate; rifle range; rush and run

RR railroad; recovery room; research report; Rolls Royce; rural route

R&R rest and recreation; rock and roll

RRB Railroad Retirement Board

rr & c records, reports, and control

rrd receive, record, display

RRM renegotiable-rate mortgage

rrp recommended retail price

RRU Radio Research Unit (USA)

r/s revolutions per second

r & s research and study

RSC Royal Shakespeare Company

RSFSR Russian Soviet Federal Socialist Republic

rs & i rules, standards, and instructions

RSM reconnaissance strategic missile

RSNA Radiological Society of North America

rsp rear-screen projection

r-s ratio response-stimulus ratio

RSV Revised Standard Version (Bible)

RSVP please reply [Fr *repondez s'il vous plait*]

rswc right side up with care

rt right

RT radio telegraphy/telephone; reaction time; recreational therapy; respiration therapist; return ticket; rocket target

R/T radio telegraphy

R & T research and technology

RTA reciprocal trade agreements

rtb return to base

rtcp radio transmission control panel

rtd returned

RTDS real time data system (computer)

rte route

r-t-e ready to eat

RTE Research Training and Evaluation

Rt Hon right honorable

RTL Right-to-Life

rtm registered trademark

RTN registered trade name

rto radio-telephone operator

rtol restricted take off and landing

rtor right turn on red (traffic rule)

Rt Rev right reverend

RTSA Retail Trading Standards Association

RTSRS Real-Time Simulation Research System

RTU returned to unit (mil)

RTV reentry test vehicle

RTW ready to wear; road tank wagon

rtz return to zero

Ru ruthenium (chem)

RUM remote underwater manipulator

Rus Russia, Russian

rush remote use of shared hardware

rv rear view; recreational vehicle; reentry vehicle; relief valve; right ventricle

RV rateable value (fin); research vessel; revised version

R/V rendezvous; research vessel

RVA Regular Veterans' Association of the United States

rvc random vibration control; relative velocity computer

Rvp Reid vapor pressure

RVR runway visual range

rw radiological warfare; runway

r/w read/write; right-of-way

rwh radar warning and homing

rwi read, write, initial; real world interval; remote weight indicator

r/w memory read/write memory

r/w storage read/write storage

rwt read, write, tape

rwy railway

r/x receiver

Rx prescription; recipe

rxs radar cross section

Ry railway

rym refer to your message

ryt reference your telegram; reference your telex

–S–

s school; sea; second, time interval unit; second of arc; section; see; semi; set; shilling; snow (met); south; spades; steel; stem; stock; stratus (met); substantive; symmetrical (chem)

s. half [L *semi*]; left [L *sinister*]

S Sabbath; saint; Saturday; Saxon; scalar (math); secondary; secret; secretary; section; siemens; silver; singular; slow; society; south; staff; strangeness (phys); statute; sulphur (chem); sun; Sunday; Sweden

s.a. by skill (med) [L *secundum artem*]; undated [L *sine anno*]

SA Salvation Army; Saudi Arabia; Secretary of the Army; South Africa; South America; special agent; supply assistant

Sab Sabbath

SABMIS seaborne antiballistic missile intercept system

SABMS safeguard antiballistic missile system

sac sacrifice

SAC Scientific Advisory Council; State Athletic Commission; Strategic Air Command

SACAD stress analysis and computer-aided design (computer)

Sacr Sacrament

SAE Society of Automatic Engineers

saec. century [L *saeculum*]

SAF Secretary of the Air Force; Strategic Air Force

SAG Screen Actors Guild; Scientific Advisory Group

SALT Strategic Arms Limitation Treaty/Talks

salv salvage

Salv Salvador

1 Sam 1 Samuel (Bible)

2 Sam 2 Samuel (Bible)

SAM surface to air missile

San.D. Doctor of Sanitation

sar search and rescue; semi-automatic rifle

SAR search and rescue center; Sons of the American Revolution; South African Republic; standardized abnormality ratio

SASE self-addressed stamped envelope

Sask Saskatchewan

sat. saturate; satellite

Sat Saturday; Saturn

SAT Scholastic Aptitude Test

SATCO signal automatic air traffic control system

SATCOMA satellite communications agency

SATEX semi-automatic telegraph exchange

sav sale/stock at valuation

sb single breasted; small bore; small business; smooth bore; south bound; stilb; substantive; switch board

s/b should be; surface based

Sb antimony (chem) [L *Stibium*]

S.B. Bachelor of Science

SBA Small Business Administration

SBN standard book number

SBO secure base of operation

sc scene; science; slow call; small caps

sc. namely [L *scilicet*]

Sc scandium (chem)

SC South Carolina; Security Council; Supreme Court

Sc.D. Doctor of Science

sch schedule

sch. note [L *scholium*]

sci science; single column inch

sci-fi science fiction

SCLC Southern Christian Leadership Conference

Scot. Scotland

SCOTUS Supreme Court of the United States

scr scrip; scruple

Scrip scriptural; scripture

SCRL signal corps radar laboratory

Sc & T Science and Technology

SCUBA self contained underwater breathing apparatus

sd safe deposit; said; same date; second defense; several dates; sound

s.d. without date [L *sine die*]

SD South Dakota; Secretary of Defense; special delivery; standard deviation; State Department; submarine detector

S.D. Diploma in Statistics

SDA Seventh-Day Adventist; source data automation; Students for Democratic Action

S Dak South Dakota

S Doc senate/state document

SDP Social Democratic Party

SDS Students for a Democratic Society

se special equipment; spherical equivalent; standard error; straight edge

Se selenium (chem)

SE southeast; standard English

S/E stock exchange

SEATO Southeast Asia Treaty Organization

sec secant; second; secretary; section; sector; security

sec. according to [L *secundum*]

SEC Securities and Exchange Commission

Sec Gen secretary general

Secy secretary

sed sedative; sediment

seg segment

Seg follows, comes after (mus)

sem semicolon; seminary

Sen senate; senator; senior; Senegal

Sen Rept Senate Report

sent. sentence

sep separate; separation

Sept September

SEPTA Southeast Pennsylvania Transit Authority

seq sequel; sequence

seq. the following [L *sequens*]; it follows [L *sequitur*]

ser serial; series; sermon

sess session

SET Selective Employment Tax

sext sextant

sf safety factor; salt free; signal frequency; single feed; sinking fund (fin);

spinal fluid; standard form; standard frequency; stress formula

s-f science fiction

SF San Francisco

sfc spinal fluid count

Sfc sergeant, first class

S1c seaman, first class

s-ft second-foot

SFU signals flying unit

sg specific gravity; steel girder

s-g subgenus; subgeneric

S Gauge Standard Gauge

sgd signed

SGHWR steam generating heavy water reactor

sgl single

SGN Surgeon General of the Navy

Sgt sergeant

Sgt Maj sergeant major

sh second hand; surgical hernia; social history

SHAEF Supreme Headquarters, Allied Expeditionary Forces

SHAPE Supreme Headquarters, Allied Powers in Europe

she signal handling equipment; standard hydrogen electroid

SHEX Sundays and Holidays excepted

shf superhigh frequency

shoran short range (radio)

shp shaft horsepower

shpt shipment

shr share (fin)

SHRAM Short Range Air to Surface Missile

shrap shrapnel

shv solenoid hydraulic valve

s & i stocked and issued

Si silicon (chem)

SI International System of Units [Fr *Systeme International d'Unites*]; Smithsonian Institute

sibs siblings

SIBS Salk Institute for Biological Studies

sic thus [L]

SIC Scientific Information Center; specific inductive capacity; standard industrial classification

sicbm super continental ballistic missile

S-in-C Surgeon-in-Chief

sid sudden ionospheric disturbance

SID standard instrument departure; sudden infant death

SIDS sudden infant death syndrome

sig signal; signature; signifies

sig. let it be labeled (med) [L *signetur*]

SIG signature of engraver present (numis)

sim similar; similarly; simile

sin sine

sing. singular

sinh hyperbolic sine (math)

SIO satellite in orbit; Scripps Institute of Oceanography; senior intelligence officer; small income relief

si op. sit if necessary [L *si opus sit*]

siq superior internal quality

SIS Secret Intelligence Service; Submarine Integrated Sonar

sisp sudden increase of solar particles

SISS submarine integrated sonar system

SIT spontaneous ignition temperature

SITC standard international trade classification

sitcom situation comedy

SITPRO simplification of international trade procedures

SIZ security identification zone

s.j. under legal consideration [L *sub judice*]

S.J. Society of Jesus (Jesuit Order)

SJC Standing Joint Committee; Supreme Judicial Court

Skt Sanskrit

sl sales letter; sea level; support line

s.l. according to law [L *secundum legem*]; no place of publication [L *sine loco*]

SL salvage loss; scout leader; sea level; search light; security list; southern league; supplementary list

S&L savings and loan

sla single line approach

SLAM supersonic low-altitude missile

SLBM submarine launched ballistic missile

sl & c shipper's load and count

sld sailed; sealed; sold; solid; specific learning disability

slf straight line frequency

s.l.p. without lawful issue [L *sine legitime prole*]

SLP Socialist Labour Party

SLR self loading rifle; Statute Law Revision Act; single lens reflex

slto sea level takeoff

sm small; streptomycin; sustained medication; systolic murmur; syzygy mathematics

Sm samarium (chem)

SM sales manager; senior magistrate; sergeant-major; service module; shipment memorandum; silver medallist; Sisters of Mercy; soldier's medal; stage manager; state militia; station master; strategic missile

sma subject matter area

sm caps small capitals (typo)

SMD submarine mine depot; superintendent of mine design

s mi statute mile

sml simulate; simulation; simulator; small

smm standard method of measurement

smog smoke-laden fog

SMS sequence milestone system; synchronous meteorological satellite

smsa standard metropolitan statistical area

smt ship's mean time

SMUS Soviet Mission to the United States

SMW standard metal window

s m w d sep single, married, widowed, divorced, separated

sn serial/series/service number

s.n. according to nature [L *secundum naturam*]; without name [L *sine nomin*]

Sn tin (chem) [L *stannum*]

S/N shipping note; signal to noise ratio

SNAFU situation normal, all fouled up

SNCC Student Non-Violence Coordinating Committee

SNF system noise figure

sng synthetic natural gas

Sng Singapore

Soc Dem social democrat

sociol sociology

sonar sound navigation ranging

Song of Sol Song of Solomon (Bible)

SOP standard operating procedure

SOS wireless distress signal

sota state of the art

SOTIM sonic observation of the trajectory and impact of missiles

sov sovereign

Sov Soviet

SOWETO Southwestern Townships (South Africa)

sp self-propelled; selling price; space; space character (data processing); special; special purpose; species; specific; specimen; speed; spelling; spirit; sport

s.p. without issue [L *sine prole*]

s & p systems and procedures

SP shore patrol

SPAN Solar Particle Alert Network

SPANDAR space and range radar

Spansule space plus capsule

SPAR Coast Guard Women's Reserve; super precision approach radar

SPC stored program control

SPCA Society for the Prevention of Cruelty to Animals

SPCC Society for the Prevention of Cruelty to Children

spd subject to permission to deal (fin)

sp del special delivery

spec special; specific; specification; specimen; spectrum; speculation

specs specifications; spectacles

sp gr specific gravity

sp ht specific heat

SPI selected period investment (fin)

SPM short particular meter (mus)

spp. species

SPQR the senate and people of Rome [L *senatus populusque romanus*]

SPRI Scott Polar Research Institute

SPRING solid propellant rocket intercept missile

sp surf. specific surface

sptg. sporting

SPUR space power unit reactor; source program utility routines (computer)

sq squadron; square

Sq Square

sq ft square foot

sq in square inch

sq m square meter/mile

sq rd square rod

sq yd square yard

sr scientific research; self raising; sex ratio; shipping receipt; short rate; slow release; steradian; stimulus response

Sr senior; strontium (chem)

SRBM short range ballistic missile

SRBP synthetic resin bonded paper

SRC sample return container

srf self resonant frequency; solar radiation flux; submarine range finder

SRIC Southwest Research and Information Center

SRM short range missile; speed of relative movement

SRO single-room occupancy; standing room only

ss simplified spelling; single strength; sworn statement

ss. namely (law) [L *scilicet*]

SS Secretary of State; secret service; secondary school; stainless steel; standard size; steamship

S.S. Holy Scripture [L *Sacra Scriptura*]

S/S same size; self shank (buttons); silk screen; station to station;

S to S ship to shore

SSA Social Security Administration

SSB Social Security/Selective Service Board

ssc station selection code (data processing)

S.Sc.D. Doctor of Social Science

SSG guided missile submarine

SSI supplemental security income

SSM single sideband modulation; surface to surface missile

SSR Soviet Socialist Republic

SSS Selective Service System

SSSI sites of specific scientific importance

SST supersonic transport/travel

st select time; short ton; stanza; state; statement; static thrust; statute; stem; stitch; stone; street; strophe; syncopated time

St Saint; Street

ST shipping ticket; shock troops; spring tide; standard/summer time; surtax

S & T supply and transport

sta station

STANAG Standard NATO Agreement

stand. standard

staph staphycoccus

START Strategic Arms Reduction Talks

stat. immediately (med) [L *statim*]

stats statistics

stbd starboard

STC satellite test center; sensitivity time control

std standard; started

stdft³ standard cubic foot (feet)

steno stenographer; stenography

ster stereotype; sterling

stet let it stand (proofreading)

s & ti scientific and technical information

stip stipend

stk stock

STM Scientific, Technical, and Medical; short term memory; special test missile; System Training Mission

STO senior technical officer; standing order

STOL short take off and landing

STP standard temperature and pressure

STRAC strategic air command/army corps

Strad Stradivarius violin

STRAD signal transmitting, receiving and distribution

strep. streptococcus

STRICOM U.S. Strike Command

STS serological test for syphillis

stwy stairway

su service unit; set up; strontium unit

Su Sunday

SU Soviet Union

sub subaltern; sub editor; subject; subjunctive; subscription; subsidiary; subsistence; substantive; substitute; suburb; subway

subch subchapter

subd subdivision

subj subject; subjunctive

subpar subparagraph

subpt subpart

subsec subsection

substand substandard

suf suffix

sug suggestion

sum summary

SUM surface to underwater missile

Sun Sunday

SUN symbolic unit number (computer)

SUNS sonic underwater navigation system

sup superficial; superfine; superior; supreme

sup. above [L *supra*]

supp supplement, supplementary

supr superior; supervisor; supreme

supra cit. cited above [L *Supra citato*]

Supt superintendent

Surg surgeon

Surg Gen surgeon general

Sus Susanna (Bible/Apocrypha)

susp suspend; suspension

s.v. under a specified word [L *sub verbo/sub voce*]; spirits of wine (med) [L *spiritus vini*]

SV sailing vessel

S/V surrender value (fin)

svg saving

SVTP sound, velocity, temperature, pressure

SW secretary of war; senior warden; Ship's Warrant; southwest; south westerly; standard weight; static water

SWACS space warning and control system

SWAT special weapons & tactics

Swaz Swaziland

SWB short wheel base

swbd switchboard

Swe Sweden

Switz Switzerland

SWL safe working load

swp safe working pressure

SWR serum Wassermann reaction

SWS static water supply

SXT sextant

syl syllable; syllabus

sym symbol; symbolic; symmetrical; symmetry; symphony

syn synchronize; synonym; synonymous; synthetic

SYNCOM synchronous communication satellite

synec synecdoche

Syr Syria

syst system; systematic

systran systems analysis translator

sz size

–T–

t table; teaspoon; teaspoonful; tempo (mus); tense; terminal; territory; time; ton; tonne (metric ton); transit; transitive; troy; turn

T surface tension (phys); tea; teacher; telegraph; telephone; temperature (med); temporary; tera (prefix, 1 trillion); terms

(math); torpedo; township; transaction; transport; transportation; transverse; tritium (chem); Tuesday

ta tablet; target area; test accessory; third attack (lacrosse); transit authority; travel allowance; true altitude

t/a trading as

t of a terms of agreement

Ta tantalum (chem)

TA table of allowances (tax); teacher's assistant; telegraphic address; territorial army; traffic agent/auditor; training advisor; turbulence amplifier

T/A temporary assistant

tab. tablet; tablet; tabulate; tabulation

TAC Tactical Air Command (USAF); Technical Assistance Committee (UN)

TACAN tactical air navigation

TACG Tactical Air Control Group

tach tachometer

tachygraphy (shorthand)

TACMAR tactical multi-function array radar

tacnav tactical navigation

TAG telegraphist air gunner

Tal Talmud

TALUS transportation and land use study

tan. tangent (math)

Tan. Tanzania

tanh hyperbolic tangent

TAO Technical Assistance Operations (UN)

TAOC Tactical Air Operations Center

TAP Technical Assistance Program

tarmac tar macadam

TARS Technical Assistance Recruitment Service (UN)

TASR terminal area surveillance radar

TASS telegraph agency of the Soviet Union

TAT tetanus antitoxin; Transatlantic Telephone Cable

TAUN Technical Assistance of the United Nations

taut. tautology

tb temporary buoy; terminal board; title block; trial balance; true bearing

t & b top and bottom

Tb terbium (chem)

TB torpedo boat/bomber; training battalion; treasury bill; tuberculosis

tba to be announced

tbd to be determined

T-bill Treasury bill

tbp true boiling point

tb & s top, bottom and sides

tbsp tablespoonful

tc temperature control; terra cotta; till cancelled; time check; tropic tides; true course

Tc technetium (chem)

TC Tank Corps (mil); Tariff Commission; tax cases; technical college; tennis club; town clerk; training center/college/corps; transport command; traveler's check

tcb take care of business

TCC Temporary Council Committee (NATO); Transport and Communications Commission (UN); Troop Carrier Command

TCH Trans Canada Highway

TCO test control officer

TCR total controlled return

TCS tactical air control system; target cost system

TCT total controlled tabulation

tctl tactical

TCTO time compliance technical order (USAF)

TCUS Tax Court of the United States

td tank destroyer; technical/test data; third defense (lacrosse); time delay/deposit; tod (28 lb. of wool); touchdown; tractor-drawn; tool design; trust deed; turbine drive

t & d taps and dies

TD tactical division; teaching diploma; technical development; traffic director; Treasury Department

TDB Total Disability Benefit

TDC top dead center

TDN total digestible nutrients

TDP technical development plan

tds temperature, depth, salinity

te task element; thermal efficiency; trial and error; turbine engine

t/e time expired; twin engined

Te tellurium (chem)

TE telecommunications engineering; topographical engineer; trade expenses

T & E test and evaluation; travel and entertainment

TEE telecommunications engineering establishment; Trans Europe Express

teg top edge gilt (book binding)

tel telephone

telecom telecommunications

telex teletype exchange

Tel no. telephone number

tem temperature; tempered; template

temp temperance; temperate; temperature; temporal; temporary

ten. tenant

Tenn Tennessee

Ter Terrace

TERCOM terrain contour matching

term. terminal; terminate; termination; termonology; termite

tert tertiary

test. testament; testator; testatrix; testimonial; testimony

TEST *Thesaurus of Engineering and Scientific Terms*

tet tox tetanus toxin

Teut Teuton; Teutonic

Tex Texas

text. rec. the received text [L *texturs receptus*]

tf tabulating form; tax free; thin flim; till forbidden; training film

TF task force; territorial force

tfa total fatty acids

tfc traffic

tfg typefounding

tfr transfer

Tft³ trillion cubic feet

TFX tactical fighter experimental

TG Tate Gallery; Theater Guild; training group; Translators' Guild

TGIF Thank God It's Friday!

T-Group training group

Tgt target

Th theater; theology; thermal; thorium (chem); Thursday

Thai. Thailand

Th.B. Bachelor of Theology

THC tetrahydrocannabinol

Th.D. Doctor of Theology

theat theater; theatrical

theol theologian; theological; theology

therm thermometer; thermometric

1 Thess 1 Thessalonians (Bible)

2 Thess 2 Thessalonians (Bible)

THI temperature humidity index

thm therm

thp thrust horsepower

Thru Thruway

Thuc Thucydides

Thurs Thursday

THz tetrahertz

ti target identification; temperature indication; tricuspid insufficiency

Ti titanium (chem)

TI technical inspection; technical institute; temperature indication/indicator; Texas Instruments (USA); textile industry; Treasure Island

T/I target identification/indicator

TIB tourist information board

tid task initiation date

t.i.d. three times day [L *tres in die*]

1 Tim. 1 Timothy (Bible)

2 Tim. 2 Timothy (Bible)

TIMM thermionic integrated micromodule

TIN transaction identification number

TIROS television and infrared observation satellite

tit title; titular

Tit Titus (Bible)

TKO technical knockout (boxing)

tkt ticket

tl test link; time loan; title list; total load/loss

t/l total loss

Tl thallium (chem)

TL torpedo lieutenant; trade-last

TLC tender loving care

tle theoretical line of escape

TLI translunar injection/insertion

tlo total loss only

TLV threshold limit value

tm temperature meter; trade mark; trench mortar; true mean

t & m test and maintenance

Tm thulium (chem)

TM tactical missile; tactical nuclear missile; technical manual; test manual; tone modulation; trademark; traffic manager; transcendental meditation

tma total material assets

TML tetramethyl lead; three mile limit

TMO telegraph money order

TN Tennessee; true north

tnpk turnpike

TNT trinitrotoluene (dynamite)

tntc too numerous to count

tn wp thermonuclear weapon

to. time opening; tool order; traditional orthography; turn over

t/o take off

TO technical officer; telegraphic order; telegraph/telephone office; telephone order; trained operator; transport officer

Tob Tobit (Bible)

TOC technical order compliance; table of contents

TOET Test of Elementary Training

TOEFL Test of English as a Foreign Language

TOES tables of organization and equipment; trade-off evaluation system

TOGA Tests of General Ability

tohp take off horsepower

tonn tonnage

too. time of origin

TOP temporarily out of print

tor time of receipt

tos terms of service

TOSCA Toxic Substances Control Act

tot. total

TP third party

tpd tons per day

tph tons per hour

TPI terminal phase initiation

tpr temperature, pulse, respiration

tr trace; track; tragedy; train; transaction; transfer; transitive; translate; translator; transport; transpose (typo); treasurer; treble; troop; truck; trust; trustee

tr. tincture (med) [L *tinctura*]

Tr trainee

TR target rifle; tariff reform; taxations reports; test run; tons registered; tracking radar

T/R transmitter/receiver

TRAAC transit research and altitude control satellite

TRACALS traffic control and landing system

trach trachia; tracheotomy

trad tradition; traditional

TRADEX target resolution and discrimination experiment

trans translation; translator; transport; transportation; transpose; transaction; transfer; transistorize; transitive; transitory; translate; transposition; transverse

transp transportation

Treas Treasurer

TRECOM transportation research command

trf tuned radio frequency

TRH Their Royal Highnesses

TRIAL Technique for Retrieving Information from Abstracts of Literature

trig trigonometric; trigonometry; trigonometrical

TRIGA trigger reactor

TRLFSW tactical range landing force support weapon

trn technical research note

TRO temporary restraining order

Trop Can Tropic of Cancer

Trop Cap Tropic of Capricorn

TRS tetrahedral research satellite; ticket reservation system

ts temperature switch; tensile strength; test summary; till sale; turbine steamship; twin screw; typescript; type specification

TS Tourette's syndrome

T & S transport and supply

tsa tax sheltered annuity; total survey area

TSD Tay Sachs Disease

tsfr transfer

T Sgt top sergeant

TSH Their Serene Highnesses

tsi tons per square inch

tsp teaspoonful

tss typescripts

TSS time sharing system; turbine steamship; twinscrew ship/steamer/steamship

tstr tester

tt tank technology

TT technical training; teetotal; telegraphic transfer; tetanus toxoid; torpedo tube; transit time; tuberculin-tested

TTAB Trademark Trial and Appeal Board

TTC technical training command

TTL transistor-transistor logic

TTM two-tone modulation

TTS teletypesetting

TTY teletypewriter

TU thermal/toxic unit; trade union; transmission unit

Tues Tuesday

Tur Turkey

turb turbine

turboprop turbine propelled

tus. cough (med) [L *tussi*]

TV television

TVA Tennessee Valley Authority

tvq top visual quality

TVR temperature variation of resistance

tw tail wind

Twad twaddell

twb twin with bath

T2g technician, second grade

twp township

TWPD tactical and weapons policy division

TWR Trans World Radio

TWS timed wire service

TWT transonic wind tunnel; traveling-wave tube

TWU Transport Workers Union

tx tax; taxation

TX Texas

typ type

typo typographer; typographic; typographical; typographical error; typography

–U–

u unified atomic mass (phys); unit; unknown; upper

U uncle; union; union (math); unionist; unite; universal (film); university; uranium (chem); Utah

ua under age

U/a underwriting account

UADPS Uniform Automatic Data Processing System

UAE United Arab Emirates

UAHC Union of American Hebrew Congregations

UAM underwater-to-air missile

uap unexplained atmospheric phenomenon

uas upper air space

UAW United Auto Workers

U-Boat submarine [Ger *Unterseeboot*]

uc upper case (typo)

UCC Uniform Commercial Code

UCCC uniform consumer credit code

ucd usual childhood diseases

UCD upper critical depth (ocean)

ucl upper cylinder lubricant (eng)

UCMJ uniform code of military justice

ucr unconditioned response

ucs unconditional stimulus; unconscious

udc universal decimal classification

UDC Urban Development Corporation; United Daughters of the Confederacy

UDI unilateral declaration of independence

udw ultra deep water

ue uexpired; unit equipment

u/f urea-formaldehyde resin

U factor measure of insulating power

ufn until further notice

UFO unidentified flying object

ufp unemployed full pay

u/g underground

Ug Uganda

ugf unidentified growth factor

ugt urgent

uh upper half

uhf ultra high frequency

uhp ultra high purity

uhs ultra high speed

uht ultra high temperature

uhv ultra high vacuum/voltage

ui ultrasonic industry; unemployment insurance

u.i. as below [L *ut infra*]

u/i under instruction; unit of issue

UJA United Jewish Appeal

UK United Kingdom

UL Underwriters' Laboratory; universal league; university library; upper limb

ulb universal logic block

ulc unsafe lane change; upper left center

u & lc upper and lower case (typo)

ULCA United Lutheran Church of America

ulf ultra low frequency; upper limiting frequency

ULLV unmanned lunar logistics vehicle

ulm ultrasonic light modulator; universal logic module

ULMS undersea long-range missile system

uls unsecured loan stock (fin)

ulv ultra low volume

UMFC United Methodist Free Churches

U Mi Ursa Minor (astron)

ump umpire

UMS universal military service

UMT universal military training

UMTA Urban Mass Transportation Administration

UMTS universal military training service/system

UMW United Mine Workers

UN United Nations

UNA United Nations Association

unab unabridged

UNAC United Nations Appeal for Children

UNACC United Nations Administrative Committee and Coordination

unan unanimous

UNARCO United Nations Narcotics Commission

unauth unauthorized

UNB universal navigation beacon

unbd unbound

UNC uncirculated (numis); United Nations Command

UNCF United Nations Children's Fund; United Negro College Fund

uncir uncirculated

unclass unclassified

uncond unconditioned

uncor uncorrected

und under

UNDP United Nations Development Program

UNEDA United Nations Economic Development Administration

UNEF United Nations Emergency Force

UNESCO United Nations Educational, Scientific, and Cultural Organization

UNETAS United Nations Emergency Technical Aid Service

ung. ointment (med) [L *unguentum*]

UNHQ United Nations Headquarters

UNICEF United Nations Children's Fund

UNIDO United Nations Industrial Development Organization

Unit Unitarian; Unitarianism

univ universal; universalist; university

Univ University

UNIVAC universal automatic computer

unkn unknown

unm unmarried

UNO United Nations Organization

unop unopposed

unpd unpaged; unpaid

UNPOC United Nations Peace Observation Commission

unpub unpublished

UNREF United Nations Refugee Emergency Fund

unsat unsatisfactory; unsaturated

UNTA United Nations Technical Assistance

u & o use and occupancy

uoc ultimate operating capability

UOD ultimate oxygen demand (water conservation)

uov unit of variance

up. under proof (spirits); upper

UP Union Pacific; United Presbyterian; United/University Press;

UPC Universal Product Code; Unesco Publications Center; United Presbyterian Church;

UPD united port district; urban planning directorate

UPI United Press International

UPR Union Pacific Railroad

ups uninterrupted power supply

UPS United Parcel Service

UPU Universal Postal Union

Ur Uruguay

urg urgent

Urol urology

u.s. as above [L *ut supra*]

u/s unserviceable

US United Service; United States; Uncle Sam (USA); under secretary; uniform system of lens aperture (photo);

USA United States Army

U.S.A. United States of America

USAAC United States Army Air Corps

USAC United States Air Corps

USAEC United States Atomic Energy Commission

USAF United States Air Force

USAFA United States Air Force Academy

USAID United States Agency for International Development

USAR United States Army Reserve

USAT United States Army Transport

USBC United States Bureau of the Census

USBM United States Bureau of Mines

usc under separate cover

USC United States Code/Congress; up stage center (theater)

USCA United States Code Annotated

USCC United States Circuit Court

USCCA United States Circuit Court of Appeals

USCG United States Coast Guard

USCGA United States Coast Guard Academy

USCGR United States Coast Guard Reserve

USDA United States Department of Agriculture

USES United States Employment Service

USF United States Forces

USG United States Government

USGS United States Geological Survey

USIA United States Information Agency

USIS United States Information Service

USM United States Mail/Marines/Mint

USMA United States Military Academy

USMC United States Marine Corps/Maritime Commission

USN United States Navy

USNA United States Naval Academy

USNG United States National Guard

USNR United States Naval Reserve

USO United Service Organizations

USP United States Patent/Pharmacopoeia

USPO United States Post Office

USPS United States Postal Service

USS Under Secretary of State; United States Senate/Ship/Steamer/Steel

USSB United States Savings Bonds

USSC United States Supreme Court

USSR Union of Soviet Socialist Republics

USVH United States Veterans' Hospital

usw ultra short wave; underwater sea warfare

USWB United States Weather Bureau

USWI United States West Indies

Ut Utah

UT   Utah; Universal Time

ut dict.   as directed [L *ut dictum*]

uti   urinary tract infection

ut inf.   as below [L *ut infra*]

utop   utopian

ut sup.   as above [L *ut supra*]

U2   high altitude photographic aircraft

uv   ultraviolet

uvl   ultraviolet light

u/w   underwater

U/w   underwriter

UXB   unexploded bomb

–V–

v   unusual visibility (met); vacuum; valley; valve; vertical; vector (math); vein; ventilator; ventral; verb; verse; version; very; vicar; village; virus; viscosity; visibility; vision (med); vocative; voice; volcano; voltage; voltmeter; volume; vowel

v.   against [L *versus*]; by way of [L *via*]; or [L *vel*]; in place of [L *vice*]; left-hand page of open book [L *verso*]; see [L *Vide*]

V   potential energy (math); vanadium (chem); velocity (phys); Venerable; version; very (in titles); vespers; vice (in titles); victory; Viscount; Viscountess; volt

va   value analysis; verb active; verbal adjective; vinyl acetate; voltampere (elec)

v.a.   lived ... years [L *vixit ... annos*]

VA   Veterans' Administration; Virginia; Voice of America; voltampere; volunteer artillery; Volunteers of America

Va   Virginia

V/A   voucher attached

V and A   Victoria and Albert Museum (London)

VAb Van Allen belt (astron)

VABM vertical angle bench mark

vac vacancy; vacant; vacation; vacuum; volts alternating current

VAC vector analog computer

vacc vaccination; vaccine

vac dist vacuum distilled

vag vagabond; vagina; vagrancy; vagrant

VAH Veterans' Administration Hospital

va & i verb active and intransitive

val valley; valuation; value; valvular

valid. validate; validation

VAMP visual acoustic magnetic pressure; visual approach for management planning

van. vanguard; vanilla

Vanc Vancouver (Canada)

Vapi visual approach path indicator

var variable; variant (math); variation; variety; various

VAR visual-aural radio range

var cond variable condenser

var dial. various dialects

var ed & tr various editions and translations

varistor variable resistor

varsity university

vas vasectomy

vasc vascular

Vasi visual approach slope indicator

vas vit. glass vessel [L *vas vitreum*]

Vat Vatican

VAT value added tax

VATE versatile automatic test equipment

Vat Sta Vatican State

vaud vaudeville

v aux verb auxiliary

vb verb; verbal

vba verbal adjective (participle)

vbl verbal

vc valuation clause; vehicular/visual communication; vinyl chloride

v.c. for example [L *verbi causa*; seen cultivated [L *visum cultum*]

VC Vatican City; vice-chairman/chancellor/consul; Victoria Cross; Vietcong

VCA vinylene carbonate (chem); virtual crystal approximation

VCCS voltage controlled current source (elec)

VCG vertical center of gravity; vice-consul general

VCI volatile corrosive inhibitor

VCO voltage controlled oscillator

VCR video cassette recorder

VCXO voltage controlled crystal oscillator

vd vapor density; various dates; verbal discrimination; void

VD venereal disease

V Day victory day

v def verb defective

v dep verb deponent

VDH valvular disease of the heart

VDI vegetation drought index

VDR variable diameter rotor

VDS variable depth sonar

vdt variable density wind tunnel; video display terminal

VDT video display terminal

VDU visual display unit

VE valve engineer; vocational education

veb variable elevation beam

vec vector

VE Day Victory in Europe

veg vegetable; vegetarian; vegetation

vel vellum (bookbinding); velocity

ven veneer; venereal; ventral; ventricle

Ven Venerable; Venetian; Venezuela; Venice; Venus

vent. ventilate; ventilation

vent fib ventricular fibrillation

ver verification; verify; verse; version

VERA versatile experimental reactor assembly; vision electronic recording apparatus

vern vernacular

verso reverso, left hand page of open book

vert vertebra; vertical/vertigo

verticam vertical camera

ves. in the evening [L *vespere*] (med); vessel; vestry

vet. veteran; veterinarian; veterinary; veterinary surgeon

VET Verbal Test

Vet Admin Veteran's Administration

Vet.M.B. Bachelor of Veterinary Medicine

Vet.Sci. Veterinary Science

Vet.Surg. Veterinary Surgeon

vf very fair/fine

VF video/voice frequency; visual field

v-f band voice-frequency band

VFC voltage-to-frequency converter

VFO variable frequency oscillator

VFP variable factor programming (computer)

VFR visual flight/flying rules

VFU Vertical Format Unit (computer)

VFW Veterans of Foreign Wars

v.g. for the sake of [L *verbi gratia*]

Vg   Virgin

VG   velocity gravity; very good; Vicar General

vgc   viscosity gravity constant

VGPI   visual glide path indicator

vhf   very high fidelity/ frequency

vhf/uhf   very high and ultra high frequency

VHO   very high output

VHP   very high performance

vi   verb instransitive

VI   Vancouver Island; vertical interval (cartog); Virgin Islands; viscosity index; volume indicator

via   virus inactivating agent

vias   voice interference analysis system

VIB   vertical integration building

Vic   Victoria

Vice Adm   vice admiral

Vien   Vienna (Austria)

vii   viscosity index improver

vil   village

v imp   verb impersonal

v imper   verb imperative

vin   vehicle identification number

vini   viniculture

VIP   value improvement project; variable/versatile information processing (USN); very important person

VIPRE   visual precision

Vir   Virgo

V.I.R.   Victoria Empress and Queen [L *Victoria Imperatrix Regina*]

Vir Is   Virgin Islands

vis   viscosity; visible; visibility; visual

Vis   viscount; viscountess

VISTA   Volunteers in Service to America

vit   vitreous

VIT   vertical interval test

VITA Volunteers for International Technical Assistance

VITAL variably initialized translator for algorithmic languages

vitr glass [L *vitreum*]

vit stat vital statistics

vivi vivisection

vix. he/she lived [L *vixit*]

viz. namely [L *videlicet*]

VJ Day Victory over Japan day

vk vertical keel; volume kill

VL vice-lieutenant; vulgar latin

vla very low altitude

vlf very low frequency

VLR very long range (aircraft)

vltg voltage (elec)

vlv valve; valvular

V/m volts per meter/mile

VM velocity modulation; Viet Minh

vmap video map equipment

VMC visual meteorological conditions

VMD vertical magnetic dipole

vn verbal noun

VN Vietnam; Vietnamese

vo. left-handed page [L *verso*]

VO valuation officer; verbal order; veterinary officer; Victorian Order; voice-over

VOA Voice of America

voc vocal; vocalist; vocation; vocative

VOC vehicle observer corps

vocab vocabulary

VOD velocity of detonation

vodacom voice data communication

VODAT voice-operated device for automatic transmission

vol volatile; volume; voluntary; volunteer

volum volumetric

VOTEM voice-operated typewriter employing morse

vp vanishing point; vapor pressure; variable pitch; various pagings

VP vice-president

vpd vehicles per day

v ph vertical photography

vpm vehicles per mile; vendor part modification; volts per mil

vpn vendor part number

V Pres vice-president

vps vibrations per second

vr variant/various reading; verb reflexive; voltage regulator (elec); vulcanized rubber

VR variety reduction; vertical retort; volunteer reserve;

V.R. Queen Victoria [L *Victoria Regina*]

VRA Vocational Rehabilitation Administration

v refl verb reflexive

vri visual rule instrument land (aircraft)

vs variable speed; vital signs

vs. against [L *versus*]

V.S. Veterinary Surgeon

vsb verbal substantive

VSD vendor's shipping document; ventricular septal defect

VSI vertical speed indicator; very seriously ill

VSM vestigial sideband modulation

VSMF visual search microfilm file

VSO very superior old

VSOP very special old pale (cognac)

VSQ very special quality

VSR very short range; very special reserve

VSTOL vertical and short take-off and landing

VSWR voltage standing wave ration (elec)

vt transitive verb

v & t volume and tension (med)

Vt Vermont

VT Vermont

VTL variable threshold logic (computer)

VTO vertical take-off

VTOHL vertical take-off and horizontal landing

VTOL vertical take-off and landing

VTOVL vertical take-off vertical landing

VTR video-tape recording

VTU volunter reserve training unit, US Coast Guard

vtvm vacuum tube volt meter

vu volume unit

vul vulgar

vv interchanged [L *vice versa*]; spoken loudly [L *viva voce*]

v/v volume per volume

VVO very, very old

VVS very, very superior

VWG vibrating wire gauge

Vx vertex

vy very

–W–

w waist; wall; war; warm; waste; water; watt (elec); weather; weight; west; western; wet; wet dew (met); white; width; wife; wind; wire; with; woman (size); won; word; work; wrong

W gross weight; tungsten (wolfram) (chem); very wide; Wales; warden; Waterloo; watt; Wednesday; Welsh; west; western; widow; widower; work (phys)

Wa. Washington

WA Washington; Welfare Administration; West Africa; Western Australia

WAAC Women's Army Auxiliary Corps

WAAF Women's Auxiliary Air Force

WAB Wage Adjustment Board

WAC Women's Army Corps; World Aeronautical Chart

WACSM Women's Army Corps Service Medal

WADF Western Air Defense

WADS wide area data service

wae when actually employed

WAEC War Agricultural Executive Committee

WAF Women in the Air Force

WAFFLE wide angle fixed field location equipment

WAG Writer's Action Group

WAIS Wechsler's Adult Intelligence Scale (psych)

Wall. Wallace, U.S. Supreme Court Reports

w Am white American male

WAM words a minute; work analysis and measurement

war. warrant

War. Warsaw

warn. warning

warr warranty

Wash. Washington (state)

Wass Wassermann (blood test)

WAT weight, altitude and temperature; Word Association Test (psych)

WATS Wide-Area Telephone Service

WAVES Women Accepted for Volunteer Emergency Service

wb wage board; waste/water ballast; wave band; west bound; wheel base

Wb weber

WB water board; weather bureau; weekly benefits (ins); wet bulb; World Bank for Reconstruction and Development (UN); World Brotherhood

W/B way bill

WBA World Boxing Association of America

WBC white blood cell/corpuscle/count; World Boxing Council

WBD *Webster's Biographical Dictionary*

WBGT wet bulb globe temperature/thermometer

wbi will be issued

WBIT Wechsler-Bellevue Intelligence test (psych)

wbo wide band oscilloscope; wide bridge oscillator

wbp weather and boil proof

wbs walking beam suspension

WBT wet bulb temperature

wc watch committee; water closet/cock; wheel chair; will call; without charge

WC water closet; war cabinet; working capital; workmen's compensation

WCAA West Coast Athletic Association

WCC War Crimes Commission; White Citizens' Council; World Council of Churches

WCF World Congress of Faiths

WCP World Council of Peace

WCT World Championship Tennis

WCTU Women's Christian Temperance Union

wd ward; warranted; weed; wood; word; would; wound

w/d well developed

WD war/water department; works department

W/D wind direction

Wed Wednesday

WES waterways experiment station

WESO Weapons Engineering Standardization Office

WEU Western European Union

wf wrong font (typo)

WF Wells Fargo and Company; wing forward

w factor will factor (psych)

WFL Women's Freedom League

WFP World Food Program

WFPA World Federation for the Protection of Animals

WFTU World Federation of Trade Unions

wg water gauge; weighing; weight guaranteed; wing; wire gauge

WGI World Geophysical Interval

W Ger West Germany

wh wharf; which; white

w/h withholding

Wh watt hour (elec)

WH water heater; White House; wing half

whap when or where applicable

WHO White House Office; World Health Organization

whsle wholesale

WI West Indies; Windward Islands; Wisconsin

wia wounded in action

wid widow; widower

WILCO will comply

WILPF Women's International League for Peace and Freedom

WIN Work Incentive (program)

W Ind West Indies

Wind I Windward Islands

wip work in progress

Wis Wisconsin

Wisd of Sol Wisdom of Solomon (Bible/Apocrypha)

WM watt/wave meter; white metal; wire mesh

WMC Ways and Means Committee

W/(m-K) watt per meter kelvin

wndp with no down payment

WNL within normal limits

w/o without

WO War Office; warrant officer; welfare officer; wireless operator; written order

wob washed overboard

woc without compensation

woe without equipment

Women's Lib Women's Liberation (movement)

WOO western operations office (NASA); World Oceanographic Organization

woool words out of ordinary language

WORSE word selection

wosac worldwide synchronization of atomic clock

WOSD weapons operational systems development

wot wide open throttle

WP word processing

WPC World Petroleum Congress

WPCA Water Pollution Control Administration

WPCF Water Pollution Control Federation

wpi wholesale price index

wpm words per minute

WPN World Press News

WPRS Water and Power Resources Service

WPs Warsaw Pact Members

WRAP weapons readiness analysis program

WRC water-retention coefficient

w ref with reference to

w reg with regard to

WRI War Resisters International

WS Wallops Station (NASA); water soluble; weapon system

W Sam Western Samoa

wsd working stress design

WSED weapons systems evaluation division

WSEG weapons systems evaluation group

WSJ Wall Street Journal

wsp water supply point

W/sr watt per steradian

W/(sr-m²) watt per steradian square meter

wt warrant; watertight; weight; without

WT watch time; withholding tax

WTD war trade department

WTMH watertight manhole

WTO Warsaw Treaty Organization

WTP weapons testing program

wu work unit

WU Western Union

wv water valve

w/v weight in volume; weight/volume

WV West Virginia

W Va West Virginia

wvt water vapor transfer/transmission

wvtr water vapor transmission rate

w/w weight for weight; weight/weight

WW Who's Who; worldwide

WWCTU World Women's Christian Temperance Union

WWD Women's Wear Daily

WWF World Wildlife Fund

WWI World War One

WWII World War Two

WWO wing warrant officer

WWSSN worldwide standard seismograph network

WY Wyoming

Wyo Wyoming

–X–

x extra

X experiment; explosive; extension

xaam experimental air to air missile

XACT X (unnamed computer) automatic code translation

xan xanthic; xanthene

xasm experimental air to surface missile

x cut cross cut

xcy cross country

xd x-dividend, not including right to dividend

x'd executed

x'd out crossed out

Xe xenon (chem)

xf extra fine

xfa cross fired acceleration

xfer transfer

xfmr transformer

xg crossing

xgam experimental guided air missile

Xh experimental helicopter (USN)

xhr extra high reliability

xin without interest

XING crossing

XM experimental missile

Xmas Christmas

xmit transmit

xmsn transmission

xmtr transmitter

Xn Christian

Xnty Christianity

x-out cross out

xp express paid

XP represents Christ/Christianity

xpd expedite

xper without privileges

XPS x-ray photoemission spectroscopy

XQ cross question

XRD x-ray diffraction

X rds cross roads

x ref cross reference

x sec extra sec (dry champagne)

Xt Christ

xtal crystal

xtrans experimental language (computer)

xtry extraordinary

Xty Christianity

XUV extreme ultraviolet

xw experimental warhead

xxx international urgency signal

–Y–

y yacht; yard; year; yellow; young; youngest; admittance (elec); altitude; dry air (met); lateral axis; ordinate

Y hypercharge; Yen; yttrium (chem); Yugoslavia

YA young adults

Yb ytterbium (chem)

yd yard

yd² square yard

yd³ cubic yard

ydi yard drain inlet

YH youth hostel

Yid Yiddish

yl yield limit

YLJ *Yale Law Journal*

YMCA Young Men's Christian Association

YMHA Young Men's Hebrew Association

yo year old

yob year of birth

yod year of death

yom year of marriage

yr year; younger; your

yrs yours

ys yard superintendant; yield strength

YU Yale University

Yump young upwardly mobile professional

Yuppie Young urban professional

YWCA Young Women's Christian Association

YWHA Young Women's Hebrew Association

–Z–

z dust haze (met); third unknown quantity (math); zenith; zenith distance; zero; zone

Z atomic number; impedance (elec)

ZAC zinc ammonium chloride

Zam Zambia

ZAP zero anti-aircraft potential

ZAS zero access storage

zd zenith description/ distance; zero defect

ZEBRA zero energy breeder reactor assembly

Zech Zechariah (Bible)

zen zenith

ZENITH Zero energy nitrogen heated thermal reactor

Zeph Zephaniah (Bible)

zero-g zero gravity, weightlessness

ZETA zero energy thermonuclear apparatus/ assembly

ZETR zero energy thermal reactor

ZF zero frequency; zone of fire

Z Hr zero hour

zig zero immune globulin

Zimb Zimbabwe

ZIP + 4 9-digit ZIP Code

ZIP Code Zone Improvement Plan Code (Postal Service)

zl freezing drizzle (met)

Zn zinc (chem)

Zod Zodiac

Zoo Zoological Gardens

zool zoological; zoologist; zoology

ZPG zero population growth

zr freezing rain (met)

Zr zirconium (chem)

zsg zero-speed generator

ZT Zone Time

ZUM Zone Usage Measurement

Zur Zurich

zwl zero wave length

Common Words/ Acronyms and Abbreviations

–A–

abbreviated **abbr; abbrev**

ablative **abl**

able-bodied seamen **AB**

about **a; ab; abt**

above **abv**

above named **an.**

above sea level **asl**

abridge **abr**

absent **abs**

absent with leave **awl**

absent without official leave **awol**

absolute **a; abs; absol**

abstract **abs; abstr**

accelerando (mus) **accel**

acceleration **acc**

acceleration of gravity **g**

accent **acc**

acceptance **acc; acpt**

accompanied **acc; ac-comp**

according **acc**

according to value [L *ad valorem*] **ad val.**

account **A/C; acc; acct**

accountant **acct**

account of **a/o**

accounts receivable **A/R**

accredited **accred**

accusative **acc; accus**

acetone-dicarboxylic acid **ADA**

acquire **acq**

Acquired Immune Deficiency Syndrome **AIDS**

acquittal **acq**

acre **a; ac**

acronym **acron**

acting **act**

actinium (chem) **Ac**

action variable **J**

active **a; act.**

active duty **AD**

activities of daily living **adl**

Acts of the Apostles (Bible) **Acts**

actual cash value **acv**

actual gross weight **agw**

actual time of departure **ATD**

actuary **act.**

additional **add.; addit; addl**

address **add.**

adenosine diphosphate **ADP**

adjacent **adj**

adjective **adj**

adjourned **adj**

adjustable rate mortgage **ARM**

adjusted gross income **AGI**

adjustment **adj**

adjutant **Adj**

adjutant general **Adj Gen**

administration **admin**

admiral **Adm**

admission **adm**

adrenocorticotropic hormone (anti-rheumatic drug) **ACTH**

advance **adv**

advanced capabilities radar **ACR**

advanced data processing **ADP**

advanced placement **AP**

advance ratio **J**

advantage **ad**

Advent **Adv**

adverb **adv**

advertisement **adv**

advocate **Adv**

aeronautic **aero**

affidavit **afft**

affiliate **aff**

affirmative **aff**

Afghanistan **Afg**

Africa **Afr**

African **Afr**

African Methodist Episcopal **AME**

African National Congress **ANC**

Afrikaans **Afrik**

after **aft.**

afternoon **aft.**

against [L *contra*] **con.**

age **a**

aged [L *aetatis*] **aet.**

Agency for International Development **AID**

agent **Ag; agt**

aggregate **agg**

agnostic **agnos**

agreed **agd**

agreement **Ag; agt**

Agricultural and Industrial **A & I**

Agricultural Credit Corporation **ACC**

agriculture **Ag**

aid to dependent children **ADC**

aid to families with dependent children **AFDC**

aide-de-camp **ADC**

AIDS-related-complex **ARC**

airborne warning and control system **AWACS**

air-conditioning **A/C**

Air Corps **AC**

aircraft **A/C**

aircraft accident report **aar**

air cushion vehicle **acv**

Air Defense Command **ADC**

air defense identification zone **ADIZ**

air defense warning **ADW**

Air Force Base **AFB**

air interception **AI**

airman, first class **A1c**

airport surveillance radar **ASR**

air raid precautions **ARP**

air traffic control officer **ATCO**

Alabama **AL; Ala**

Alaska **AK**

Albania **Alb**

Alberta **AB**

Alcoholics Anonymous **AA**

algebra **alg**

Algeria **Alg**

alkaline **alk**

all but dissertation **ABD**

all concerned notified **acn**

all-points bulletin (law enforcement) **APB**

alphabetical **alph**

also known as **aka**

alteration **alt**

alternate **alt**

alternating current **ac; AC**

altitude **alt**

aluminium (chem) **Al**

amalgamated **amal**

Ambassador **Amb**

amendment **amend.**

America **A; Amer**

American **Amer**

American Automobile Association **AAA**

American Bar Association **ABA**

American Basketball Association **ABA**

American Civil Liberties Union **ACLU**

American College Test/ Testing **ACT**

American Dental Association **ADA**

American Indian **AmerInd**

American Institute of Architects **AIA**

American League **AL**

American Library Association **ALA**

American Medical Association **AMA**

American National Red Cross **ANRC**

American Red Cross **ARC**

American Samoa **Amer Samoa**

American Sign Language **ASL**

American Society for the Prevention of Cruelty to Animals **ASPCA**

American Standard Code for Information Interchange **ASCII**

American Stock Exchange **Amex**

americium (chem) **Am**

among other things [L *inter alia*] **in. al.**

amount **amt**

ampere **A**

ampere-hour **Ah**

ampere per meter **A/m**

ampere-turn **At**

amphibious **amph**

amplitude modulation **AM**

analogy **anal**

anatomy **anat**

and elsewhere [L *et alibi*] **et al.**

and following page (pages) **f; ff**

Andorra **And.**

and others [L *et alii*] **et al.**

and so forth [L *et cetera*] **etc.**

and the following [L *et sequentia*] **et seq.**

Angola **Ang**

angstrom **A**

annotate **annot**

annual percentage rate **APR**

annulment **annul.**

anonymous **a; anon.**

answer **a; ans**

Antarctica **Ant.**

anthology **anthol**

anthropology **anthrop**

antiballistic missile **ABM**

antimony [L *Stibium*] **Sb**

antique **ant.**

antonym **ant.**

apartment **Apt**

apocrypha **Apoc**

apostrophe **apos**

apothecary **ap**

apothecary pound **lb ap**

appeal **app; appl**

appendix **app**

applicable **appl**

appointment **appt**

appositive **appos**

approval **app**

approximate **app; approx**

approximately [L *circa*] **c**

April **Ap; Apr**

archaic **arch.**

archduke **Arch.**

archipelago **arch.**

architecture **arch.**

Arctic **Arc**

area **a**

Argentina **Arg**

argon (chem) **Ar**

arithmetic **arith**

Arizona **Ariz; AZ**

Arkansas **AR; Ark**

Army Air Corps **AAC**

Army Air Force **AAF**

army intelligence **AI**

Army of the United States **AUS**

Army post office **APO**

arrangement **arr**

arrive **arr**

arsenic (chem) **As**

article **art.**

as above [L *ut supra*] **u.s.**

as below [L *ut infra*] **u.i.**

as directed [L *ut dictum*] **ut. dict.**

aspirin, phenacetin, caffeine **APC**

assembly **ass.**

asset value **av**

assistant **Asst**

associate **assoc**

Associate in Applied Science **A.A.S.**

Associate in Arts **A.A.**

Associated Press **AP**

association **ass.; assn; assoc**

as soon as possible **ASAP**

astatine (chem) **At**

astonomical units **au**

astrology **astrol**

astronomy **astron**

Atlantic **Atl**

Atlantic Nuclear Force **ANF**

Atlantic standard time **AST**

Atlantic time **AT**

at length [L *in extenso*] **in ex.**

atmosphere (technical) **at; atm**

Atomic Energy Commission **AEC**

Atomic Energy Control Board **AECB**

atomic number **Z; at. no.**

atomic weight **A; at. wt**

at, or near, the end [L *ad finem*] **fin.**

at pleasure [L *ad libitum*] **ad lib.**

attached **att**

at the beginning [L *ad initium*] **ad init.**

at the place [L *ad locum*] **ad loc.**

at the suit of [L *ad sectam*] **ad s.**

attorney general **AG**

audio frequency **AF**

audiovisual **A/V**

August **A; Aug**

Australia **A; Aust**

Austria **Aus**

authentic **auth**

author **auth**

authorize **auth**

author's alterations **AA**

author's proof **ap**

automated data processing **ADP**

automated teller machine **ATM**

automatic amplitude control **AAC**

automatic digital calculator **ADC**

automatic frequency control **afc**

automatic phase control **APC**

Avenue **Av; Ave**

average **av; avg**

average annual rainfall **aar**

average body dose (radiation) **abd**

average crop yield **acy**

avoirdupois **avdp**

avoirdupois pound **lb avdp**

–B–

bachelor **B**

Bachelor of Agricultural Science **B.A.S.; B.A.Sc.**

Bachelor of Agriculture **B.Agr.**

Bachelor of Applied Arts **B.A.A.**

Bachelor of Applied Science **B.A.S.; B.Sc.App.; B.A.Sc.**

Bachelor of Architecture **B.Arch.**

Bachelor of Arts **A.B.**

Bachelor of Arts and Architecture **B.A.A.**

Bachelor of Business Administration **B.B.A.**

Bachelor of Canon Law [L *juris canonici baccaulaureus*] **J.C.B.**

Bachelor of Chemical Engineering **B.Ch.E.**

Bachelor of Chemistry **Ch.B.**

Bachelor of Civil Engineering **B.C.E.**

Bachelor of Civil Law **B.C.L.**

Bachelor of Commerce **B.Comm.**

Bachelor of Dental Science **B.D.Sc.**

Bachelor of Divinity **B.D.**

Bachelor of Education **B.Ed.; Ed.B.**

Bachelor of Electrical Engineering **B.E.E.**

Bachelor of Engineering Science **B.E.S.**

Bachelor of Fine Arts **B.F.A.**

Bachelor of Humane Letters **L.H.B.**

Bachelor of Journalism **B.J.**

Bachelor of Juridical and Social Science **B.Jur. & Soc.Sc.**

Bachelor of Law **B.L.**

Bachelor of Laws **LL.B.; J.B.** [L *jurum baccalaureus*]

Bachelor of Letters **B.Lit(t).; L.B.**

Bachelor of Literature **B.Lit(t).**

Bachelor of Medical Technology **B.M.T.**

Bachelor of Music **B.M.**

Bachelor of Science **B.S.; B.Sc.; B.Sci.**

Bachelor of Science in Education **B.S.Ed.**

Bachelor of Surgery **B.Ch.**

Bachelor of Surgery (GB) **B.S.**

Bachelor of Theology **B.Th.**

Bachelor of Veterinary Science **B.V.Sc.**

bacillus **b**

background **bg; bkgd**

background information **BI**

back order **b/o**

back stage **bs**

backward **bkd; bwd**

bacon, lettuce and tomato **BLT**

Bahamas Islands **Ba I**

bail bond **BB**

balance **bal**

balance sheet **bs; B/S**

ball bearing **bb**

ballistic missile defense **BMD**

ballistic missile weapon system **BMWS**

Bangladesh **Bngl**

bank draft **b/d**

Bank for International Settlements **BIS**

banking **bkg**

bank rate **BR**

bankrupt **bkrpt**

Baptist **Bapt**

bar **B**

Barbados **Barb**

barium (chem) **Ba**

barometer **bar.; brm**

baron **B**

baronet **Bart; Bt**

barrel **bar; bbl**

barrister **Bar.**

baryon scale **b**

basal metabolic rate **BMR**

basal metabolism **BM**

base address register (computer) **BAR**

base exchange **BX**

baseline **BL**

basement **bsmt**

base unit **bu**

basic **bsc**

Basic Assembly Language **BAL**

Basic Educational Opportunity Grant **BEOG**

basic training **BT**

basso **b**

battalion **bat.; bn; btn**

battle **bat.**

battleship **BB**

Baume **B**

Baume scale (chem) **Be**

bay **b**

Bay Area Rapid Transit (San Francisco subway system) **BART**

beachhead **bhd**

beacon **bn**

bearer bonds **bb**

bearing **br; brg**

beat **bt**

beautiful people **BP**

bed and board **b&b**

bed and breakfast **b&b**

bed, breakfast and bath **bbb**

bedroom **BR**

bedtime **BT**

been **bn**

before [L *ante*] **a.**

before Christ **B.C.**

before Christ [L *ante Christum*] **A.C.**

before meals (med) [L *ante cibum*] **A.C.**

before noon [L *ante meridiem*] **a.m.**

before the common era **B.C.E.**

before the present **B.P.**

Beginners' All-Purpose Symbolic Instruction Code (computer lang) **BASIC**

beginning **beg**

Behold the Man [L *Ecce Homo*] **Ecc. Hom.**

bel **B**

Belgian-Netherlands-Luxembourg Committee **BENELUX**

Belgium **Bel**

bench mark **BM**

Benevolent & Protective Order of Elks **BPOE**

benzene hexachloride **BHC**

benzoyl (chem) **Bz**

berkelium (chem) **Bk**

beryllium (chem) **Be**

Better Business Bureau **BBB**

between **bet.; btwn**

beverage **bev**

Bible **B**

bibliography **bibl; bibliog**

bicarbonate of soda **bicarb**

big close-up **BCU**

Big Man on Campus **BMOC**

bill book **BB**

bill discounted **b/d**

bill of health **B/H**

bill of lading **B/L**

bill of rights **BR**

bill of sale **bs; B/S**

bills receivable **B/R**

bin **B**

binary (math) **bin.**

binary digit (computer) **BIT**

biography **biog**

biology **biol**

birthplace **bp; bpl**

bishop **B; Bp**

bismuth (chem) **Bi**

bits per inch (computer) **bpi**

black and white **B/W**

black letter **BL**

Blessed Mary the Virgin **B.M.V.**

blood alcohol level **BAL**

blood pressure **BP**

blue book **BB**

blueprint **BP**

board **bd**

board foot **bd ft; fbm**

board foot measure **fbm**

board measure **bm**

Board of Civil Service Examiners **BCSE**

Board of Education **B of E**

Board of Public Works **BPW**

Board on Geographic Names **BGN**

body odor **bo**

body of law [L *corpus juris*] **C.J.**

boiling point **bp; b pt**

boldface (typo) **bd; bf; bld**

Bolivia **Bol**

bombardier **br**

bomb disposal squad **BDS**

bond **bd**

bonus point **BP**

bookkeeping **bkg**

book of reference **BR**

books **bb**

book value **BV**

born **b; bn**

boron (chem) **B**

borough **bor**

botany **bot**

Botswana **Bots**

bottle **bot; btl**

bottom **bot**

boulevard **Blvd**

bound **bd**

bowel movement **BM**

box **bx**

box office **bo**

Boy Scouts of America **BSA**

brake horsepower **bhp**

Brazil **Braz**

breakwater **brkwtr**

breech-loading rifle **blr**

brevet **bvt**

bridge **brg**

brief **bf; br; brf**

brig **br**

brigade **br**

brigade headquarters **BHQ**

brigadier **Brig**

brigadier general **BG; Brig Gen**

brightness **B**

Britain **Brit**

British Broadcasting Corporation **BBC**

British Columbia **BC**

British Empire Medal **BEM**

British Expeditionary Forces **BEF**

British Museum **BM**

British Petroleum **BP**

British Railways **BR**

British Standards Institute **BSI**

British thermal unit **Btu**

British Virgin Islands **BVI**

British West Indies **BWI**

broad **bd**

Broadcast Music Incorporated **BMI**

bromide **brom**

bromine (chem) **Br**

Brooklyn **Bklyn**

Brooklyn and Manhattan Transit (NYC Subway) **BMT**

brother **b; br; Bro**

brotherhood **b**

brought down **b/d**

brown **br; brn**

Browning automatic rifle **BAR**

Brunei **Brun**

building **bldg**

building line **BL**

built **blt**

Bulgaria **Bul**

bulletin **bull.**

bureau **bu; bur**

Bureau of Indian Affairs **BIA**

Bureau of Labor Statistics **BLS**

Bureau of Land Management **BLM**

buried **bur**

Burma **Burm**

bursar **burs**

bushel **bsh; bu**

business **bus.**

button **btn**

by virtue of office [L *ex officio*] **e.o.; ex off.**

bytes per second **bps**

Byzantine **Byz**

—C—

cadmium (chem) **Cd**

calcium (chem) **Ca**

calculate **calc**

calculus **calc**

caliber **cal**

California **Ca; CA; Cal; Calif**

californium (chem) **Cf**

calorie **C; cal**

Cambodia **Camb**

Cameroon **Cam**

Canada **Ca; Can**

Canal Zone **CZ**

cancelled **canc**

cancer **CA**

candela **cd**

candidate **cand**

candle hour **ch; chr**

candle (phys) **c**

candlepower **cp**

canon **can**

capacitance (elec) **C**

capacity **c; cap**

capital gains tax **cgt**

capital letter **cap.**

captain **Capt; cpt**

caption **capt**

carat **c; car.; ct; kt**

carbonate **carb**

carbon (chem) **C**

carbon copy **cc**

cardiac arrest **CA**

cardiopulmonary resuscitation **CPR**

carried forward (accounting) **c/f**

carton **ctn**

cases (legal) **ca.**

cash before delivery **cbd**

cash discount **cd**

cash management account **CMA**

cash on delivery **c.o.d.**

cash on hand **c.o.h.**

casualty **cas**

cataloging in publication **CIP**

cataloging in source **CIS**

catalogue **cat.**

catechism **cat.**

cathode **c; cath**

cathode-ray tube **CRT**

Catholic **C; Cath**

caveat **cav**

Celsius **C; Cel**

center fielder **cf**

center forward **cf**

center of pressure **cp**

Centers for Disease Control **CDC**

Centigrade **C; cent.**

centigrade heat unit **CHU**

centigram **cg**

centiliter **cL**

centimeter **cm**

centimeters per second **cm ps**

centipoise **cP**

Central African Republic **CAR; Cen Afr Rep**

Central America **CA**

Central Intelligence Agency **CIA**

central processing unit **CPU**

central standard time **CST**

central time **CT**

Central Treaty Organization **Cento**

century **c; cent.**

cerebral palsy **CP**

cerium (chem) **Ce**

certificate of deposit **CD**

certified **cert**

certified public accountant **CPA**

cesium (chem) **Cs**

Chamber of Commerce **CoC**

chancellor **C; Ch**

Channel Island **CI**

chapter **ch**

character **char.**

characters per second (computer) **cps**

charge **chg**

charter **chtr**

chartered accountant **CA**

check **Ch; ck**

chemical and biological warfare **CBW**

Chemical Engineer **C.E.; Chem.E.**

chemically pure **cp**

chemical warfare **CW**

chemistry **chem**

Chicago **Chi**

chief executive officer **CEO**

chief inspector **CI**

Chief Justice **CJ**

Chinese Communist Party **CCP**

chlorine (chem) **Cl**

Christ **C**

Christian **C**

Christ (symbol) **XP**

chromium (chem) **Cr**

chronicle **chron**

1 Chronicles (Bible) **1 Chron**

2 Chronicles (Bible) **2 Chron**

chronometry **chron**

church **Ch**

church warden **CW**

circa **c.; ca.**

circuit **C; circ; ct**

circuit breaker **CB**

Circuit Court of Appeals **CCA**

circulation **circ**

circumference **C; circ; circum**

citation **cit**

citizen **cit**

citizens' band (radio) **CB**

city **c**

civil **civ**

Civil Aeronautics Board **CAB**

Civil Air Regulations **CAR**

civilian **civ**

civilization **civ**

civil procedure **CP**

clinical **clin**

clockwise **C; CW**

closed circuit television **CCTV**

coast guard **CG**

cobalt (chem) **Co**

cocaine **C**

Code of Federal Regulations **CFR**

codicil **cod.**

codification **cod.**

coefficient of association (math) **q**

collaborate **collab**

collection **col**

collective **collect**

college **col**

college fraternity **frat**

colloquialism **colloq**

Colombia **Col**

colon **col**

colonel **Col**

colony **col**

Colorado **CO; Colo**

Colossians (Bible) **Col**

columbium (chem) **Cb**

column **col**

combination **comb.**

combined blood count **cbc**

comedy **com**

command **comm**

commander **Cdr; Comdr**

Commander-in-Chief **CIC; C-in-C**

commanding officer **CO; C/O**

commentary **comm**

commercial bill of lading **cb/l**

commissioner **com; comm**

committee **com**

Commodity Credit Corporation **CCC**

Commodity Futures Trading Commission **CFTC**

common **com; comm**

Common Business Oriented Language (computer lang) **COBOL**

common era **C.E.**

common prayer **CP**

communication satellite **Comsat**

Communist International **Comintern**

Communist Party **CP**

community access television **CATV**

compact disc **CD**

compact disc read only memory **CD-ROM**

company **Co; comp**

compare, or see [L *confer*] **cf.**

compilation **comp**

composition **comp**

comprehensive **comp**

computer-assisted design **CAD**

computer-based information system **CBIS**

computer generated imagery **CGI**

computerized axial tomagraphy **CAT-scan**

computerized emission tomogram **CET**

concentration **con**

concerning **con**

conclusion **con**

condense **cond**

conditional **cond**

conductance (elec) **G**

conductivity **cond**

conductor **c; cond**

confirm **cfm**

Congo **Con**

congregation **cong**

Congress **C**

conjugation **conj**

conjunction **conj**

Connecticut **Conn; CT**

connection **con**

conquer **conq**

conscientious objector **CO; C/O**

consecrate **cons**

consecutive **cons**

conservation **cons**

conservative **Cons**

consignment **cons; consgt**

consolidated **cons**

consonant **cons**

constant **c; const**

constant pressure **cp; CP**

constituency **const**

constitution **const**

construction **cons; const; constr**

construe **constr**

consul **c; con; cons**

consult **cons**

Consumer Price Index **CPI**

contained **contd**

contemporary **contemp**

contents **cont**

continent **cont**

continued **con; cont; contd**

continuum **cont**

contract **cont; contr**

contraction **cont; contr**

contralto **c**

control **cont; contr**

Control Program/Microcomputers **CP/M**

convention **conv**

conventional foot of water **ftH₂O**

conventional inch of mercury **inHg**

conventional inch of water **inH2O**

converter **conv**

convertible **conv**

cooperative **co-op**

copper (chem) **Cu**

copy **c**

1 Corinthians (Bible) **1 Cor**

2 Corinthians (Bible) **2 Cor**

corollary **coroll**

coronary care unit **CCU**

coroner **cor**

corporal **corp; cpl**

corporation **corp**

corpus **cor**

correct **cor; corr**

correlative **cor; corr; correl**

correspondence **corr**

corresponding **corresp**

corrupt **cor**

Costa Rica **CR**

cost-of-living adjustment **COLA**

coulomb **C**

counselor-at-law [L *Iuris-consultus*] **ictus.**

counter clockwise **ccw**

county **co**

county clerk **CC**

court **Ct**

court of appeal **CA**

Court of Claims **CCls**

Court of Customs and Patents Appeals **CCPA**

credit **cr**

criminal **crim**

criterion **crit**

critical **crit**

criticism **crit**

crown **cr**

cubic **c; cu**

cubic centimeter **cc; cm³**

cubic feet per hour **cfh**

cubic feet per minute **cfm**

cubic foot **cf; cft; cu ft; ft³**

cubic inch **cu in; in³**

cubic meter **m³**

cubic millimeter **mm³**

cubic yard **yd³**

cum dividend (fin) **cd; cdiv**

curie **Ci**

curium (chem) **Cm**

currency **c**

current density **J**

current (elec) **i**

custom house **CH**

customs assigned numbers **CAN**

customs declaration **C/D**

cyanide **Cy**

cycle (radio) **c**

cycles per minute **c/m**

cylinder **cyl**

Cyprus **Cyp**

Czechoslovakia **Czech**

–D–

Dahomey **Dah**

Daniel (Bible) **Dan**

darcy **D**

database **DB**

data processing **DP**

date **d**

dated **dd; dtd**

dative **dat**

datum **dat**

daughter **d; dau**

Daughters of the American Revolution **DAR**

day **d**

daylight saving time **DST**

daylight time **DT**

dead **d**

dead on arrival **DOA**

deadweight tons **dwt**

debenture **deb**

debit **deb; dr**

debtor **dr**

debutante **deb**

decade **dec.**

deceased **d; dec; decd**

December **D; Dec**

decibel **dB**

decibel unit **dBu**

decigram **dg**

deciliter **dL**

decimal **dec**

decimeter **dm**

declaration **decl**

declension **dec; decl**

decompression **decomp**

decorative **dec**

decrease **dec**

dedicated **dd; ded**

defeated **d**

defendant **def**

defense **def**

Defense Intelligence Agency **DIA**

deficit **def**

definite **def**

definite article **def art.**

definition **def**

degree **d; deg**

degree Fahrenheit **F**

deka (prefix, 10) **da**

dekagram **dag; dkg**

dekaliter **daL; dkl**

dekameter **dam**

Delaware **DE; Del**

delayed action **DA**

delayed broadcast **DB**

delegation **del; deleg**

delete **d; del**

delirium tremens [L] (med) **dt**

delivered **dd; Dld**

delivery **d; del; D/y**

demilitarized zone **DMZ**

democracy **dem**

Democrat **D; Dem**

Democratic Party **DP**

demonstration **demo**

denier **den**

Denmark **Den**

denomination **denom**

denotation **den**

density **d**

dentist **den**

deoxyribonucleic acid **DNA**

depart **d; dep**

department **dep; dept; dpt**

Department of Commerce **DOC**

Department of Defense **DOD**

Department of Health, Education and Welfare **HEW**

Department of Housing and Urban Development **HUD**

Department of Motor Vehicles **DMV**

Department of National Defense **DND**

Department of Public Works **DPW**

Department of the Army **DA**

Department of the Navy **DON**

Department of the Treasury **DOT; DT**

Department of Transportation **DOT**

departure **dep**

dependant **dep**

deponent **dep; dept; dpt**

deposit **dep; dpt**

deposit account **DA**

deposit receipt **D/R**

depot **dep; dpt**

depth **d**

deputy **dep; dept; dpty**

derivation **deriv**

dermatology **derm**

descendant **desc**

describe **desc**

desert **des**

design **des; dsgn**

designate **des; desig**

design requirements **dr**

destination **destn; dstn**

destroyer **D**

detach **det**

detail **det**

determine **det**

deuterium (chem) **D**

deuteron **d**

Deuteronomy (Bible) **Deut**

Deutsche Mark **DM**

development **dev**

deviation **dev**

Dewey Decimal Classification **DDC**

dexter **d**

diagnose **diag; Dx**

diagonal **diag**

diagram **dia; diag**

dialect **dial.**

dialogue **dial.**

diameter **d; dia; diam**

dichlorodiphenyltrich-
loroethane (pesticide)
DDT

dictionary **dic**

didymium (chem) **Di**

died **d**

dietary **diet**

difference **diff**

differential **diff**

digital audio tape **DAT**

digital-to-analog convert-
or **DAC**

dilatation and curettage
(surgical procedure)
D&C

dilute **dil**

dime **d**

dimension **dim; dmn**

diminish **dim**

diminutive **dim; dimin**

diocese **dioc**

diphthong **diphth**

Diploma in Clinical Pa-
thology **D.C.P.**

Diploma in Medical Jur-
isprudence **D.M.J.**

Diploma in Ophthalmic

Medicine and Surgery
D.O.M.S.

Diploma in Psychological
Medicine **D.P.M.**

diplomat **dip; dipl**

direct current **dc**

direction **dir**

direct order **d/o**

Disabled American Vet-
erans **DAV**

disbursement **disb**

disciple **dis; disc**

disc jockey **DJ**

discontinue **dis**

disc operating system
(computer) **DOS**

discount **dis; disc**

discovery **disc**

disease **d**

dishonorable discharge
DD

dispensary **disp**

dispense **dis; disp**

dispersion **disp**

displaced person **DP**

displacement **displ**

dissertation **diss**

distance **d; dis; dist**

distant early warning (DEW line) **DEW**

distilled **dist**

distributed data processing **DDP**

distributive **dist**

district attorney **DA**

District Court **Dist Ct**

District of Columbia **DC**

(ditto), the same **do.**

dividend **div**

division **div; divn**

divorced **d; div**

docket **dkt**

doctor **D; doc; Dr**

Doctor of Arts **Art.D.**

Doctor of Business Administration **D.B.A.**

Doctor of Canon and Civil Law [L *Juris utriusque Doctor*] **J.U.D.**

Doctor of Chemistry **Ch.D.; Dr. Chem.**

Doctor of Civil Law **D.C.L.; J.C.D.**

Doctor of Commercial Law **D.Com.L.**

Doctor of Dental Science **D.D.S.; D.D.Sc.**

Doctor of Dental Surgery **D.D.S.**

Doctor of Divinity **D.D.**

Doctor of Economics **D.Ec.; D.Econ.**

Doctor of Education **D.Ed.; Ed.D.**

Doctor of Engineering **D.E.**

Doctor of Fine Arts **D.F.A.**

Doctor of Humane Letters **D.H.L.; L.H.D.**

Doctor of Jurisprudence **D. Jur.;** [L *jurum doctor*] **J.D.**

Doctor of Law [L *Candidatus juris*] **Cand.jur.;** [L *juris doctor*] **J.D.;** [L *juris doctor*] **Jur. D.**

Doctor of Laws **LL.D.**

Doctor of Letters **D.Lit(t).; L.D.; Litt.D.**

Doctor of Literature **D.Lit(t).**

Doctor of Ophthalmology **D.O.**

Doctor of Philosophy **D.Ph.; Ph.D.**

Doctor of Psychology **D.Psych.**

Doctor of Public Health **D.P.H.**

Doctor of Theology **D.T.**

Doctor of the Science of Laws **J.S.D.**

Doctor of Zoology **D.Zool.**

document **doc**

doing business as **dba**

dollar **d; dol**

Dominican Republic **Dom Rep**

dormitory **dorm**

dose **d**

dowager **D; dow**

Dow Jones Industrial Average **DJIA**

down **dn**

dozen **dn; doz; dz**

dram **dr**

dramatist **dram**

drawing **dwg**

drilled **dd**

drill instructor **Di**

Drive **Dr**

driving while intoxicated **DWI**

Drug Enforcement Administration **DEA**

dubious **dub**

due date **DD**

Dun and Bradstreet **D & B**

duplicate **dup**

duration **d**

dust jacket **dj**

dwelling **dwg**

dyne **dyn**

dysprosium (chem) **Dy**

–E–

each **ea**

earned run average **era**

ear, nose and throat **ENT**

earth **E**

Earth Resources Observation Systems **EROS**

east **E**

easterly **e**

eastern daylight time **EDT**

Eastern European Time **EET**

eastern standard time **EST**

eastern time **ET**

East Germany **E Ger**

east longitude **E long**

east-southeast **ESE**

Ecclesiastes (Bible) **Eccles**

Ecclesiasticus (Bible/ Apocrypha) **Ecclus**

ecclesiastic **eccl**

ecological **ecol**

ecology **ecol**

Economic Commission for Asia and the Far East **ECAFE**

Economic Commission for Europe **ECE**

economics **econ**

economist **econ**

economy **econ**

Ecuador **Ec**

Edinburgh **Edin**

edited **ed; edit**

edition **e; ed; edit; edn**

editor **ed; edit**

editorial **edit**

Editor in Chief **Ed in Ch**

educated **ed; educ**

education **ed**

educational quotient **EQ**

Egypt **Eg**

einsteinium (chem) **Es**

elasticity **e**

elected **el**

election **elec**

elector **elec**

electoral **elec**

electric **el; elec**

electrical charge **q**

electricity **el; elec**

electrocardiogram **ECG; EKG**

electroencephalogram **EEG**

electromagnetic unit **emu**

electromotive force **emf**

electromotive force of cell **e**

electromyography **EMG**

electron **e; elec**

electron bombardment induced conductivity **EBICON**

electronic computer-originated mail **E-COM**

electronic data processing **EDP**

electronic delay-storage automatic computer **EDSAC**

electronic funds transfer system **EFTS**

electronic numerical integrator and calculator (computer) **ENIAC**

electronvolt **eV**

electrostatic unit **esu**

element **el; elem**

elementary **elem**

elevated railway **el**

elevation **el; elev**

elongation **el**

emergency room **ER**

Eminence **Em**

Emperor **Emp**

Empire **Emp**

Employee Retirement Income Security Act **ERISA**

employment ownership plan **EOP**

Empress **Emp**

enclosed **enc; encl**

enclosure **enc; encl**

encyclopedia **ency; encyc**

end of month **eom**

endorse **end**

endorsement **end**

engine **eng**

engineer **e; eng**

engine (railway) **f**

England **E; Eng**

English **E; Eng**

English as a second language **ESL**

English shilling (numis) **E**

English-Speaking Union **ESU**

engrave **eng**

ensign **Ens**

entomology **ent**

envelope **env**

Environmental Protection Agency **EPA**

environs **env**

epilogue **Epil**

Episcopalian **Epis; Episc**

equal **eq**

Equal Credit Opportunity Act **ECOA**

Equal Employment Opportunity Commission **EEOC**

Equal Rights Amendment **ERA**

equals [L *aequales*] **aeq.**

equate **eq**

equation **eq**

equator **E; eq**

Equatorial Guinea **Equat Gui**

equipment **eq**

equitable **eq**

equity **eq**

equivalent **eq; equiv**

equivalent air speed **EAS**

erbium (chem) **Er**

ergonomics **ergon**

erroneous **erron**

error **e; err.**

1 Esdras (Bible/Apocrypha) **1 Esd**

2 Esdras (Bible/Apocrypha) **2 Esd**

Eskimo **Esk**

especially **esp**

Esquire **Esq**

essence **ess**

establish **est; estab**

estate **est**

Esther (Bible/Apocrypha) **Est**

estimate **est**

estimated air speed **EAS**

estimated time of arrival **ETA**

estimated time of departure **ETD**

estimation **est**

estuary **est**

Ethiopia **Eth**

ethyl (chem) **et**

etymology **ety; etym**

Europe **Eur**

European **Eur**

European Atomic Energy Community **Euratom**

European Common Market (European Economic Community) **Euromarket**

European Economic Community (Common Market) **EEC**

European Environmental Bureau **EEB**

European Free Trade Association **EFTA**

European Plan (no meals) (travel) **EP**

European Railway Passenger (ticket) **Eurailpass**

European Recovery Program **ERP**

European Theater of Operations **ETO**

europium (chem) **Eu**

evolution **evol**

evolutionary **evol**

example **ex**

Excellency **Exc**

except **ex**

exception **ex**

exchange **ex; exch**

exchequer **exch**

exclude **ex**

excluding interest (fin) **ex int**

exclusive **ex**

execute **ex; exec**

execution time (computer) **E-time**

executive **ex; exec**

Executive Office of the President **EOP**

executive order **EO**

executor **ex; exec**

exempt **ex**

exhibit **exhib**

exhibitioner **exhib**

Exodus (Bible) **Exod**

exponential (math) **exp**

export **ex**

express **ex**

extend **ext**

extended binary coded decimal interchange code (computer) **EBCDIC**

extension **ex; ext**

extent **ext**

exterior **ext**

external **ext**

extinct **ext**

extra **ex; ext**

extract **ex**

extraction **ext**

extract (med) [L *extractum*] **ext**

extraordinary and plenipotentiary (dipl) **EP**

extrasensory perception **ESP**

extreme **ext**

extremely high frequency **ehf**

Ezekiel (Bible) **Ezek**

Ezra (Bible) **Ez**

–F–

facing **f**

facsimile **fac; fs**

facsimile transmission **FAX**

factor **fac**

faculty **fac**

Fahrenheit **F**

fair **f**

Fair Labor Standards Act **FLSA**

Falkland Islands **Falk Is**

familiar **fam**

family **fam**

Family Planning Association **FPA**

farad **F**

Faraday **Far.**

Farm Credit Administration **FCA**

Farmers Home Administration **FmHA**

Farm Security Administration **FSA**

father **f**

Father **Fr**

fathom   **f; fath**

favor   **fav**

favorite   **fav**

February   **F; Feb**

federal   **fed.**

Federal   **Fed**

Federal Aviation Administration   **FAA**

Federal Bureau of Investigation   **FBI**

Federal Communications Commission   **FCC**

Federal Crop Insurance Corporation   **FCIC**

Federal Deposit Insurance Corporation   **FDIC**

Federal Election Commission   **FEC**

Federal Emergency Management Agency   **FEMA**

Federal Energy Administration   **FEA**

Federal Highway Administration   **FHWA**

Federal Home Loan Bank Board   **FHLBB**

Federal Home Loan Mortgage Corporation (Freddie Mac)   **FHLMC**

Federal Housing Administration   **FHA**

Federal Information Processing Standards   **FIPS**

Federal Insurance Contributions Act   **FICA**

Federal Maritime Commission   **FMC**

Federal National Mortgage Association (Fannie Mae)   **FNMA**

Federal Power Commission   **FPC**

Federal Radiation Council   **FRC**

Federal Radio Commission   **FRC**

Federal Republic of Germany (West Germany)   **FRG**

Federal Reserve   **Fed**

Federal Reserve District   **FR Dist**

Federal Reserve System   **FRS**

Federal Savings and Loan Insurance Corporation   **FSLIC**

Federal Security Administration **FSA**

Federal Supply Service **FSS**

Federal Trade Commission **FTC**

federated **fed.**

federation **fed.**

feet **f**

feet per minute **fpm**

feed per second **fps**

feet per second per second **fpsps**

Fellow **F; Fell**

female **f; fem**

feminine **fem**

femtometer **fm**

femto (prefix, one-quadrillionth) **f**

fermium (chem) **Fm**

feudal **feud.**

feudalism **feud.**

fiction **fict**

fictional **fict**

fictitious **fict**

figure **fig**

film optical sensing device (computer) **FOSDIC**

final **fin.**

finance **fin.**

financial **fin.**

financier **fin.**

Finland **Fin**

fire department **FD**

first edition [L *editio princeps*] **e.p.**

first filial offspring resulting from crossing animals/plants F_1

first in, first out (system of inventory) **FIFO**

first in, last out (system of inventory) **FILO**

fiscal year **FY**

Fish and Wildlife Service **FWS**

Flanders **Fl**

fleet post office **FPO**

Flemish **Fl; Flem**

flexible **flex.**

flight research center (NASA) **FRC**

Florida **FL; Fla**

florists telegraph delivery service **FTD**

fluid **f**

fluid ounce(s) **fl oz**

fluorescent **fluor**

fluoridation **fluor**

fluoride **fluor**

fluorine **F**

folio **f; fo; fol**

follow **fol**

following **f; ff; fol**

Food and Agriculture Organization (UN) **FAO**

Food and Drug Administration **FDA**

Food and Nutrition Service **FNS**

foot **f; ft**

footcandle **fc**

footlambert **fL**

footnote **fn**

foot per minute **ft/min**

foot per second **ft/s**

foot per second cubed **ft/s³**

foot per second squared **ft/s²**

foot-pound **ft-lb**

foot poundal **ft-pdl**

foot pound-force **ft-lbf**

foot/pound/second **fps**

foot second **ft sec**

force **f**

foreign exchange **FX**

Foreign Press Association **FPA**

foreign rights **for. rts**

Forest Service **FS**

for example [L *exempli causa*] **e.c.**; [L *exempli gratia*] **e.g.**

Formula Translation (computer language) **FORTRAN**

Fort **Ft**

for the sake of the honor [L *honoris causa*] **h.c.**

forward **fwd**

for your information **fyi**

founded **f**

four times a day (med) [L *quater in die*] **QID**

four-wheel drive **FWD**

franc **F**

France **F; Fr**

Franciscan (religious order) **Franc**

francium (chem) **Fr**

free on board **fob**

freeway **fwy**

freezing drizzle (met) **zl**

freight **frt; frgt**

French **F; Fr**

French-Canadian **Fr Can**

frequency **f; F; Freq**

frequency modulation **FM**

frequency rate **FR**

frequent **freq**

frequently **freq**

friar **F**

friction **fric**

frictional **fric**

Friday **F; Fri**

from **fr**

from the beginning [L *ab initio*] **ab init.**

frontispiece **front**

front-wheel drive **FWD**

function **f**

furlong **f; fur.**

furnace **furn**

furnish **furn**

furniture **furn**

further **fur.**

future **fut**

Future Farmers of America **FFA**

–G–

gadolinium (chem) **Gd**

Gaelic **Gael.**

Galatians (Bible) **Gal**

gallium (chem) **Ga**

gallon **gal**

gallon [L *congius*] **C**

gallons per minute **gal/min**

gallons per second **gal/s**

galvanic **galv**

galvanized **galv**

Gambia **Gam**

Gamblers Anonymous **GA**

gas constant (chem) **R**

gauge **g**

gauss **G; gs**

gazette **gaz**

gazetteer **gaz**

geiger counter **GM counter**

gelding **g**

gender **g; gen**

genealogy **gen**

general **g; gen**

General **Gen**

General Accounting Office **GAO**

general agent **GA**

General Agreement on Tariffs and Trade **GATT**

general assembly **GA**

general average (ins) **g/a, g/av; gen av**

General Delivery **GD**

general factor **g**

general headquarters **GHQ**

general issue **GI**

general manager **gen mgr**

General Motors **GM**

general (movie rating) **G**

General Post Office **GPO**

general practitioner **GP**

general purpose (GP) vehicle **Jeep**

general quarters **GQ**

General Services Administration **GSA**

general staff officer **GSO**

generator **gen**

generic **gen**

Genesis (Bible) **Gen**

genetic **gen**

genital **gen**

genitive **g**

gentleman **gent**

genuine **gen**

genus **gen**

geodesy **geod**

geodetic **geod**

geographer **geog**

geography **geog**

geologic **geol**

Geological Survey **GS**

geologist **geol**

geology **geol**

geometric **geom**

geometry **geom**

geophysics **geophys**

Georgia **Ga; GA**

German **G; Ger**

German Democratic Republic (East Germany) **GDR; Ger Dem Rep**

germanium (chem) **Ge**

Germany **G; Ger**

gerund **ger**

Giga electron volt **GeV**

gigahertz (gigacycle per second) **GHZ**

giga (prefix, 1 billion) (phys) **G**

gilbert (phys) **Gb**

gill **gi; gl**

Girls Clubs of America **GCA**

Girl Scouts of America **GSA**

glossary **gloss.**

gold (chem) [L *aurum*] **Au**

gold standard **GS**

goods **gds**

gothic **goth.**

government **govt; gvt**

government issue **GI**

Government National Mortgage Association (Ginnie Mae) **GNMA**

Government Printing Office **GPO**

Governor **Gov**

grade **gr**

grade point average **GPA**

gradient **grad**

grading **grad**

graduate **grad**

graduated-payment adjustable-rate mortgage **GPARM**

graduated payment mortgage **GPM**

Graduate Management Admissions Test **GMAT**

Graduate Record Examination **GRE**

grain **gr**

gram **g; gm; gr; grm**

grammar **gr; gram.**

grammarian **gram.**

grammatical **gram.**

grammar school **GS**

gram molecule **gm mol; M**

gram per cubic centimeter **g/cm³**

grams per liter **g/l**

grand ($1,000) **G**

Grand Army of the Republic **GAR**

Grand Old Party (Republican Party) **GOP**

grand theft auto **GTA**

gravitation constant (phys) **G**

gravity **g; gr**

Great Britain **GB; Gt Br; Gt Brit**

greater **gtr**

greater common factor (math) **gcf**

greatest common divisor (math) **gcd**

Greece **Gr; Gre**

Greek **Gk; Gr**

Greenwich civil time **GCT**

Greenwich mean astronomical time **GMAT**

Greenwich mean time **GMT**

gross **gr; gro**

gross domestic product **GDP**

gross national product **GNP**

gross tons **gr tons**

gross weight **gr wt; W**

gross weight vehicle **GVW**

ground **gr**

ground to air **g/a**

group **gp; gr; grp**

Guam **GU**

guarantee **guar**

guaranteed **gtd**

guider **g**

guinea (British currency) **g; gm**

gynecologist **gyn**

–H–

Habakkuk (Bible) **Hab**

habeas corpus [L] may you have the body (law) **hab. corp.**

habitat **hab**

habitation **hab**

hafnium (chem) **Hf**

Haggai (Bible) **Hag**

hail (met) **h**

half **hf**

hallmark **hm**

halogen **hal**

Hamiltonian (phys) **H**

hand **hd**

handbook **hdbk; hnbk**

handling **hdlg**

hand made **hm**

Hanover **Han**

harbor **h**

hardness **h**

hardness (pencils) **H**

hardship **hdsp**

harmonic **harm**

harmony **harm**

Hawaii **Ha; HI**

Hawaiian **Ha**

Hawaiian Islands **HI**

head **hd**

headmaster **hm**

headmistress **hm**

head office **HO**

headquarters **HQ; hdqrs**

Health and Human Resources (Department of) **HHS**

Health Maintenance Organization **HMO**

hearts (cards) **h**

heat **h; ht**

heat of combustion of an element under constant pressure (chem) **HCp**

heat of combustion of an element under constant volume (chem) **HCv** heat transfer unit **HTU**

heavy **h; hvy**

heavy hydrogen (chem) **HH**

Hebraic **He; Heb**

Hebrew **He; Heb**

Hebrews (Bible) **Heb**

hectare **ha**

hecto (prefix, 100) **h**

hectogram **hectog; hg**

hectoliter **hectol; hL**

hectometer **hm**

he did it himself [L *ipse fecit*] **i.f.**

height **h; hgt; ht**

helicopter **hcptr**

helium (chem) **He**

hemoglobin **Hb; hem.**

hemorrhage **hem.**

henry **H**

heraldry **her**

herbaceous **herb.**

herbalist **herb.**

herbarium **herb.**

heredity **hered**

here is buried [L *hic sepultus* or *situs*] **H.S.**

here lies [L *hic iacet*] **H.I.**

here lies [L *hic jacet*] **H.J.**

here lies buried [L *hic jacet sepultus*] **H.J.S.**

here rests in peace [L *hic requiescit in pace*] **H.R.I.P.**

Her/His Exalted Highness **HEH**

Her/His Grace **HG**

Her/His Highness **HH**

Her/His Imperial Highness **HIH**

Her/His Majesty **HM**

Her/His Serene Majesty **HSM**

herniated nucleus pulposus (herniated disc) **HNP**

herpetologist **herp**

herpetology **herp**

hertz (cycles per second) **Hz**

hexachlorocyclohexane (insecticide) **HCH**

hexachord **hex**

hexagon **hex**

hexagonal **hex**

Hibernian **Hib**

hieroglyphics **hier**

high **Hi**

high altitude photographic aircraft **U2**

high command **Hi Com**

high commissioner **Hi Com**

highest common factor (math) **hcf**

high fidelity **hi fi**

high frequency **HF**

high frequency current **hfc**

high frequency gas **HFG**

high frequency oscillator **hfo**

High German **HG**

high school **hs**

high vacuum **hv**

high velocity **hv**

high voltage **hv**

highway **hwy**

Hindi **Hi; Hind**

Hindu **Hind**

His/Her Eminence **HE**

His/Her Excellency **HE**

His/Her Majesty's Ship **HMS**

His/Her Royal Highness **HRH**

His Holiness **HH**

His Honor **HH**

historian **hist**

historic **hist**

history **hist**

hit **h**

Hittite **Hitt**

Holland **Holl**

holmium (chem) **Ho**

Holy Ghost **HG**

Holy Roman Church **HRC**

Holy Roman Emperor **HRE**

Holy Roman Empire **HRE**

home economics **home ec**

Home Guard **HG**

home office **HO**

homeopath **homeo; homo**

homeopathic **homeo; hon.o**

home run **hr**

homestead **hmstd**

homosexual **homo**

honor **hon**

honorable **hon**

honorary **hon**

honors **hons**

horizon **hor**

horizontal **h; hor**

horizontal force of earth's magnetism **H**

horizontal take off and land **HTOL**

horology **hor**

Horse Guards **HG**

horsepower **hp**

horsepower-hour **hph**

horticulture **hort**

Hosea (Bible) **Hos**

hospital **hosp**

hour **h; hr**

hour at which a military operation is to begin **H-hour**

hours, minutes, seconds **hms**

house **hse**

House of Commons **HC**

House of Lords **HL**

House of Representatives **HR**

House Un-American Activities Committee **HUAC**

human **hum.**

human immuno-deficiency virus **HIV**

humanities **hum.**

humanity **hum.**

humidity index **Hi**

humorous **hum.**

hundred **h; hund**

hundred [L *centum*] **C**

hundredweight **cwt**

Hungary **Hung**

husband **h; husb**

husbandry **husb**

hybrid **hyb**

hydrate **hyd**

hydraulic **hyd**

hydrochloric acid (chem) **HCl**

hydroelectric unit **heu**

hydrogen (chem) **H**

hydrogen-ion concentration **pH**

hydrographic **hyd**

hydrostatics **hyd**

hygiene **hyg**

hypodermic **hyp**

hypotenuse **hyp**

hypothesis **hyp; hypoth**

hypothetical **hyp; hypoth**

—I—

Iceland **Ice.**

Icelandic **Ice.**

ichthyology **ichth**

Idaho **ID; Ida.**

identification **ID; ident**

identification card **ID card**

identify **ident**

ignition **ign**

illegitimate **illegit**

illinium (chem) **Il**

Illinois **IL; Ill**

illiterate **illit**

illumination **E**

illustrate **ill; illus**

illustration **ill; illus**

illustrator **ill; illus**

imaginary **imag**

imaginary unit (math) **i**

imagination **imag**

imagine **imag**

imitate **imit**

imitation **imit**

imitative **imit**

Immigration and Naturalization Service **INS**

immunity **immun**

immunization **immun**

immunology **immun**

imperative **imp.; imper**

imperfect **imp.; imperf**

imperforate (stamps) **im-perf**

imperial **imp.**

imperial bushel **ibu**

imperial gallon **igal**

impersonal **imp.; impers**

implement **imp.**

import **imp.**

important **imp.**

importer **imp.**

impression **imp.**

inaugurate **inaug**

in care of **c/o**

inch **in**

inch per hour **in/h**

inch per second **in/s; in/sec**

inch-pound **in-lb**

incidence rate **IR**

incline **incl**

include **inc; incl**

inclusive **inc; incl**

incognito **incog**

income **inc**

Incorporated **Inc**

incorrect **incorr**

increase **inc; incr**

increment **incr**

incunabula **incun**

indefinite **indef**

independent **ind**

Independent **I; Ind**

Independent Labor Party **ILP**

Independent Liberal **Ind L**

Independent Methodist **I Meth; Ind Meth**

Independent Order of Odd Fellows **IOOF**

Independent Subway Line (NYC Subway) **IND**

index **ind**

index correlation **ic**

Index Register **IR**

India **In; Ind**

Indian **In**

Indiana **IN; Ind**

indicated horsepower **ihp**

indication **ind**

indicative **ind; indic**

indicator **indic**

indirect **ind**

indium (chem) **In**

individual **indiv**

individual retirement account **IRA**

Indo-European **IE; Indo-Eur**

Indo-German **Indo-Ger**

induction **induc**

industrial dynamics **ID**

Industrial Workers of the World **IWW**

industry **indust**

infantry **inf**

infantry reserve corps **IRC**

infectious disease **ID**

inferior **inf**

infinitive **inf; infin**

infirmary **infirm.**

influence **inf**

information **inf; info**

information department **ID**

information processing language **IPL**

information retrieval **ir**

infrared **ir**

inhabitant **inhab**

initial velocity **iv**

ink blot test **ib test**

innings **inn.**

in original place [L *in situ*] **in s.**

input/output **I/O**

input preparation unit (computer) **IPU**

inquiry **inq**

inscribe **inscr**

inscription **inscr**

inside diameter **id**

insoluble **insol**

insolvent **insolv**

inspect **insp**

inspection **insp**

inspector **insp**

Inspector General **Insp Gen**

instance **inst**

instant **inst**

Institute **I; Inst**

Institute for Defense Analysis **IDA**

Institute of Civil Engineers **ICE**

Institute of Radio Engineers **IRE**

institution **inst; instn**

Institution **Inst**

instruction **inst**

instructor **I; inst**

instrument **inst**

instrument correlation **ic**

Instrument flight rules **IFR**

instrument reading **ir**

insurance **ins**

integrated circuit **ic**

intelligence **int**

Intelligence **I**

intelligence department **ID**

intelligence quotient **IQ**

intensive **intens**

intensive care unit **ICU**

Inter-American Defense Board **IADB**

Interborough Rapid Transit (NYC Subway) **IRT**

intercommunication **intercom**

intercontinental ballistic missile **ICBM**

interest **i; int**

Intergovernmental Maritime Consultative Organization **IMCO**

interior **int**

interjection **int; interj**

intermediate **int; inter**

intermediate frequency **IF**

intermediate range ballistic missile **IRBM**

Intermediate-range Nuclear Forces **INF**

intermittent precipitation (met) **i**

internal **int**

internal combustion **ic**

Internal Revenue Service **IRS**

international **int; intl**

International Air Transport Association **IATA**

International Atomic Energy Agency **IAEA**

International Bank for Reconstruction and Development **IBRD**

International Bureau of Weights and Measures **IBWM**

International Business Machines Corporation **IBM**

International Civil Aviation Organization **ICAO**

International Committee of the Red Cross **ICRC**

International Communication Agency **ICA**

International Criminal Police Organization **Interpol**

International Date Line **IDL**

International Development Association (UN) **IDA**

International Development Bank **IDB**

International Finance Corporation (UN) **IFC**

International Fund for Agricultural Development **IFAD**

International Labor Office (UN) **ILO**

International Labor Organization **ILO**

International Ladies Garment Workers' Union **ILGWU**

International Law Commission (UN) **ILC**

International Maritime Committee **IMC**

International Maritime Organization **IMO**

International Monetary Fund **IMF**

International Olympic Committee **IOC**

International Pharmacopeia **P.I.**

international practical temperature scale **ipts**

International Red Cross **IRC**

International Refugee Organization **IRO**

International Scientific Vocabulary **ISV**

International Standard Serial Number **ISSN**

International Standards Organization **ISO**

International Telecommunication Union **ITU**

International Telephone and Telegraph Company **ITT**

International Trade Commission **ITC**

International Trade Organization **ITO**

International Transport Workers' Federation **ITWF**

International Typographical Union **ITU**

international units **IU**

International Word Processing Association **IWPA**

International Youth Hostels Federation **IYHF**

interpreter **interp**

interrogative **inter.; interrog**

Interstate Commerce Commission **ICC**

in the beginning [L *in initio*] **in init.**

in the beginning [L *in principio*] **in pr.**

in the Hebrew year **A.H.**

in the meantime [L *ad interim*] **a.i.; ad int.**

in the place cited [L *loco citato*] **loc. cit.**

in the same place [L *ibidem*] **ibid.**

in the world of or according to [L *apud*] **ap.**

in the year [L *anno*] **ann.**

in the year of our Lord [L *anno Domini*] **A.D.**

in the year of the Hegira **A.H.**

in the year of the world [L *anno mundi*] **A.M.**

in this month [L *hoc mense*] **h.m.**

in this place [L *hoc loco*] **h.l.**

intramuscular **IM**

intransitive **i; int; intr**

intrauterine contraceptive device **IUCD**

intrauterine device **IUD**

invention **inv**

inventor **inv**

inversion **inv**

invert **inv**

investigational new drug **IND**

invoice **inv**

invoice value **iv**

iodine (chem) **I**

Ionic **Ion**

ionium (chem) **Io**

Iowa **Ia; IA**

I owe you **IOU**

Iranian **Iran.**

Ireland **I; Ir; Ire**

iridescent **irid**

iridium (chem) **Ir**

Irish **I; Ir**

Irish Republican Army **IRA**

iron (chem) **Fe**

irredeemable (fin) **irr**

irregular **irr; irreg**

Isaiah (Bible) **Is; Isa**

Islam **Is**

Islamic **Is**

island **i; is.; Is**

isolate **isol**

isolation **isol**

isopin **I**

isoprene rubber **IR**

Israel **Is; Isr**

Israeli **Is**

Israel Labor Party **ILP**

issue **iss**

Italian **I; It**

italics **ital**

Italy **I; It**

itinerary **itin**

–J–

Jacobean **Jac**

Jacobian determinant (math) **J**

January **J; Ja; Jan**

Japan **Jap**

Japanese **Jap**

jargon **jarg**

Jehovah **JHVH**

Jehovah's Witness **JW**

Jeremiah (Bible) **Jer**

jeroboam **jerob**

Jersey **Jer**

Jerusalem **Jer**

Jesus **Jes.**

Jesus Christ **J.C.**

Jesus Christ [L *Iesus Christus*] **I.X.**

Jesus of Nazareth, King of the Jews [L *Iesus Nazarenus Rex Iudaeorum*] **INRI**

Jesus Savior of Man [L *Jesus Hominum Salvator*] **J.H.S.**

jet-assisted takeoff **jato**

Jet Propulsion Laboratory (NASA) **JPL**

Jewish Defense League **JDL**

Job Training Partnership Act **JTPA**

joint account **J/A**

Jonah (Bible) **Jon**

Joshua (Bible) **Josh**

joule per degree **J/deg**

joule (phys) **J**

journal **j; jour**

Journal **Jl; Jnls; Jr**

Journal of the American Medical Association **JAMA**

journeyman **jour**

Judaism **Jud**

Judea **Jud**

judge **j**

Judge-Advocate **JA**

Judge Advocate General **JAG; Judge Adv Gen**

Judges (Bible) **Judg**

judgment **jud**

judicial **jud**

Judith (Bible/Apocrypha) **Jth.**

Julius Caesar **J.C.**

July **Jl; Jy**

junction **jn; junc**

June **Jn; Jn.; Ju**

junior **Jr**

junior high school **JHS**

junior varsity **JV**

Jupiter **J; Jup**

jurisdiction **jurisd**

jurisprudence **juris**

juror **jr**

jury **jy**

justice **j; jus**

Justice Department **JD**

Justice of Appeal **JA**

Justice of the Peace **JP**

juvenile **juv**

juvenile court **JC**

juvenile delinquent **jd**

juxtaposition **jux**

–K–

Kansas **Kans; KS**

Kansas City **KC**

karat **k**

kayser **K**

kelvin (phys) **K**

Kentucky **Ky; KY**

kick off **KO**

killed in action **KIA**

kilocalorie **kcal**

kilocycle **kc**

kiloelectronvolt **keV**

kilogauss **kG**

kilogram **k; kg; kilo**

kilogram-force **kgf**

kilohertz (kilocycles per second) **kHz**

kilo-ohm **k**

kiloliter **kL**

kilometer **k; km**

kilometer per hour **km/h**

kilometers per hour **kph**

kilopound-force **klbf**

kilo (prefix, 1,000) **k**

kiloton **kt**

kilovar **kvar**

kilovolt-ampere **kVA**

kilovolt (elec) **kV**

kilowatt **kW**

kilowatthour **kWh**

kinetic potential symbol **L**

king (chess) **K**

king's knight (chess) **KKt**

king's pawn (chess) **KP**

king's rook's pawn (chess) **KRP**

kitchen patrol **KP**

kitchen police **KP**

Knight **Kt**

Knight Commander of the Order of the British Empire **KBE**

Knight of the Order of Malta **KOM**

Knight of the Order of the Garter **KG**

Knight of the Red Cross **KRC**

Knight (or Dame) Grand Cross Order of the British Empire **GBE**

Knights of Columbus **K of C**

Knights of Labor **K of L**

Knights of Pythias **K of P**

Knight Templar **KT**

knit **K**

knock-out (boxing) **KO**

knot **k; kt**

knots indicated air speed **kias**

knot (speed) **kn**

Koran **Kor**

Korea **Kor**

krypton (chem) **Kr**

Ku Klux Klan **KKK**

–L–

label **lab**

labor **lab**

laboratory **lab**

Labor Department **LD**

Labor Party **LP**

Labor Zionist Organization of America **LZOA**

Labrador **LB**

lacquer **lac**

lactation **lac**

lactobacillus **L**

Ladies' Professional Golf Association **LPGA**

lading **ldg**

lady **l**

lagoon **lag; lg**

lake **l**

lambda **l**

lambert **L**

Lamentations (Bible) **Lam**

laminar air flow **laf**

laminate **lam**

land **l; ld**

landing **ldg**

landing report **lr**

landing ship **ls**

landing zone **LZ**

land mine **lm**

land utilization survey **LUS**

lane **Ln**

language **lang**

lanthanum (chem) **La**

laparotomy **lap.**

Lapland **Lap.**

large **l; lg; lge**

large close-up (photo) **LCU**

large grain **LG**

large post **LP**

largest vessel **LV**

laryngology **laryngol**

last in, first out **LIFO**

last in, last out **LILO**

last paid **lp**

last year's model **lym**

late **l**

Late Hebrew **L Heb**

Late Latin **L Lat**

latent period **lp**

lateral **l; lat**

lateral axis **y**

Latin **L; Lat**

Latin America **LA**

Latin Old Style **LOS**

latitude **l; lat**

latitude and longitude indicator **lli**

Latter-Day Saints (Mormons) **LDS**

Latvia **Lat**

Laureate in English Literature **L.E.L.**

lavatory **lav**

law **l**

Law-Latin **Law-L**

lawrencium (chem) **Lr**

Law School Admission Test **LSAT**

Law Society **LS**

lead **ld**

lead (chem) [L *plumbum*] **Pb**

leading **ldg**

leading edge **le**

leaf **l**

leaflet **lft**

league **lge**

leakage and breakage **lkg & bkg**

lean body mass **lbm**

least common multiple **lcm**

least fatal dose **lfd**

leave **lv**

leave and liberty **l & l**

leaves **ll**

ledger account **L/A**

ledger folio **lf**

Leeward Islands **LI**

left back (sport) **lb**

left hand **lh**

left (in stage directions) **L**

left [L *laevus*] **laev.**

left to right **L/R**

left upper entrance (theater) **lue**

legal **leg.**

Legal Affairs department of UN **LEG (UN)**

Legal Aid Society **LAS**

Legal Service Corporation **LSC**

legal weight **leg wt**

legation **leg.**

Legion of Merit **LM**

legislation **leg.; legis**

legislature **leg.**

legitimate **l**

length **l; lgth**

length overall (shipping) **loa**

Leo **L**

lethal dose **ld**

let it be made (med) [L *fiat*] **F.**

let it be printed [L *imprimatur*] **imp.**

letter **let; ltr**

letter of credit **LC; loc**

letterpress **L/P**

leucine **leu**

Levant **Lev**

level crossing **LC**

Leviticus (Bible) **Lev**

lexicon **lex**

liaison officer **lo**

liberal **lib**

Liberia **Lib**

liberty **lib**

library **lib**

Library Association **L/A**

library catalogue **lib cat.**

Library Club of America **LCA**

library edition **le**

Library Journal **LJ**

Library of Congress **LC; Lib Cong; L of C**

Library of Congress Catalogue Card **LCCC**

libretto **lib**

Licensed Physical Therapist **LPT**

Licensed Practical Nurse **LPN**

Licensed Surveyor **LS**

Licentiate in Divinity **L.D.; L. Div.**

Licentiate in Medicine **Lic. Med.; L.M.**

Licentiate of the College of Physicians and Surgeons of America **L.C.P.& S.A.**

Licentiate of the Institute of Physics **L. Inst. P.**

Lieutenant **Lieut; Lt**

Lieutenant Colonel **Lt Col**

Lieutenant Commander **Lt Comdr**

Lieutenant Governor **Lt Gov**

Lieutenant Junior Grade **Lt jg**

life policy **LP**

liftup door **lud**

ligament **lig**

light **Lt**

light amplification by stimulated emission of radiation **laser**

light detection and ranging **LIDAR**

light difference **ld**

light emitting diode **LED**

light equipment **le**

lighter than air **lta**

lightface (typo) **lf**

light observation helicopter **LOH**

light output ratio **LOR**

light weight **LW**

lignite **l**

limit **lim**

limited **ltd**

limited edition **le**

limited signed edition **lse**

Limited Test Ban Treaty **LTBT**

line **l**

linear **lin**

linear foot **lin ft**

linear force **lft**

linear programming **lp**

line feed character (data processing) **lf**

line of sight **LOS**

lines **lin; ll**

lines per inch **lpi**

lines per minute **lpm; l/m**

lines per second **lps; l/s**

linguistics **ling**

link **li**

liquid **liq**

liquid curing media **lcm**

liquid hydrogen **LH^2**

liquid metal **lm**

liquid oxygen **LO^2; lox; loxygen**

liquid ozone **loz**

liquid petroleum **LP**

liquified natural gas **LNG**

liquified petroleum gas **LPG**

lira **L**

list processor (computer) **lisp.**

liter **L**

literary **lit**

literature **lit**

lithium (chem) **Li**

lithograph **li; litho**

little **lit**

Little League Baseball **LLB**

live load **ll**

living and well **l and w**

Lloyd's Register of Shipping **LRS**

load **ld**

loading **ldg**

load limit **ld lmt**

loans and discounts **L&D**

local **loc**

local acquisition radar **lar**

local board **LB**

local standard time **LST**

local time **LT**

location **loc; locn**

locative **loc**

locator at outer marker (compass) **lom**

locus **l**

logarithm (math) **log**

logic **log**

logical language **loglan**

logistic **log**

Logistic Support Squadron **LSS**

London **L**

long-acting **LA**

long distance call **ldc**

long distance xerography **LDX**

Long Island **LI**

Long Island Railroad Company **LIRR**

longitude **long.**

longitudinal **longl**

longitudinal center of buoyancy **lcb**

longitudinal center of flotation **lcf**

longitudinal center of gravity **lcg**

long playing record **LP**

long range **lr**

long range accuracy **LORAC**

long range active detection **LORAD**

long range ballistic missile **lrbm**

long range navigation **LORAN**

long range planning **LRP**

long reduced rate (tax) **LRR**

long run **lr**

long sight **ls**

long ton **lg tn; Lt**

Lord **L**

Los Angeles **LA**

loss and damage **L&D**

loss of signal (space) **LOS**

lot tolerance percent defective **LTPD**

Louisiana **La; LA**

low altitude **L/A**

low blood pressure **lbp**

low cost production **LCP**

low density **LD**

low density lipoprotein **ldl**

lowercase **lc**

lower dead center **ldc**

lower left **ll**

lower limit **ll**

lowest common denominator **lcd**

lowest common factor **lcf**

lowest common multiple **lcm**

lowest operating frequency **lof**

low explosive **le**

low fat diet **lfd**

low frequency **lf**

low pressure **lp**

low pressure chamber **lpc**

low speed **ls**

low speed logic **LSL**

low tension **lt**

low tension battery (elec)
  ltb

low water **LW**

low wave **LW**

lubrication **lub**

Luke (Bible) **Lk**

lumbar **lum**

lumen **lm**

lumen hour (phys) **l hr;
  lm hr; lu h**

lumen second **lm-s**

luminous **lum**

lunar excursion module
  LEM

lunar module (space) **LM**

luteinizing hormone **LH**

lutetium (chem) **Lu**

Lutheran **Luth**

lux **lx**

luxurious **lux**

lymphatic **lym**

lyric **lyr**

lysergic acid diethyla-
  mide **LSD**

–M–

1 Maccabees (Bible/Apoc-
  rypha) **1 Macc**

2 Maccabees (Bible/Apoc-
  rypha) **2 Macc**

machine language **ml**

Mach number (phys) **M**

magnesium (chem) **Mg;
  mag**

magnetic **mag**

magnetic bearing **mb**

magnetic detection indi-
  cator **mdi**

magnetic north **MN**

magnetic resonance im-
  aging **MRI**

main battery **mb**

main distributing frame
  (data processing) **mdf**

Maine **Me; ME**

main landing gear **mlg**

main line of resistance
  mlr

Major **Maj**

Major General **Maj Gen**

Major League Baseball Players Association **MLBPA**

Malachi (Bible) **Mal**

Malaysia **Mal**

male **m**

Malta **Mal**

management **mgmt; mgt**

management control data system **MCDS**

manager **man.; mgr**

manganese (chem) **Mn**

Manitoba **Man; MB**

Manpower Development and Training Act **MDTA**

manual **m; man.**

manufacturing **mfg**

manuscript **ms**

map analysis **ma**

March **Mar**

margin **marg**

marine **mar**

marine biological laboratory **MBL**

marine corps **MC**

maritime **mar; marit**

market value **mv**

married **m**

Martinique **Mart; Mqe**

Maryland **Md; MD**

masculine **m; masc**

mass (phys) **m**

Massachusetts **MA; Mass**

mass unit **mu**

Master of Administration **M. Admin.**

Master of Applied Arts **M.A.A.**

Master of Architecture **M.Arch.**

Master of Arts **A.M.; M.A.**

Master of Business Administration **M.B.A.**

Master of Ceremonies **emcee; MC**

Master of Dental Science **M.Dent.Sc.; M.D.Sc.**

Master of Divinity **M. Div.**

Master of Economics **M.Ec.; M.Econ.**

Master of Education **Ed.M.; M.Ed.**

Master of Engineering [L *Magister in Arte Ingeniaria*] **Ma.E.; M.E.; M.A.I.**

Master of Fine Arts **M.F.A.**

Master of Hospital Administration **M.H.A.**

Master of Laws **LL.M.; M.L.**

Master of Letters **M.L.; M.Litt.**

Master of Liberal Arts **L.M.A.; M.L.A.**

Master of Literature **M.Litt.**

Master of Medical Science **M.Med.; M.S.M.; M.S. Med.**

Master of Medicine **M.Med.**

Master of Music **Mus.M.**

Master of Philosophy **M.Ph.**

Master of Science **M.Sc.**

Master of Teaching **M.T.**

Master of Theology **M.Th.**

masurium (chem) **Ma**

mate **m**

materia medica **mat. med.**

maternity **mat.; matern**

mathematics **math**

matriculate **matric**

Matthew (Bible) **Matt**

Mauritania **Maur**

maximum **max**

maximum gross weight **mgw**

maximum permissible dose **MPD**

maxwell (phys) **Mx**

mean blood pressure **mbp**

mean body temperature **mbt**

mean effective pressure **mep**

mean indicated pressure **mip**

mean low water (tides) **mlw**

mean radial error **mre**

mean sea level **msl**

mean square error **mse**

mean variation **mv**

measure **m; meas**

measure of insulating power **U factor**

mechanical **mech**

mechanical engineer **ME**

median **med**

medical **m; med**

medical certificate **MC**

medical college admission test **MCAT**

medical corps **MC**

medical evacuation **medevac**

medicine **med**

Mediterranean **Med**

medium **m; med**

medium frequency **mf**

medium high frequency **mhf**

medium internal radiation dose **MIRD**

mega (prefix, 1 million) **M**

megacycle **Mc; meg**

megahertz **MH; MHz**

megaton **meg; Mt**

megawatt **meg; MW**

megohm **M**

melting point **mp**

member **mem**

member of Congress **MC**

Member of Parliament **MP**

Member of the Order of the British Empire **MBE**

memorandum **mem; memo**

memory error **ME**

memory module **MM**

mendelevium (chem) **Md; Mv**

merchandise **mdse; mer**

merchant marine **MM**

Mercury **Mer**

mercury (chem) [L *hydrargyrum*] **Hg**

meridian **m; mer**

messenger **msgr**

metal (chem) **M**

metallurgical **met.;
metal.**

metallurgical engineer
Met. E.

metaphor **met.; metaph**

metaphysical **met.**

metastasis **metas**

meteorological **met.**

meter **m**

Methodist Church **MC**

Methodist Episcopal
Church **MEC**

method of operation [L
modus operandi] **MO**

metronome (mus) **met.**

metropolitan **met.; met-
rop**

metropolitan statistical
area **MSA**

Mexico **Mex**

Micah (Bible) **Mic**

Michigan **MI; Mich**

microbiology **microbiol**

micron *mu*

microwave amplification
by stimulated emission
of radiation **MASER**

midday **m**

middle **m; mid**

midnight **mid**

mile **m**

mile(s) per gallon **mi/gal;
mpg**

mile(s) per hour **mi/h;
mph**

mile (statute) **mi**

military **mil**

Military Cross **MC**

military intelligence **MI**

military observers **MOs**

military police **MP**

milli (prefix, one-thou-
sandth) **m**

milliampere **mA**

millibar **mb; mbar**

millicuries **mc**

millicycle **mc**

millifarad **mF**

milligram **mg**

millihenry **mH**

millihertz **mHz**

milliliter **mL**

millimeter **mm**

milliohms **mohms**

million **m**

millisecond **ms**

millivolt **mV**

milliwatt **mW**

minimal effective dose **med**

minimum **m; mnm**

minimum annual income **mai**

minimum daily requirement **mdr**

minimum effective dose **MED**

minimum weight **min wt**

Minnesota **Minn; MN**

minor **min**

minute (time) **m; min**

miscellaneous **misc; msc**

missing **m**

missing in action **MIA**

Missing Persons Bureau **MPB**

Mississippi **Miss; MS**

Missouri **Mo; MO**

mister **Mr.**

mistress **Mrs.**

mixture **m; mixt**

mobile army surgical hospital **MASH**

moderate **m; mod**

modern **mod**

Modern Language Association **MLA**

modified **mod**

modulated continuous wave **mcw**

modulator/demodulator **MODEM**

molar (chem) **M**

molar (dental) **m**

molecular weight **mol wt**

mole (unit of substance) **mol**

molybdenum (chem) **Mo**

Monaco **Mon**

Monday **Mon**

money order **MO**

money supply **M**

Mongolia **Mong**

mononucleosis **mono**

monosodium glutamate **MSG**

Montana **Mont; MT**

Morocco **Mor**

morphology **morph**

mortgage **mort; mtg**

most favored nation **MFN**

most valuable player **MVP**

mothers against drunk driving **MADD**

motor vehicle **MV**

mountain daylight saving time **MDST**

mountain standard time **MST**

mountain time **MT**

Mozambique **Moz**

multilateral (nuclear) force **MLF**

multiple independently targetable reentry vehicle **MIRV**

multiple sclerosis **MS**

multiplication **mult**

muscular dystrophy **MD**

mutual **mut**

mutual assured destruction **MAD**

mutual inductance (phys) **M**

muzzle velocity **mv**

mycology **myc**

mythology **myth.**

–N–

Nahum (Bible) **Nah**

name **n**

nanoampere **nA**

nanofarad **nF**

nano (prefix, one-billionth) **n**

nanosecond **ns**

nanowatt **nw**

national **N; nat; natl**

National Academy of Design **NAD**

National Academy of Engineering **NAE**

National Academy of Sciences **NAS**

National Advisory Council **NAC**

National Aeronautics and Space Administration **NASA**

National Air and Space Museum **NASM**

National Association for Mental Health **NAMH**

National Association for the Advancement of Colored People **NAACP**

National Association of Book Editors **NABE**

National Association of Broadcasters **NAB**

National Association of Performing Artists **NAPA**

National Association of Securities Dealers **NASD**

National Association of Securities Dealers Automated Quotations **NASDAQ**

National Association of Women's Clubs **NOWC**

National Basketball Association **NBA**

National Boxing Association **NBA**

National Boys' Club **NBC**

National Bureau of Economic Research **NatBurEconRes; NBER**

National Bureau of Standards **NBS; NtBurStnds**

National Cancer Institute **NCI**

National Center for Disease Control **NCDC**

National Center for Health Statistics **NCHS**

National Collegiate Athletic Association **NCAA**

National Conference of Christians and Jews **NCCJ**

National Congress of American Indians **NCAI**

National Council for Civil Liberties **NCCL**

National Council of Catholic Women **NCCW**

National Council of Women, US **NCWUS**

National Council to Control Handguns **NCCH**

National Debt **ND**

National Defense Education Act **NDEA**

National Defense Research Committee **NDRC**

National Democratic Club **NDC**

National Education Association **NEA**

National Education Television **NET**

National Electrical Code Standards **NECS**

National Emergency Relief Administration **NERA**

National Federation of Women's Institutes **NFWI**

National Football League **NFL**

National Foundation on the Arts and the Humanities **NFAH**

National Geographic Society **NGS**

National Health Insurance **NHI**

National Hockey League **NHL**

National Industrial Recovery Act **NIRA**

National Institute for the Deaf **NID**

National Institute of Education **NIE**

National Institute of Oceanography **NIO**

National Institutes of Health **NIH**

nationalist **nat**

National Labor Board **NLB**

National Labor Relations Board **NLRB**

National League **NL**

National Liberation Front **NLF**

National Maritime Board **NMB**

National Mediation Board **NMB**

National Mental Health Association **NMHA**

National Oceanic and Atmospheric Administration **NOAA**

National Ocean Service **NOS**

National Office of Vital Statistics **NOVS**

National Opinion Research Center **NORC**

National Organization of Women **NOW**

National Park Service **NPS**

National Peace Council **NPC**

National Press Club **NPC**

National Public Radio **NPR**

National Recovery Administration **NRA**

National Retail Credit Association **NRCA**

National Rifle Association **NRA**

National Science Foundation **NSF**

National Scientific Register **NSR**

National Security Council **NSC**

National Security Resources Board **NSRB**

National Society for Medical Research **NSMR**

National Standards Reference Data System **NSRDC**

National Teacher Corps **NTC**

National Television Standards Committee **NTSC**

National Travelers Aid Association **NTAA**

National Trust for Historic Preservation **NTHP**

National Urban Coalition **NUC**

National Volunteer Force **NVF**

National War College **NWC**

National Weather Records Center **NWRC**

National Weather Satellite Center **NWSC**

National Weather Service **NWS**

National Welfare Fund **NWF**

National Welfare Rights Organization **NWRO**

National Wildlife Federation **NWF**

National Wildlife Refuge **NWR**

National Women's Political Caucus **NWPC**

native **nat**

natural **nat**

Natural History **Nat Hist**

nautical **naut**

nautical mile **nmi**

naval **nav**

naval air station **NAS**

Naval Air Transport Services **NATS**

naval attache **N Att**

naval base **NB**

Naval Officer Candidate School **NAVOCS**

Naval Training Research Laboratory **NTRL**

navigation **N; nav**

navigational satellite **NAVSAT**

navigator **nav**

Navy Shore Patrol Administration **NSPA**

near (optics) **N**

Nebraska **NE; Nebr**

necessary **nec; necy**

negation **neg**

negative **n; neg**

negotiate **neg**

Nehemiah (Bible) **Neh**

neodymium (chem) **Nd**

neologism **neol**

neon (chem) **Ne**

Nepal **Nep**

Neptune **Nept**

neptunium (chem) **Np**

net **n; nt**

net annual gain **nag**

net asset value (fin) **nav**

net assimilation rate **nar**

net book value **nbv**

Netherlands **Neth; NL**

net payment in 30 days **n/30**

net present value (fin) **npv**

net proceeds **np**

net registered tonnage **NRT**

net weight **nwt; net wt; nt wt**

neurology **neurol**

neuter **n; neut**

neutral **n**

neutron **n**

neutron velocity selector **nvs**

Nevada **Nev; NV**

New Brunswick **NB**

New Economic Policy **NEP**

New England **NE; N Eng**

New English Bible **NEB**

Newfoundland **NF; Nfd**

New General Catalogue (astrony) **NGC**

New Guinea Territory **N Gui**

New Hampshire **NH**

New Jersey **NJ**

New Latin **NL**

New Mexico **NM; N Mex**

New South Wales **NSW**

New Testament (Bible) **New Test.; NT**

newton **N**

New York **NY**

New York City **NYC**

New York Commodity Exchange **COMEX**

New York Stock Exchange **NYSE**

New Zealand **NZ**

Nicaragua **Nic**

nickel (chem) **Ni**

Nielsen Television Index **NTI**

Nigeria **Nig**

night **n**

niobium (chem) **Nb**

nitrogen (chem) **N**

nitroglycerine **nitro**

nitrous oxide **NOx**

nobelium (chem) **No**

no charge **N/C**

no date **ND**

nominative **n; nom; nomin**

noncommissioned **non com.**

noncommissioned officer **NCO**

non resident **non res**

nonstandard **nonstand**

noon **n**

noon [L *meridies*] **M.**

no par value (fin) **npv**

norm **n**

normal **n; norm.**

normal temperature and pressure **ntp**

north **N**

North Africa **N Afr**

North America **NA; N Am**

North Atlantic **N At**

North Atlantic Treaty Organization **NATO**

North Carolina **NC**

North Dakota **ND; N Dak**

northeast **NE**

Northern Ireland **NI**

Northern Territory **NT**

north-northwest **NNW**

northwest **NW**

Northwest Territories **NWT**

Norway **Norw**

not applicable **n/a; NA**

notary public **NP**

not available **n/a; NA**

note well [L *nota bene*] **n.b.**

not known **NK**

noun **n**

noun plural **npl**

Nova Scotia **NS**

November **Nov**

nuclear **nuc**

nuclear detection (radiation monitoring device) **nu-tec**

Nuclear Regulatory Commission **NRC**

nuclear ship **NS**

nuclear testing **N-test**

nucleus **nuc**

nullity (legal) **N**

number **n; No; num**

Numbers (Bible) **Num**

numismatic **numis**

–O–

Obadiah (Bible) **Obad**

obituary **obit**

object **obj**

objection **obj**

objective **obj**

obligation **obl**

oblige **obl**

oblique **obl**

obscure **obs**

observatory **obs**

observed vehicle **ov**

Observer Corps **OC**

obsessive compulsive disorder **OCD**

obsolete **obs**

obstetric **obs**

obstetrician **OB; obs**

obstetrician gynecologist **Ob-Gyn**

obverse **obv**

occasional **o**

Occupational Safety and Health Administration **OSHA**

occupational therapy **OT**

Ocean Data Station **ODS**

Oceanic Air Traffic Control **OATC**

oceanographic facility **OF**

Ocean Research Institute **ORI**

Ocean Resources Conservation Association **ORCA**

ocean station **os**

ocean station vessel **OSV**

ocean transportation **OT**

ochre **och**

octane number **ON**

octave (mus) **O; oct**

octavo **o; oct**

October **Oct**

off Broadway **OB**

offer **off.**

office **off.**

office copy **oc**

office hours **oh**

Office of Aerospace Research **OAR**

Office of Civil Defense **OCD**

Office of Civilian Requirements **OCR**

Office of Economic Opportunity **OEO**

Office of Education **OE**

Office of Management and Budget **OMB**

Office of Manned Space Flight **OMSF**

Office of Personnel Management **OPM**

Office of Price Administration **OPA**

Office of Public Affairs **OPA**

officer of the deck **OOD**

Office of the Secretary of Defense **OSD**

Office of the Secretary of the Air Force **OSAF**

Office of the Secretary of the Army **OSA**

Office of the Secretary of the Navy **OSN**

Office of the Treasurer of the United States **OTUS**

Office of Water Resources Research **OWRR**

Office of World Weather Systems **OWWS**

officer **off.**

Officer Candidate School **OCS**

officer of the day **OD**

Officer of the Order of the British Empire **OBE**

officer of the watch **OOW**

officers' association **OA**

officers' training school **OTS**

official classification **oc**

official receiver **OR**

official referee **OR**

Official Secrets Act **OSA**

official use **OU**

off time **OT**

Ohio **O; OH**

Oklahoma **OK; Okla**

old account **OA**

Old-Age and Survivors Insurance **OASI**

old age pensioner **OAP**

Old-Age, Survivors, Disability, and Health Insurance **OASDHI**

Old English **OE**

old face type **OF**

Old Style **OS**

Old Style Latin **OSL**

Old Testament (Bible) **OT; Old Test.**

Olympic **OL**

omissions excepted **OE**

omnicardiogram **ocg**

on account **O/A**

on active service **OAS**

on center **oc**

on demand **O/D**

one price only **opo**

on hand **oh**

on job training **ojt**

on-line communications drive **OCD**

online computer **OLC**

on line programming system **OLPS**

on line real time (computer) **OLRT**

on line system driver (computer) **OSD**

only child **oc**

only son **os**

on or about **O/A**

on order **o/o**

on sale **o/s**

Ontario **ON**

on the way [L *in transitu*] **in trans.**

open charter **oc**

open end **oe**

operating characteristic **OC**

operating room **OR**

operation analysis **OA**

operational, executive, and administrative personnel **OPEX**

operational forces **OF**

operational ground equipment **oge**

operational training unit **OTU**

operations **ops**

operations and engineering **O & E**

operations and management **O & M**

opinion **opn**

opportunity **opp; oppy**

opposite **opp**

opposition **opp**

optical character recognition (computer) **OCR**

optical density **od**

optical detection and ranging **OPDAR**

optics **opt.**

optimal **opt.**

optimum **opt.**

optimum earth re-entry corridor (space) **OERC**

optimum working frequency **OWF**

option **opn; opt.**

optional **opt.**

oral polio virus **opv**

orange juice **oj**

orbital launched ballistic missile **OLBM**

Orbiting Astronomical Observatory **OAO**

Orbiting Geophysical Observatory **OGO**

orbiting radio beacon ionospheric satellite **ORBIS**

orbiting solar observatory **OSO**

orbiting space station **oss**

orbiting vehicle **ov**

orchestra **orch**

ordain **ord**

order **ord**

ordered, adjudged, and decreed **OAD**

order of **o/o**

Order of Merit **OM**

Order of the Red Cross **ORC**

ordinal **ord**

ordinance **ord**

ordinary **ord**

ordinary neap tide **ont**

ordinary seaman **OS**

ordinate **y**

ordnance **ord; ordn**

ordnance board **Ord Bd**

ordnance department **Ord Dept**

Ordnance Survey **OS**

ordnance weapons command **OWC**

Oregon **OR; Oreg**

organ **org**

organic **org**

Organic Brain Syndrome **OBS**

organic heart disease **OHD**

organism **org**

organization **org**

organization and method **O & M**

Organization for Economic Cooperation and Development **OECD**

Organization for Trade Cooperation **OTC**

Organization of African Unity **OAU**

Organization of American States **OAS**

Organization of Central American States **OCAS**

Organization of Petroleum Exporting Countries **OPEC**

origin and destination **o & d**

original error **OE**

ornament **orn**

ornithology **orn**

orthography **orth**

orthopedic **orth**

osmium (chem) **Os**

osteopathy **osteo**

other people's **OP**

other ranks (mil) **OR**

ounce (avoirdupois) **oz**

out of order **o/o/o**

out of print **OP**

out of range **or.**

out of stock **o/s**

outpatients' clinic **OPC**

output per man shift **oms**

output secondary **OS**

outside **os**

outside continental United States **OCON-US**

outside diameter **od**

outside purchase **osp**

outsize **o/s**

outstanding **o/s**

overall **OA**

overcast sky (met) **o**

overcharge **o/c**

overdose **OD**

overdraft **O/D**

overdrawn **O/D**

overflow level **ol**

overhaul and repair **or.**

overhead **ovhd**

overhead projector **OVH**

override **ovrd**

overseas command **OC**

Overseas Development Administration **ODA**

Overseas Press Club of America **OPCA**

Overseas Research Council **ORC**

overseas trade **OT**

over the counter **otc**

overtime **OT**

owner's risk **OR**

Oxford **Ox.; Oxon.**

Oxford English Dictionary **OED**

oxygen (chem) **O**

–P–

Pacific **Pac**

Pacific daylight saving time **PDST**

Pacific daylight time **PDT**

Pacific Orient Express **POE**

Pacific standard time **PST**

Pacific Stock Exchange **PSE**

Pacific time **PT**

pack **pk**

package **pkg**

page **p**

paid **pd**

Pakistan **Pak**

Palestine Liberation Organization **PLO**

palladium (chem) **Pd**

Palo Alto Research Laboratory **PARL**

Pan African Congress **PAC**

Panama **Pan.**

Panama Canal **PC**

Panama Canal Zone **PCZ**

Pan American Congress **PAC**

Pan American Health Organization **PAHO**

Pan American Medical Association **PAMA**

Pan American Railway Congress Association **PARCA**

Pan American Union **PAU**

Papanicolaou Test (for cervical cancer) **Pap smear**

para-aminobenzoic acid **PABA**

paragraph **p; par; para**

Paraguay **Para; Parag**

parallax second **parsec**

parallel **par.; para**

parenthesis **paren**

parent-teachers' association **PTA**

parity (phys) **P**

parkway **Pkwy**

parole officer **PO**

part **p; pt**

partial **part.**

partial loss **PL**

participate **part.**

participial adjective **pa**

participle **p; part.**

particle **p; part.**

partnership **part.**

parts per million **p/m; ppm**

pascal **Pa**

passenger airlines reservation system **PARS**

passenger **pass.**

passive **pas; pass.**

passive participle **pp**

past **p**

past medical history **pmh**

patent **pat.**

patented **patd**

patent office **Pat. Off.; PO**

patent pending **pat. pend.**

pathology **path.**

pawn (chess) **P**

pay as you earn **PAYE**

paying guest **pg**

payroll **P/R**

peace be with you [L *pax vobiscum*] **pax**

peace corps volunteers **PCV**

pedestrian **P; ped**

penitentiary **Pen.**

Pennsylvania **Pa; PA**

Pentagon **Pent.**

Pentateuch **Pent.**

per **p**

percent **pct**

perfect **perf**

perforated **perf**

per gross ton **pgt**

pericardial cavity **P sac**

period **P; per.**

permanent **perm**

permanent address **pa**

per man hour **pmh**

permissible error **PE**

permission **perm**

permutation **perm**

perpendicular **perp**

perpetrator **perp**

perpetual **perp**

perquisite **perk**

person **per.; pers**

personal appearance **pa**

personal computer **PC**

personal identification number **PIN**

person in need of supervision **PINS**

personnel officer **PO**

perspective **pers**

pertain **pert.**

1 Peter (Bible) **1 Pet**

2 Peter (Bible) **2 Pet**

petty cash **P/C**

petty officer **PO**

pharmaceutical chemistry **Pharm Chem**

pharmacopoeia **ph**

phase **ph**

phencyclidine (angel dust) **PCP**

Phi Beta Kappa **PBK**

Philemon (Bible) **Philem**

Philippians (Bible) **Phil**

Philippine Islands **Phil I**

philosophy **ph; phil**

phonetics **phon**

phosphorus (chem) **P**

photoelectric cell **PEC**

physical education **PE; Phys Ed**

physical science **Phys Sc**

physical therapist **PT**

physician **phys**

Physician's Desk Reference **PDR**

physics **phys**

pick-up and deliver **p & d**

pico (prefix, one-trillionth) **p**

picoampere **pA**

picofarad; water-holding energy **pF**

picosecond **ps**

picowatt **pW**

pint **p; pt**

Place **Pl**

Planck's constant **h**

Planned Parenthood Federation of America **PPFA**

plate **pl**

platinum (chem) **Pt**

please note **pn**

plenipotentiary **Plen**

plural **pl**

plutonium (chem) **Pu**

pneumonia **pneum**

poetic **poet.**

Poets, Playwrights, Essayists, Editors and Novelists (Club) **PEN**

point of purchase **POP**

point of sale **POS**

Poland **Pol**

police department **PD**

political action committee **PAC**

political science **poli sci**

polonium (chem) **Po**

polyacrylic acid (chem) **PAA**

population **pop.**

port of call **PC; poc**

port of embarkation **P/E; POE**

port side out, starboard home **POSH**

Portugal **P; Port.**

position **pos; posn**

positive **pos**

positron emission tomography **PET**

postage **P**

postage due **pd**

postal district **PD**

postcard **pc**

post dated **pd; p/d**

posterior **P**

post master general **PMG**

post mortem **p.m.**

post office **PO**

postpaid **ppd**

postscript [L *post scriptum*] **P.S.**

potassium (chem) [NL *Kalium*] **K**

potential difference (elec) **pd**

pound **lb; pd**

pounds per square inch **psi**

pound sterling **L**

power assisted steering **pas**

power factor **PF**

power of attorney **P/A**

praseodymium (chem) **Pr**

pre-menstrual syndrome **pms**

precinct **pct**

precipitation **pptn**

prefabricated **prefab**

preface **pref**

preferred (fin) **pfd**

prefix **pfx**

preliminary **prelim**

premature baby **preemie**

premedical student **pre-med**

preparation for operation **pre-op**

preparatory **prep**

Presbyterian **P; Pres**

present **pres**

present participle **pres part**

president **Pres**

pressure (phys) **P**

pressurization control unit **pcu**

previous **prev**

price current **P/C**

price-earnings ratio (fin) **P/E**

Prime Minister **PM**

Prince Edward Island **PEI**

principal and interest **p & i**

prior notice required **pnr**

prisoner of war **POW**

private **pvt**

private first class **Pfc**

probable error (math) **PE**

Problem Oriented Languages (computer) **POLS**

professional-amateur **pro-am**

Professional Golfers Association **PGA**

profit and loss **P & L**

profit before tax (fin) **pbt**

proletarian **prole**

promethium (chem) **Pm**

promissory note **P/N**

pronoun **pron**

pronunciation **pron**

proof **pf**

protactinium (chem) **Pa**

Protestant **P; Prot**

Protestant Episcopal Church **PEC**

proton **p**

Proverbs (Bible) **Prov**

Province of Quebec **PQ**

Provost **Pr**

Psalms (Bible) **Ps**

pseudonym **pseud**

psychology **psych**

public address system **PA**

Public Broadcasting Service **PBS**

Public Buildings Administration **PBA**

Public Health Service **PHS**

Public Interest Research Group **PIRG**

public library **PL**

public relations **PR**

public school (with number) **PS**

public service commission **PSC**

public works administration **PWA**

Puerto Rico **PR**

pulse amplitude modulation **pam**

pulse duration modulation **pdm**

pulse frequency modulation **pfm**

pulse position modulation **ppm**

purchase order **PO**

purl **P**

–Q–

quadrangle **quad**

quadrant **quad**

quadrat (typo) **quad**

quadrilateral **quad**

quadrillion **Q**

quadrillion (10^{15}) **quad**

quadruplicate **quad**

qualification **qual**

qualification approval **QA**

qualitative **qual**

quality **qual**

quality assurance **QA**

quality assurance data system **QADS**

quality control **QC**

quality control engineering **QCE**

quality control technology **QCT**

quality indices **qi**

quantity **Q; qnty; qt; qty**

quantity not sufficient **QNS**

quantum electronics **QE**

quarantine **quar**

quarantine station **QS**

quart **qt**

quarter **qtr; quar**

quarterback **qb**

quarterly **quar**

quartermaster **Q.**

quartermaster corps **QC; QMC**

quartermaster-general **QMG; QM Gen**

quartermaster-sergeant **QMS; QM Sgt**

quarters allowance **QA**

quarter section **QS**

quarto **Q; qto**

Quebec **Qbc; Que**

queen (chess) **Q**

Queen's Bench **QB**

queen's bishop (chess) **QB**

queen's bishop's pawn (chess) **QBP**

Queen's College **QC**

Queen's Counsel **QC**

queen's knight (chess) **QKt**

queen's knight's pawn (chess) **QKtP**

Queensland **Qld**

query **Q**

question **qn**

question and answer **Q & A**

quintet **quint**

quintuplicate **quint**

quit claim **QC**

quotation **qn**

stagnation pressure **q**

–R–

rad **rd**

radar beacon **RACON**

radar cross section **rxs**

radar observer **RO**

radar planning device **rpd**

radar warning and homing **rwh**

radians per second **rad/s**

radiation **rad**

radiation absorbed dose **rad**

radiation danger zone **RDZ**

radiation resistance **rr**

radiation response **rr**

radical **rad**

radio **rad**

radio attenuation measurement **RAM**

radio detection and ranging **RADAR**

Radio Free Europe **RFE**

radio frequency amplification by stimulated emission of radiation **RASER**

radio monitoring **rm**

radio ranging **rr**

radio telegraphy **R/T**

radioactive **rada**

radioactive isotope powered pulsed light equipment **RIPPLE**

radio frequency **RF**

radiolocation **R**

radiological monitor **radmon**

radium (chem) **Ra**

radium emanation **Ra Em**

radius **r; rad**

radon (chem) **Rn**

railroad **RR**

railway **rwy; Ry**

rain (met) **r**

random access disc **RAD**

random access memory (computer) **RAM**

random access method **RAM**

range height indicator **RHI**

range mark **rm**

range of movement **rom**

Rankine **R**

rapid beam deflector **RBD**

rapid-eye movement (in sleep) **REM**

rateable value (fin) **RV**

rated horsepower **rhp**

rate of exchange **r/e**

rating **rat.**

rations **rat.**

raw material **rm**

reaction time **RT**

read bit feedback (computer) **RBF**

read only memory (computer) **ROM**

read, write, initial **rwi**

ready to eat **r-t-e**

ready to wear **RTW**

real estate investment trust **REIT**

real time data system (computer) **RTDS**

real world interval **rwi**

rear view **rv**

recapitulate **recap**

receipt **rec**

receive **rec**

receiving office/order **RO**

recipe **Rx**

reciprocal **recip**

reciprocal trade agreements **RTA**

recommend **recom**

recommended daily allowance **RDA**

reconciliation **recon**

recondition **recon**

reconnaissance **recon**

record **rec**

recorded **recd**

recovery room **RR**

recreation **rec**

recreational vehicle **rv**

recto **r; ro**

red **r**

red blood cell **rbc**

Red Cross **RC**

reentry vehicle **rv**

reentry vehicle (space) **REV**

reference **ref**

refer to your message **rym**

reflexive **refl**

regent **reg**

regiment **reg; regt**

registered **r; reg; regd**

registered nurse **RN**

registered trademark **Reg TM; rtm; RTM**

registry **reg**

regular **R; reg**

regular army **RA**

regulation **reg**

regulator **reg**

regulatory **reg**

reinforce **reinf**

reinforced concrete **rc**

relative **rel**

relative centrifugal force **rcf**

relative humidity **rh; rel hum**

relative pronoun **rel pron**

relief valve **rv**

remaining on board (ship) **ROB**

remedial occupational therapy **ROT**

remote access computing system **RACS**

remote control unit **RCU**

remote underwater manipulator **RUM**

remote use of shared hardware **rush**

remote weight indicator **rwi**

rendezvous radar **rr**

repair **rep**

repertory **rep**

reply paid **rp**

reporter **rep**

reporting in and out **RIO**

reports and memoranda **r & m**

repossession **repo**

represent **repr**

representative **rep; repr**

reproduced **repro**

Republic of Korea **ROK**

request **req**

request for quotation **RFQ**

require **req**

required **reqd**

required delivery date **rdd**

requisition **req**

research **res**

research and development **R&D**

research and technology **R & T**

research, development, testing, and evaluation **RDT&E**

reserved **res**

Reserve Officers' Training Corps **ROTC**

resistance ohm (elec) **r**

resolution **res**

respiration **resp**

respiration therapist **RT**

respiratory rate **rr**

responsibility **resp**

rest and recreation **R&R**

Rest in Peace **R.I.P.**

restricted take off and landing **rtol**

retain **ret**

retired **ret**

retired on full pay **rfp**

returned **rtd**

returned to unit (mil) **RTU**

return on investment **ROI**

return on market value **romv**

return ticket **RT**

return to base **rtb**

Revelations (Bible) **Rev**

revenue **rev**

Reverend **Rev**

reverse **rev**

revise **rev**

revised edition **rev ed**

revolutions per hour **rph**

revolutions per minute **r/min; rpm**

revolutions per second **rps; r/s**

rhenium (chem) **Re**

rheostat **rheo**

Rhesus (blood factor) **Rh**

Rhode Island **RI**

Rhodesia **Rh**

rhodium **Rh**

rhythm and blues (mus) **R&B**

ribonucleic acid (chem) **RNA**

rifle range **rr**

right **r; rt**

right ascension (astron) **R.A.**

right field **rf**

right hand **rh**

right hand page [L *folio recto*] **f.r.**

right of admission reserved **ROAR**

right of way **ROW**

right opening **ro**

Right Reverend **Rt Rev**

right side up with care **rswc**

Right to Life **RTL**

rises **r**

river **r**

Road **Rd**

rock and roll **R&R**

rocket-assisted takeoff **rato**

roentgen **R**

roentgen equivalent man **rem**

roentgen equivalent physical (phys) **rep**

Roman Catholic **RC**

Romans (Bible) **Rom**

roman type **rom**

rook (chess) **R**

room **rm**

root [L *radix*] **rad.**

root mean square **rms**

rotary combustion **rc**

rough opening **ro**

round **rd**

route **rte**

routine execution selection table (computer) **REST**

rubber (cards) **r**

rubidium (chem) **Rb**

rules, standards, and instructions **rs & i**

run out **ro**

runs batted in **rbi**

runway visual range **RVR**

rural free delivery **RFD**

rural route **RR**

rush and run **rr**

Russia **Rus**

Russian Soviet Federal Socialist Republic **RSFSR**

ruthenium (chem) **Ru**

–S–

safe deposit **sd**

safeguard anti ballistic missile system **SABMS**

safety factor **sf**

safe working load **SWL**

safe working pressure **swp**

saint **S; St**

salt free **sf**

Salvador **Salv**

salvage **salv**

samarium (chem) **Sm**

same date **sd**

1 Samuel (Bible) **1 Sam**

2 Samuel (Bible) **2 Sam**

San Francisco **SF**

satellite **sat.**

saturate **sat.**

Saturday **S; Sat**

Saturn **Sat**

Saudi Arabia **SA**

savings and loan **S&L**

saybolt universal second(s) **Sus**

scandium (chem) **Sc**

Scholastic Aptitude Test **SAT**

science **sc; sci**

science fiction **sci-fi; s-f**

scientific and technical information **s & ti**

scientific research **sr**

scripture **Scrip**

sea **s**

sea level **sl**

sea level takeoff **slto**

seaman, first class **S1c**

search and rescue **sar**

secant **sec**

second **sec**

second (time interval unit) **s**

secretary **S; sec; secy**

secretary general **Sec Gen**

Secretary of Defense **SD**

Secretary of State **SS**

Secret Service **SS**

Securities and Exchange Commission **SEC**

Security Council **SC**

sedative **sed**

sediment **sed**

segment **seg**

Selective Service System **SSS**

selenium (chem) **Se**

self-addressed stamped envelope **SASE**

self-propelled **sp**

self raising **sr**

self resonant frequency **srf**

semi-automatic rifle **sar**

semicolon **sem**

seminary **sem**

Senate **Sen**

senator **Sen**

senior **Sen; Sr**

sentence **sent.**

separate **sep**

September **Sept**

sequel **seq**

sequence **seq**

serial number **sn**

series number **sn**

service number **sn**

service unit **su**

session **sess**

Seventh Day Adventist **SDA**

sex ratio **sr**

sextant **sext**

shake before taking (med) [L *agita ante sumendum*] **agit. ante su.**

share (fin) **shr**

shipment **shpt**

shipping receipt **sr**

ship's mean time **SMT**

ship to shore **S to S**

shore patrol **SP**

short range missile **SRM**

short range (radio) **shoran**

short take off and landing **STOL**

short term memory **STM**

short ton **st**

short wheel base **SWB**

siblings **sibs**

siemens **S**

signal **sig**

signal frequency **sf**

signature **sig**

signed **sgd**

silicon (chem) **Si**

silver **S**

silver (chem) [L *argentum*] **Ag**

similar **sim**

simile **sim**

simplified spelling **ss**

simulate **sml**

sine **sin**

Singapore **Sng**

single **sgl**

single column inch **sci**

single lens reflex **SLR**

single line approach **sla**

single-room occupany **SRO**

singular **S; sing.**

situation comedy **sit-com**

situation normal, all fouled up **SNAFU**

size **sz**

slow release **sr**

small **sm; sml**

Small Business Administration **SBA**

small capitals (typo) **sc, sm caps**

smoke-laden fog **smog**

Social Security Administration **SSA**

Society for the Prevention of Cruelty to Animals **SPCA**

Society for the Prevention of Cruelty to Children **SPCC**

Society of Jesus (Jesuit Order) **S.J.**

sodium [L *Natrium*] **Na**

solar radiation flux **srf**

solid **sld**

Song of Solomon (Bible) **Song of Sol**

Sons of the American Revolution **SAR**

sound **sd**

sound navigation ranging **sonar**

south **S**

South Africa **SA**

South African Republic **SAR**

South America **SA**

South Carolina **SC**

South Dakota **SD; S Dak**

southeast **SE**

Southern Christian Leadership Conference **SCLC**

southwest **SW**

Southwestern Townships (South Africa) **SO-WETO**

Soviet Union **SU**

space **sp**

special **sp; spec**

special agent **SA**

special delivery **SD; sp del**

special purpose **sp**

species **sp; spp**

specification **spec**

specific gravity **G; sg**

specific heat **sp ht**

speed **sp**

spelling **sp**

spherical equivalent **se**

spontaneous ignition temperature **SIT**

Square **Sq**

square centimeter **cm²**

square foot **ft²; sq ft**

square foot per minute **ft²/min**

square foot per second **ft²/s**

square hectometer **hm²**

square inch **in²; sq in**

square kilometer **km²**

square meter **m²; sq m**

square mile **mi²**

square millimeter **mm²**

square yard **sq yd; yd²**

standard **stand; std**

standard book number **SBN**

standard deviation **SD**

standard error **se**

standard frequency **sf**

standard size **SS**

standard temperature and pressure **STP**

standard time **ST**

standard weight **SW**

standing order **STO**

standing room only **SRO**

starboard **stbd**

State Department **SD**

state of the art **sota**

station to station **SS**

statistics **stats**

statute **S; st**

statute mile **s mi**

steamship **SS**

stenography **steno**

steradian **sr**

stilb **sb**

stimulus response **sr**

stock at valuation **sav**

stony [L *lapideum*] **lapid.**

stop payment **sp**

stop press news **SPN**

strangeness (phys) **S**

Strategic Air Command **SAC**

Strategic Arms Limitation Talks **SALT**

street **St**

streptococcus **strep.**

strikeout (baseball) **K**

strontium (chem) **Sr**

strontium unit **su**

subchapter **subch**

subdivision **subd**

subject **sub; subj**

subjunctive **sub; subj**

submarine detector **SD**

submarine launched ballistic missile **SLBM**

subparagraph **subpar**

subscription **sub**

subsidiary **sub**

substantive **s; sb; sub**

substitute **sub**

sudden infant death syndrome **SIDS**

sulphur (chem) **S**

Sunday **S; Su; Sun**

Sundays and Holidays excepted **SHEX**

superhigh frequency **shf**

superintendent **Supt**

superior **sup; supr**

supersonic transport **SST**

supplement **supp**

supplemental security income **SSI**

supply and transport **S & T**

Supreme Court **SC**

surface based **s/b**

surface to air missile **SAM**

surface to surface missile **SSM**

surface to underwater missile **SUM**

Susanna (Bible/Apocrypha) **Sus**

suspension **susp**

Sweden **S**

syllable **syl**

symbol **sym**

symmetrical **sym**

symmetrical (chem) **s**

syncopated time **ST**

synonym **syn**

system **syst**

–T–

table **t**

table of contents **TOC**

tablespoonful **tbsp**

tablet **ta; tab.**

tabulate **tab.**

tachometer **tach**

tachygraphy (shorthand) **tachy**

Tactical Air Command (USAF) **TAC**

Tactical Air Control Group **TACG**

Tactical Air Control System **TCS**

Tactical Air Navigation **TACAN**

Tactical Air Operations Center **TAOC**

Tactical Division **TD**

Tactical Fighter Experimental **TFX**

Tactical Missile **TM**

Tactical Multi-function Array Radar **TAC-MAR**

tactical navigation **tacnav**

tactical nuclear missile **TM**

tail wind **tw**

take care of business **tcb**

take off **t/o**

Talmud **Tal**

tangent (math) **tan**

Tank Corps (mil) **TC**

tank destroyer **td**

tantalum (chem) **Ta**

Tanzania **Tan.**

target **t; tgt**

target area **ta**

target identification **ti; T/I**

task force **TF**

task initiation date **tid**

Tasmania **Tasm**

tautology **taut.**

tax **tx**

Tax Court of the United States **TCUS**

tax free **tf**

tax sheltered annuity **tsa**

Tay Sachs Disease **TSD**

tea **T**

teacher **T**

teacher's assistant **TA**

teaspoonful **t; tsp**

technetium (chem) **Tc**

Technical Assistance Committee (UN) **TAC**

Technical Assistance Program **TAP**

technical college **TC**

technical data **td**

technical institute **TI**

technical knockout (boxing) **TKO**

technical manual **TM**

teetotal **TT**

telecommunications **telecom**

telegraph **T**

telegraph agency of the Soviet Union **TASS**

telephone **T; tel**

teletype exchange **telex**

teletypewriter **TTY**

television **TV**

television and infra-red observation satellite **TIROS**

tellurium (chem) **Te**

temperance **temp**

temperate **temp**

temperature **tem; temp**

temperature control **tc**

temperature humidity index **THI**

temperature indication **ti**

temperature (med) **T**

temperature meter **tm**

temperature, pulse, respiration **tpr**

template **tem**

tempo (mus) **t**

temporary **T; temp**

temporary assistant **T/A**

temporary restraining order **TRO**

tenant **ten.**

tender loving care **TLC**

Tennessee **Tenn; TN**

Tennessee Valley Authority **TVA**

tensile strength **ts**

tera (prefix, 1 trillion) **T**

terbium (chem) **Tb**

terminal **t; term.**

terms (math) **T**

terms of service **tos**

terrace **Ter**

territorial army **TA**

tertiary **tert**

test and evaluation **T & E**

test and maintenance **t & m**

test data **td**

testimonial **test.**

testimony **test.**

test link **tl**

test manual **TM**

test run **TR**

tests of general ability **TOGA**

test summary **ts**

tetanus toxin **tet tox**

tetrahertz **THz**

Teutonic **Teut**

Texas **Tex; TX**

Thailand **Thai**

thallium (chem) **Tl**

Thank God It's Friday! **TGIF**

that is [L *id est*] **i.e.**

theater **Th; theat**

the court desires to consider (legal) [L *curia advisare vult*] **c.a.v.**

the defendant being absent [L *absente reo*] **abs. re.**

Their Majesties **TM**

theology **th; theol**

theoretical line of escape **tle**

the received text [L *texturs receptus*] **text. rec.**

therefore [L *igitur*] **igr.**

thermal efficiency **te**

thermal unit **TU**

thermometer **therm**

thermometric **therm**

thermonuclear weapon **tn wp**

the same [L *idem*] **id.**

the same as [L *idem quod*] **i.q.**

1 Thessalonians (Bible) **1 Thess**

2 Thessalonians (Bible) **2 Thess**

this is [L *hic est*] **h.e.**

this year [L *hoc anno*] **h.a.**

thorium (chem) **Th**

thousand **K**

three mile limit **TML**

Thruway **Thru**

thulium (chem) **Tm**

Thursday **Th; Thurs**

ticket reservation system **TRS**

till cancelled **tc**

time check **tc**

time delay **td**

time expired **t/e**

time of origin **too.**

time of receipt **tor**

time opening **to.**

time sharing system **TSS**

1 Timothy (Bible) **1 Tim**

2 Timothy (Bible) **2 Tim.**

tin (chem) [L *stannum*] **Sn**

titanium (chem) **Ti**

title **tit**

Titus (Bible) **Tit**

to be added **add.**

to be announced **tba**

to be determined **tbd**

Tobit (Bible) **Tob**

to infinity [L *ad infinitum*] **ad inf.**

ton **t**

tone modulation **TM**

tonne (metric ton) **t**

tons per day **tpd**

tons per square inch **t si**

too numerous to count **tntc**

top, bottom and sides **tb & s**

top dead center **TDC**

top sergeant **T Sgt**

torpedo **T**

total **tot.**

total digestible nutrients **TDN**

Total Disability Benefit **TDB**

total energy (anal. mechanics) **H**

total load **tl**

total loss **tl; t/l**

total material assets **tma**

total survey area **tsa**

touchdown **td**

tourist information board **TIB**

township **T; twp**

toxic unit **TU**

trace **tr**

tracking radar **TR**

tractor-drawn **td**

trademark **TM**

tradition **trad**

traffic agent/auditor **TA**

traffic director **TD**

traffic manager **TM**

tragedy **tr**

trainee **Tr**

training advisor **TA**

training center **TC**

training film **tf**

training group **TG; T-Group**

transaction **T; tr; trans**

transaction identification number **TIN**

Trans Canada Highway **TCH**

transcendental meditation **TM**

Trans Europe Express **TEE**

transfer **tfr; tr; trans; tsfr; xfer**

transformer **xfmr**

transistor-transistor logic **TTL**

transit **t**

Transit Authority **TA**

transitive **t; tr; trans**

translate **tr; trans**

translunar insertion **TLI**

transmission unit **TU**

transmit **xmit**

transmitter/receiver **T/R**

transport **T; tr; trans**

transport and supply **T & S**

transport command **TC**

transport officer **TO**

transpose (typo) **tr; trans**

transverse **T; trans**

travel allowance **ta**

travel and entertainment **T & E**

traveler's check **TC**

treasury bill **TB; T-bill**

Treasury Department **TD**

Treasure Island **TI**

treble **tr**

trial and error **te**

trial balance **tb**

trigger reactor **TRIGA**

trigonometry **trig**

trinitrotoluene (dynamite) **TNT**

tritium (chem) **T**

Tropic of Cancer **Trop Can**

Tropic of Capricorn **Trop Cap**

tropic tides **tc**

troy **t**

true altitude **ta**

true bearing **tb**

true boiling point **tbp**

true north **TN**

tuberculin-tested **TT**

tuberculosis **TB**

Tuesday **T; Tues**

tuned radio frequency **trf**

tungsten (wolfram) (chem)
W

turbine propelled **turboprop**

Turkey **Tur**

turn **t**

turn over **to.**

turnpike **tnpk**

twin engined **t/e**

two-tone modulation
TTM

type **typ**

typescripts **tss**

typography **typo**

–U–

ultimate operating capa-
bility **uoc**

ultimate oxygen demand
(water conservation)
UOD

ultra deep water **udw**

ultra high frequency **uhf**

ultra high purity **uhp**

ultra high speed **uhs**

ultra high temperature
uht

ultra high vacuum **uhv**

ultra high voltage **uhv**

ultra low frequency **ulf**

ultra low volume **ulv**

ultra short wave **usw**

ultrasonic industry **ui**

ultrasonic light modula-
tor **ulm**

ultraviolet **uv**

ultraviolet light **uvl**

umpire **ump**

unabridged **unab**

unanimous **unan**

unbound **unbd**

uncirculated **uncir**

uncirculated (numis) **UNC**

unclassified **unclass**

uncle **U**

Uncle Sam (USA) **US**

unconditional stimulus **ucs**

unconditioned **uncond**

unconditioned response **ucr**

unconscious **ucs**

uncorrected **uncor**

under **und**

under age **ua**

underground **u/g**

under instruction **u/i**

under proof (spirits) **up.**

undersea long-range missile system **ULMS**

under secretary **US**

Under Secretary of State **USS**

under separate cover **usc**

underwater sea warfare **usw**

underwater-to-air missile **UAM**

underwriter **U/w**

Underwriters' Laboratory **UL**

underwriting account **U/a**

undignified [L *infra dignitatem*] **infra dig.**

unemployed full pay **ufp**

unemployment insurance **ui**

Unesco Publications Center **UPC**

unexpired **ue**

unexplained atmospheric phenomenon **uap**

unexploded bomb **UXB**

unidentified flying object **UFO**

unidentified growth factor **ugf**

unified atomic mass (phys) **u**

uniform code of military justice **UCMJ**

Uniform Commercial Code **UCC**

uniform consumer credit code **UCCC**

uniform system of lens aperture (photo) **US**

unilateral declaration of independence **UDI**

uninterrupted power supply **ups**

union **U**

union (math) **U**

Union of American Hebrew Congregations **UAHC**

Union of Soviet Socialist Republics **USSR**

Union Pacific **UP**

Union Pacific Railroad **UPR**

unit **u**

Unitarian **Unit**

Unitarianism **Unit**

unite **U**

United Arab Emirates **UAE**

United Auto Workers **UAW**

United Daughters of the Confederacy **UDC**

United Jewish Appeal **UJA**

United Kingdom **UK**

United Lutheran Church of America **ULCA**

United Methodist Free Churches **UMFC**

United Mine Workers **UMW**

United Nations **UN**

United Nations Administrative Committee and Coordination **UN-ACC**

United Nations Association **UNA**

United Nations Children's Fund **UNCF; UNICEF**

United Nations Command **UNC**

United Nations Development Programme **UNDP**

United Nations Economic Development Administration **UNEDA**

United Nations Educational, Scientific and Cultural Organization **UNESCO**

United Nations Emergency Force **UNEF**

United Nations Emergency Technical Aid Service **UNETAS**

United Nations Headquarters **UNHQ**

United Nations Industrial Development Organization **UNIDO**

United Nations Narcotics Commission **UNARCO**

United Nations Organization **UNO**

United Nations Peace Observation Commission **UNPOC**

United Nations Refugee Emergency Fund **UNREF**

United Nations Technical Assistance **UNTA**

United Negro College Fund **UNCF**

United Parcel Service **UPS**

united port district **UPD**

United Presbyterian **UP**

United Presbyterian Church **UPC**

United Press International **UPI**

United Service **US**

United Service Organizations **USO**

United States **US**

United States Agency for International Development **USAID**

United States Air Corps **USAC**

United States Air Force **USAF**

United States Air Force Academy **USAFA**

United States Army Air Corps **USAAC**

United States Army Reserve **USAR**

United States Army Transport **USAT**

United States Atomic Energy Commission **USAEC**

United States Bureau of Mines **USBM**

United States Bureau of the Census **USBC**

United States Circuit Court **USCC**

United States Circuit Court of Appeals **USCCA**

United States Coast Guard **USCG**

United States Coast Guard Academy **USCGA**

United States Coast Guard Reserve **USCGR**

United States Code **USC**

United States Code Annotated **USCA**

United States Congress **USC**

United States Department of Agriculture **USDA**

United States Employment Service **USES**

United States Forces **USF**

United States Geological Survey **USGS**

United States Government **USG**

United States Information Agency **USIA**

United States Information Service **USIS**

United States Mail **USM**

United States Marine Corps **USMC**

United States Marines **USM**

United States Maritime Commission **USMC**

United States Military Academy **USMA**

United States Mint **USM**

United States National Guard **USNG**

United States Naval Academy **USNA**

United States Naval Reserve **USNR**

United States of America **U.S.A.**

United States Patent **USP**

United States Pharmacopoeia **USP**

United States Postal Service **USPS**

United States Post Office **USPO**

United States Savings Bonds **USSB**

United States Senate **USS**

United States Ship **USS**

United States Steamer **USS**

United States Supreme Court **USSC**

United States Veterans' Hospital **USVH**

United States Weather Bureau **USWB**

United States West Indies **USWI**

unit equipment **ue**

unit of inductance (H= Vs/A) **H**

unit of issue **u/i**

unit of magnetic permeability **H/m**

universal **univ**

universal automatic computer **UNIVAC**

universalist **univ**

universal military service **UMS**

universal military training **UMT**

universal military training system **UMTS**

universal navigation beacon **UNB**

Universal Postal Union **UPU**

Universal Product Code **UPC**

universal time **UT**

university **U; univ**

university library **UL**

unknown **unkn**

unmanned lunar logistics vehicle **ULLV**

unmarried **unm**

unopposed **unop**

unpaged **unpd**

unpaid **unpd**

unpublished **unpub**

unpublished [L *ineditus*] **ined.**

unsafe lane change **ulc**

unsatisfactory **unsat**

unsaturated **unsat**

unsecured loan stock (fin) **uls**

unserviceable **u/s**

until effective (med) [L *ad effectum*] **ad effect.**

until further notice **ufn**

upper **up.**

upper air space **uas**

upper and lower case (typo) **u & lc**

upper case (typo) **uc**

upper critical depth (ocean) **UCD**

upper cylinder lubricant (eng) **ucl**

upper half **uh**

upper left center **ulc**

upper limb **UL**

upper limiting frequency **ulf**

up stage center (theater) **USC**

uranium (chem) **U**

Urban Development Corporation **UDC**

Urban Mass Transportation Administration **UMTA**

urban planning directorate **UPD**

urea-formaldehyde resin **u/f**

urgent **ugt; urg**

urinary tract infection **uti**

Urology **Urol**

Ursa Minor (astron) **U Mi**

Uruguay **Ur**

US Army **USA**

US Coast Guard **USCG**

use and occupancy **u & o**

US Navy **USN**

usual childhood diseases **ucd**

Utah **U; Ut; UT**

utopian **utop**

–V–

vacancy **vac**

vacation **vac**

vaccination **vacc**

vacuum **v; vac**

vagrancy **vag**

validate **valid.**

valley **v; val**

valuation **val**

valuation clause **vc**

value **val**

value added tax **VAT**

value analysis **va**

valve **v; val**

valve engineer **VE**

valvular **val**

valvular disease of the heart **VDH**

vanadium (chem) **V**

Van Allen belt (astron) **VAb**

Vancouver (Canada) **Vanc**

Vancouver Island **VI**

vanguard **van.**

vanilla **van.**

vanishing point **vp**

vapor density **vd**

vapor pressure **vp**

variable **var**

variable condenser **var cond**

variable density wind tunnel **vdt**

variable depth sonar **VDS**

variable elevation beam **veb**

variable factor programming (computer) **VFP**

variable frequency oscillator **VFO**

variable pitch **vp**

variable resistor **varistor**

variable speed **vs**

variable threshold logic (computer) **VTL**

variant (math) **var**

variation **var**

variety **var**

vascular **vasc**

vasectomy **vas**

Vatican **Vat**

Vatican City **VC**

vaudeville **vaud**

vector analog computer **VAC**

vector (math) **v**

vegetation **veg**

vegetation drought index **VDI**

vehicle identification number **vin**

vehicles per day **vpd**

vehicles per mile **vpm**

vehicular communication
 vc

vein **v**

velocity **vel**

velocity modulation **VM**

velocity of detonation
 VOD

velocity of light **c**

velocity (phys) **V**

veneer **ven**

Venerable **V; Ven**

venereal **ven**

venereal disease **VD**

Venetian **Ven**

Venezuela **Ven**

Venice **Ven**

ventilate **vent.**

ventilation **vent.**

ventral **v; ven**

ventricle **ven**

ventricular fibrillation
 vent fib

Venus **Ven**

verb **v; vb**

verb active **va**

verb active and intransi-
tive **va & i**

verbal **vb; vbl**

verbal adjective (participle) **vba**

verbal discrimination **vd**

verbal order **VO**

Verbal Test **VET**

verb auxiliary **v aux**

verb defective **v def**

verb imperative **v imper**

verb impersonal **v imp**

verb intransitive **vi**

verb reflexive **vr; v refl**

Vermont **Vt; VT**

vernacular **vern**

verse **v**

version **v; ver**

vertebra **vert**

vertex **Vx**

vertical **v; vert**

vertical and short take-off
and landing **VSTOL**

vertical angle bench mark
 VABM

vertical camera **verticam**

vertical center of gravity; vice-consul general **VCG**

Vertical Format Unit (computer) **VFU**

vertical integration building **VIB**

vertical interval (cartog) **VI**

vertical interval test **VIT**

vertical keel **vk**

vertical magnetic dipole **VMD**

vertical photography **v ph**

vertical retort **VR**

vertical speed indicator **VSI**

vertical take-off **VTO**

vertical take-off and landing **VTOL**

very **v; vy**

very fair **vf**

very good **VG**

very high and ultra high frequency **VHF/UHF**

very high fidelity **vhf**

very high frequency **vhf**

very high output **VHO**

very high performance **VHP**

very important person **VIP**

very (in titles) **V**

very low altitude **vla**

very low frequency **vlf**

very special old pale (cognac) **VSOP**

very special quality **VSQ**

very special reserve **VSR**

very superior old **VSO**

very, very old **VVO**

very, very superior **VVS**

vespers **V**

vessel **ves**

vestry **ves**

veteran **vet**

Veterans' Administration **VA; Vet Admin**

Veterans' Administration Hospital **VAH**

Veterans of Foreign Wars **VFW**

veterinarian **vet**

veterinary officer **VO**

veterinary science **Vet Sci**

vibrating wire gauge **VWG**

vibrations per second **vps**

vicar **v**

vice admiral **Vice Adm**

vice-chairman **VC**

vice-consul general **VCG**

vice (in titles) **V**

vice-lieutenant **VL**

vice-president **VP; V Pres**

victory **V**

victory day **V Day**

Victory in Europe **VE Day**

video cassette recorder **VCR**

video display terminal **vdt; VDT**

video frequency **VF**

video map equipment **vmap**

video-tape recording **VTR**

Vienna (Austria) **Vien**

Vietcong **VC**

Viet Minh **VM**

Vietnam **VN**

village **v; vil**

viniculture **vini**

vinyl acetate **va**

vinyl chloride **vc**

Virginia **Va; VA**

Virgin Islands **VI; Vir Is**

Virgo **Vir**

virus **v**

virus inactivating agent **via**

viscosity **v; vis**

viscosity gravity constant **vgc**

viscosity index **VI**

viscosity index improver **vii**

Viscount **V; Vis**

Viscountess **V; Vis**

visibility **v; vis**

vision (med) **v**

visual **vis**

visual acoustic magnetic pressure **VAMP**

visual approach path indicator **Vapi**

visual approach slope indicator **Vasi**

visual-aural radio range **VAR**

visual communication **vc**

visual display unit **VDU**

visual field **VF**

visual flight rules **VFR**

visual meteorological conditions **VMC**

visual precision **VIPRE**

visual rule instrument land **vri**

vital signs **vs**

vital statistics **vit stat**

vitreous **vit**

vivisection **vivi**

vocabulary **vocab**

vocal **voc**

vocation **voc**

vocational education **VE**

Vocational Rehabilitation Administration **VRA**

vocative **v; voc**

voice **v**

voice frequency **VF**

voice-frequency band **v-f band**

voice interference analysis system **vias**

Voice of America **VOA**

voice over **VO**

void **vd**

volcano **v**

volt **V**

voltage **v; vltg**

voltage regulator (elec) **vr**

voltage-to-frequency converter **VFC**

voltampere **VA**

volt ampere (elec) **va**

voltmeter **v**

volts alternating current **vac**

volts per mil **vpm**

volume **v; vol**

volume and tension (med) **v & t**

volume indicator **VI**

volume per volume **v/v**

volume unit **vu**

voluntary **vol**

volunteer **vol**

volunteer reserve **VR**

Volunteers in Service to America **VISTA**

Volunteers of America **VA**

voucher attached **V/A**

vowel **v**

vulcanized rubber **vr**

vulgar **vul**

vulgar latin **VL**

–W–

Wage Adjustment Board **WAB**

wage board **wb**

waist **w**

Wales **W**

wall **w**

Wallace, U.S. Supreme Court Reports **Wall**

Wall Street Journal **WSJ**

war **w**

War Agricultural Executive Committee **WAEC**

war cabinet **WC**

War Crimes Commission **WCC**

ward **wd**

warden **W**

war department **WD**

warm **w**

warning **warn.**

War Office **WO**

warrant **war.; wt**

warranted **wd**

warrant officer **WO**

warranty **warr**

War Resisters International **WRI**

Warsaw **War.**

Warsaw Pact Members **WPs**

Warsaw Treaty Organization **WTO**

war trade department **WTD**

washed overboard **wob**

Washington **Wa; WA; Wash.**

Wassermann (blood test) **Wass**

waste **w**

waste ballast **wb**

watch time **WT**

water **w**

Water and Power Resources Service **WPRS**

water ballast **wb**

water board **WB**

water closet **wc**

water cock **wc**

water department **WD**

water gauge **wg**

water heater **WH**

Waterloo **W**

Water Pollution Control Administration **WPCA**

Water Pollution Control Federation **WPCF**

water-retention coefficient **WRC**

water soluble **WS**

water supply point **wsp**

watertight **wt**

watertight manhole **WTMH**

water valve **wv**

water vapor transfer **wvt**

water vapor transmission **wvt**

water vapor transmission rate **wvtr**

waterways experiment station **WES**

watt (elec) **w; W**

watt hour (elec) **Wh**

watt meter **WM**

wave band **wb**

way bill **W/B**

Ways and Means Committee **WMC**

Weapons Engineering Standardization Office **WESO**

weapons operational systems development **WOSD**

weapons readiness analysis program **WRAP**

weapon system **WS**

weapon system programming and control system **WSPACS**

weapons systems evaluation division **WSED**

weapons systems evaluation group **WSEG**

weapons testing program **WTP**

weather **w**

weather and boil proof **wbp**

weather bureau **WB**

weber **Wb**

Webster's Biographical Dictionary **WBD**

Wechsler-Bellevue Intelligence test (psych) **WBIT**

Wechsler's Adult Intelligence Scale (psych) **WAIS**

Wednesday **W; Wed**

weed **wd**

weekly benefits (ins) **WB**

weighing **wg**

weight **w; wt**

weight, altitude and temperature **WAT**

weight for weight **w/w**

weight guaranteed **wg**

weight in volume **w/v**

weight/volume **w/v**

weight/weight **w/w**

Welfare Administration **WA**

welfare officer **WO**

well developed **w/d**

Wells Fargo and Company **WF**

Welsh **W**

west **W**

West Africa **WA**

west bound **wb**

West Coast Athletic Association **WCAA**

western **w; W**

Western Air Defense **WADF**

Western Australia **WA**

Western European Union **WEU**

Western Operations Office (NASA) **WOO**

Western Samoa **W Sam**

Western Union **WU**

West Germany **W Ger**

West Indies **WI; W Ind**

West Virginia **WV; W Va**

wet **w**

wet bulb **WB**

wet bulb globe temperature **WBGT**

wet bulb globe thermometer **WBGT**

wet bulb temperature **WBT**

wet dew (met) **w**

wharf **wh**

wheel base **wb**

wheel chair **wc**

when actually employed **wae**

when or where applicable **whap**

which **wh**

which see [L *quod vide*] **q.v.**

which was to be demonstrated [L *quod erat demonstrandum*] **q.e.d.**

which was to be discovered [L *quod erat inveniendo*] **q.e.i.**

which was to be done [L *quod erat faciendum*] **q.e.f.**

white **w; wh**

white American male **wAm**

white blood cell **WBC**

white blood corpuscle **WBC**

white blood count **WBC**

White Citizens' Council **WCC**

White House **WH**

white metal **WM**

White Sands Missile Range (US Army) **WSMR**

wholesale **whsle**

wholesale price index **wpi**

Who's Who **WW**

wide [L *latus*] **lat.**

wide angle fixed field location equipment **WAFFLE**

wide area data service **WADS**

Wide-Area Telephone Service **WATS**

wide band oscilloscope **wbo**

wide bridge oscillator **wbo**

wide open throttle **wot**

widow **W; wid**

widower **W; wid**

width **w**

width [Fr *largeur*] **larg.**

wife **w**

will be issued **wbi**

will call **wc**

will comply **WILCO**

will factor (psych) **w factor**

wind **w**

wind direction **W/D**

Windward Islands **WI; Wind I**

wing **wg**

wing forward **WF**

wing half **WH**

wing warrant officer **WWO**

wire **w**

wire gauge **wg**

wireless distress signal **SOS**

wireless operator **WO**

wire mesh **WM**

Wisconsin **WI; Wis**

Wisdom of Solomon (Bible/Apocrypha) **Wisd of Sol**

with **w**

with [L *cum*] **c**

withholding **w/h**

withholding tax **WT**

within normal limits **WNL**

with no down payment **wndp**

without **w/o; wt**

without charge **wc**

without compensation **woc**

without date [L *sine die*] **s.d.**

without equipment **woe**

without interest **xin**

without issue [L *sine prole*] **s.p.**

without privileges **xper**

with reference to **re; w/ref**

with regard to **w/reg**

with the solo part (mus) [It *colla parte*] **C.p.**

wolfram (chem) **W**

Women Accepted for Volunteer Emergency Service **WAVES**

Women in the Air Force **WAF**

Women's Army Auxiliary Corps **WAAC**

Women's Army Corps **WAC**

Women's Auxiliary Air Force **WAAF**

Women's Christian Temperance Union **WCTU**

Women's Freedom League **WFL**

Women's International League for Peace and Freedom **WILPF**

Women's Liberation (movement) **Women's Lib**

Women's Wear Daily **WWD**

won **w**

wood **wd**

word **w; wd**

Word Association Test (psych) **WAT**

word processing **WP**

words a minute **WAM**

word selection **WORSE**

words out of ordinary language **woool**

words per minute **wpm**

work **w**

work analysis and measurement **WAM**

Work Incentive (program) **WIN**

working capital **WC**

working stress design **wsd**

work in progress **wip**

workmen's compensation **WC**

work (phys) **W**

works department **WD**

work unit **wu**

World Aeronautical Chart **WAC**

World Bank for Reconstruction and Development **WB**

World Boxing Association of America **WBA**

World Boxing Council **WBC**

World Brotherhood **WB**

World Championship Tennis **WCT**

World Congress of Faiths **WCF**

World Council of Churches **WCC**

World Council of Peace **WCP**

World Federation for the Protection of Animals **WFPA**

World Federation of Trade Unions **WFTU**

World Food Program **WFP**

World Geophysical Interval **WGI**

World Health Organization **WHO**

World Oceanographic Organization **WOO**

World Petroleum Congress **WPC**

World Press News **WPN**

World War One **WWI**

World War Two **WWII**

worldwide standard seismograph network **WWSSN**

worldwide synchronization of atomic clock **wosac**

World Wildlife Fund **WWF**

World Women's Christian Temperance Union **WWCTU**

would **wd**

wound **wd**

wounded in action **wia**

Writer's Action Group **WAG**

written order **WO**

wrong **w**

wrong font (typo) **wf**

Wyoming **WY; Wyo**

–X–

X (unnamed computer) automatic code translation **XACT**

xanthene **xan**

xanthic **xan**

x-dividend, not including right to dividend **xd**

xenon (chem) **Xe**

x-ray diffraction **XRD**

x-ray photoemission spectroscopy **XPS**

–Y–

yacht **y**

Yale Law Journal **YLJ**

yard **y; yd**

yard drain inlet **ydi**

yard superintendant **ys**

year **y; yr**

year of birth **yob**

year of death **yod**

year of marriage **yom**

year old **yo**

years [L *anni*] **ann.**

yellow **y**

Yen **Y**

Yiddish **Yid**

yield strength **ys**

young **y**

young adults **YA**

younger **yr**

youngest **y**

Young Men's Christian Association **YMCA**

Young Men's Hebrew Association **YMHA**

young upwardly mobile professional **Yump**

young urban professional **Yuppie**

Young Women's Christian Association **YWCA**

Young Women's Hebrew Association **YWHA**

your **yr**

your message received and understood **ROGER**

yours **yrs**

youth hostel **YH**

ytterbium (chem) **Yb**

yttrium (chem) **Y**

–Z–

Zambia **Zam**

Zechariah (Bible) **Zech**

zenith **z; zen**

zenith description **zd**

zenith distance **z; zd**

Zephaniah (Bible) **Zeph**

zero **z**

zero access storage **ZAS**

zero anti-aircraft potential **ZAP**

zero defect **zd**

zero energy breeder reactor assembly **ZEBRA**

zero energy nitrogen heated thermal reactor **ZENITH**

zero energy thermal reactor **ZETR**

zero energy thermonuclear apparatus **ZETA**

zero energy thermonuclear assembly **ZETA**

zero frequency **ZF**

zero gravity (weightlessness) **zero-g**

zero hour **Z hr**

zero immune globulin **zig**

zero population growth **ZPG**

zero wave length **zwl**

Zimbabwe **Zimb**

zinc ammonium chloride **ZAC**

zinc (chem) **Zn**

zirconium (chem) **Zr**

Zodiac **Zod**

zone **z**

Zone Improvement Plan Code (Postal Service) **ZIP Code**

zone of fire **ZF**

Zone Time **ZT**

zoological **zool**

Zoological Gardens **Zoo**

zoologist **zool**

zoology **zool**

Zurich **Zur**